LANGBOURNE'S LEGACY

ALAN P. LANDAU

Langbourne's Legacy (2020)
©2020 Alan P Landau

NATIONAL LIBRARY OF AUSTRALIA A catalogue record for this book is available from the National Library of Australia

The right of Alan P Landau to be identified as the moral rights author of this work has been asser by him in accordance with the Copyright Amendment (Moral Rights) Act 2000.
This book is copyrighted by the author.
Apart from any use as permitted under the Copyright Act 1968, no part may be reproduced, copied, scanned, stored in a retrieval system, recorded, or transmitted, by any form or by any mea without the prior written permission of the publisher.

ISBN: 978-0-6482493-4-4 (Paperback)
ISBN: 978-0-6482493-5-1 (Ebook)
ISBN: 978-0-6482493-7-5 (Audio Book)

Contact details for the author can be found at
www.landaubooks.com

This book is based on actual events, however it is a work of fiction.
Names, characters, places and incidents are either a product of the author's imagination or are used fictitiously and any resemblance to actual persons, living or dead, business establishments, events or locations are entirely coincidental.
The views, sentiments or expressions depicted in this book, and all books in the Langbourne Series, are fictitious and not those of the author.

Cover design : Al Packaroobie Designs
Editor : Cindy Kramer, South Africa

First published 2020

For my wonderful children, John and Cherie.
With all my love.

BOOKS IN THE LANGBOURNE SERIES :
(In sequential order.)

Langbourne

Langbourne's Rebellion

Langbourne's Empire

Langbourne's Evolution

Langbourne's Loyalty

Langbourne's Legacy

CHAPTER ONE
Bulawayo 1943

Hanna gently placed a lovingly prepared tray of tea on the small table near David. He relaxed peacefully on the wicker-woven sun lounger in the cool of the veranda. The soft clink of the exquisite china teacup caused him to open one eye lazily and look up at his sweetheart.

Hanna smiled at David. "How are you feeling, my love?"

"Tired," David said through a soft smile. "I might have a little snooze; it's such a delightful day."

Hanna sat on one of the two redwood Morris chairs and looked out into their flourishing garden, sighing contentedly. Despite the dry winter, her treasured flower beds had provided an abundance of colour amongst the rich emerald green foliage, thanks in part to the prolific deep water-well in the back garden, and Hanna's green fingers and love of gardening. Several large native trees provided a grand backdrop to their acre-sized property, giving welcome shade and cooling the air during the long hot summer months in Bulawayo.

Hanna turned her attention back to her husband. "I think you work far too hard, David. I'm worried about you. This last trip overseas was extremely stressful."

David smiled sweetly at his wife's concern. "The problem is that business is a bit of a puzzle, if you will, now that the entire world is at war ... again," David added with a sigh. "Therefore, safe international air travel is difficult, and business has slowed down to a trickle as a result. Nevertheless, I still need to get out there and buy what people want."

"Or need," Hanna added.

"Yes, what they need. We can't be buying merchandise that won't sell. That would be a sure recipe for the demise of a company like ours."

"I agree," Hanna frowned, "but your brother still puts enormous pressure on you, and your mind is unquiet. Why in heaven's name can't Morris slow down for once? Or send someone else?" she added as an afterthought.

"You know Morris," David chuckled, "he will never slow down. His entire existence is geared to doing business. It's his life. He's at his happiest when he's doing deals, outwitting business opponents, or arguing a fact."

David let his mind drift to the early days when he and Morris first arrived in Africa at the tender ages of 15 and 16; on their own, without the support of friends or family. He smiled as he contemplated how their lives had changed from sleeping on the floor of a wagon, walking through the bush for months at a time, facing hunger and avoiding hostilities. When they built their first warehouse, they would sleep on blankets at the rear of the shop because they couldn't afford to rent lodgings.

Now, today, they were wealthy, living comfortably and enjoying an enviable lifestyle. Why, he even owned one of those fancy British gasoline automobiles, the likes of which had now commandeered the streets of Bulawayo. With fond memories, he recalled their two old horses, Bruno and Splat. They were their only form of transport when they first arrived, and it didn't seem that long ago!

They had entered the right business almost the moment they set foot in Port Elizabeth, back in 1891. Morris had insisted they launch into their cigarette venture without any delay. They rolled cigarettes by day and sold them at night. The timing was just right, and in no time at all customers came to them in droves; looking for more business was unnecessary. They were hard-pressed to meet their customers' demands. Just one year later they sold the company for a handsome sum. It prompted Morris to decide they would head north, to Rhodesia, in search of greater fortune.

It was then that their lives took on entirely new dimensions, with rebellions, wars, plagues, floods, famine and, more curiously, commercial intrigue and shenanigans. He and his three brothers had to grow up fast to survive the turmoil Africa threw at them. And it came in spades.

Morris took the opportunity to summon his two remaining full brothers, Louis and Harry, to come out from Ireland without delay. Louis and Harry were barely 13 and 14 years old at the time, and reluctantly their father, Jacob, gave his permission for them to go.

For an entire year, an extraordinarily large shipment of stock that Morris had purchased on credit and loans, became lost in the African bush. However, because of the uprising, and more significantly, the outbreak of the deadly *rinderpest* plague, which virtually decimated the cattle population on the southern African continent, the value of their stock increased dramatically. Although at first a critical blow to the Langbourne brothers, which took them to the point of bankruptcy, the eventual locating of the lost wagons, completely intact, meant they could fill their warehouse to bursting point when everyone else in the settlement was suffering critical shortages. On top of that, during that year, the colony experienced severe inflation, and selling their goods at the going prices of the day meant that their profits were exceedingly healthy.

David reflected on the risks his eldest brother had taken in the business arena. Some of them were considered madness, not just by him and his siblings, but by respected businessmen in the community. The loss of the wagons was one such example, especially the sheer physical size of the shipment and risk at the time. Purchasing large quantities of hotel equipment during wartime was another and buying second-hand military boots *after* a war, turned the family name into a laughingstock. That was until the Japanese suddenly attacked the Russians and a desperate market for military footwear emerged overnight. It made them millions of pounds sterling and set the family on a course to becoming an intercontinental business conglomerate.

Morris moved his business from the wholesale trade into various other entities, such as retail, property development, shipping, procurement and financial services. He successfully invested in the London and Johannesburg Stock Exchanges and bought shares in diamond and gold mines. Morris continued to insist the brothers communicate in a time-honoured code they had perfected. Morris himself would very seldom front a business deal, preferring his younger brothers, Louis, Harry, and David in particular, to be the face of the company. Morris preferred to stay out of the limelight and manipulate the negotiations in the background, something he was exceptionally good at, causing him to become a bit of a mystery within various business circles.

Captains of industry and commerce knew about him, knew who he was and that he was the key decision-maker in the Langbourne family. Morris Langbourne was well known for his blunt social skills, his abrupt responses and almost rude habit of simply walking away from a conversation if it didn't hold his interest.

A soft breeze ruffled David's hair and brought his thoughts back to the present day and he smiled inwardly. Morris certainly was a difficult man, and it had fallen on him and his brothers to smooth a lot of ruffled feathers over the years, but the system worked well for the brothers. If a person pushed the brothers into a corner, usually someone looking for a business loan, and they needed a diplomatic way out, they would throw the blame on Morris. By merely saying he disapproved but suggesting a meeting with Morris could be further arranged, the affair usually ended abruptly.

David's thoughts shifted to his younger brother, Louis. Time had not been kind to him; he often had health issues, cheating death on more than one occasion. Nevertheless, without complaint, Louis dedicated his life to the business and his family, particularly his son, Herbert. He didn't age well; his hairline receded, thinned and greyed early, and the harsh African sun aged his face prematurely. Yet his mind was always sharp, and he always demonstrated a keen sense for business. His negotiating skills were exemplary, and his wisdom continuously sought by his fellow business associates. Louis was well respected in no less than three countries: England,

South Africa and Rhodesia.

Harry, on the other hand, had aged well. The youngest of the four brothers, he was accepted in the family as the most handsome of them all. Harry nurtured and perfected a condescending, dry, almost sarcastic manner, not just in his choice of words but also in his body language. David was quite sure this was a deliberate business ploy and not his natural character. Within their family circles, or amongst personal friends, this trait was not evident. However, put him in a business environment, even if it were in a restaurant with business associates, it could be quite taxing for those around him.

To his credit, David mused, Harry did know where to draw the line and would hold his demeanour at just the right point to keep his 'adversaries' on their toes. In this way, he controlled a meeting, and always held the upper hand. Although highly respected, especially within the Jewish quarter in which he became very involved, people did hold a particularly cautious respect for the man. The Jewish Board of Deputies in Johannesburg, of which he had been elected president for many years, held Harry in the highest regard.

Harry continued his trademark way of dressing. Wearing suspenders instead of a belt, and trousers that were slightly too long, which billowed out as they reached his highly polished brogue shoes. He married a beautiful woman, Anne, and had three lovely children: Dagmar, Sheila and William.

Much as David struggled under the demands of his eldest brother, Morris, he relished it too. His loyalty to his brothers and the business was absolute. David had travelled to the four corners of the earth buying stock and representing Langbourne Brothers, together with Langbourne Coetzee, a second family business they had launched over 50 years prior. The only difference between the two companies was that their good friend, Danie Coetzee, was a silent partner of Langbourne Coetzee and a member of that Board. Having befriended Danie when they first stepped onto African soil as young men in 1891, Morris invited Danie to join them as an arbiter should there be a family dispute or voting was split 50/50 between the brothers. Danie's services in that field were, fortunately, never required. Together they had worked as a perfect team, and as a result, all had become very wealthy.

Secretly, David felt tired now; he was 67 years old, and although his older brother showed no sign of slowing down, quite the opposite in fact, David was ready for a rest. The advent of the Second World War that had begun four years earlier had effectively forced him to slow down and stop his international travels, but with the slowdown of business, other stresses and strains had emerged. He had been tested to the limit; mentally this time, not physically.

The last few weeks had taken its toll on David, and, with Hanna's urging, he had taken a few days off to rest; a suggestion he accepted with some token objection, but nevertheless appreciated. For two days he had enjoyed lounging on his old wooden Morris chair under the comfort of a light blanket, relishing the constant pandering Hanna so lovingly provided. The garden was gentle on the eye, and the birdsong melodious. It gave him time to reflect on the adventures of his youth, which he rarely did, and the achievements of his later years.

"So, let him live his life," Hanna interrupted David's thoughts.

"I beg your pardon," David desperately pulled himself back from his thoughts, "I wasn't listening."

"I said let Morris live his life. I don't know why he has to involve you in everything he does."

"Morris is my brother," David said softly and shrugged under his thin blanket.

Hanna stood suddenly and gestured at the tray. "I've made a lovely pot of tea, David. Don't let it get cold now," she scolded with a mocking tone.

"I won't," David smiled. "Thank you, my lovely."

"I have some rose cuttings to plant in the front garden, so I'd better get along."

"Remember, the thorns on the rose stalks point downwards," David teased.

Hanna snorted with feigned irritation. "Will you ever let me live that down?"

"One day, perhaps," David chuckled softly.

Hanna gently pulled the thin blanket up under David's chin, then gave him an affectionate pat on his chest. "Call me if you need anything."

"I will do," David replied lazily, a loving smile gracing his face.

When all had gone quiet, David cast an eye at the tea tray. He was feeling so content and relaxed that the thought of sitting up and disturbing the moment felt somewhat unnecessary. Instead, he looked out into the back garden, watching some excited yellow and olive coloured masked weavers fly into a tree, chirping noisily at each other.

Although at peace in the solitude and safety of his garden, a slight frown crossed his brow as he recalled his last meeting with Morris in America some six weeks prior. There was absolutely no sign of Morris slowing down; he never stopped talking about business – ever. What concerned David more was that he found his brother becoming increasingly cantankerous with everyone and everything that crossed his path. Throughout his life, David had seemed able to keep his brother under control, but lately he was finding this quite difficult, and more to the point, quite tedious and stressful.

David could understand why Morris' resolve was tested to breaking point; the world conflict was indeed affecting their business. People were always stressed, and their characters were altered somewhat. He sighed and closed his eyes; there was nothing he could do about it now. They had done what they could under the circumstances, and all they could do was wait for the war to end. David let his thoughts drift as he listened to the noisy chattering of a flock of arrow-marked babblers that had swooped into the garden. Their incessant raspy chattering was making him smile as he listened with his eyes closed, imagining their avian conversations.

Just as he was about to drop off into another restful snooze, it crossed his mind that he really should pour himself a cup of tea; he didn't want to offend Hanna by drifting off and letting her carefully prepared beverage go cold.

A low baritone voice suddenly rumbled over David. "I see you,

Boss David."

David immediately sat bolt upright, almost tipping his lounger over. "Nguni! What are you doing here?" David exclaimed, trying to recover his dignity.

Nguni allowed a rolling laugh to flow from deep within. "I have come to find you, old man."

"And you have found the one you seek, my friend. I see you, Nguni," David laughed freely as he stood, throwing the blanket carelessly to the side and clasped the burly amaXhosa man by his forearm; a traditional greeting between good friends. "I was not expecting you."

"It seems that is so."

"A surprise indeed," David smiled sheepishly, still somewhat taken aback at the unannounced and sudden visit from his oldest friend. He was desperate to ask if there was something wrong to warrant such a visit. Still, David well knew that, in the Xhosa culture, one did not launch immediately into the crux of the matter, but etiquette dictated they must discuss lighter things first; the real reason would emerge later, as it always did. As it was, Nguni was smiling so broadly he could only be heralding good news.

"It has been a long time, my good friend," David's face was aglow with joy. "How is your family? Your wives and children?"

"They are all very well," Nguni boomed proudly. "My village is strong, and the people are happy. What of your family?"

"I have four children now. You have met my daughter, Ettie, but since then we have had three boys."

"Is that all?" Nguni jibed his friend. "The years have been kind to you, but your hair is white now. You are an old man."

"It is so," David looked at the ground in disappointed agreement, but then looked up with a wry smile. "I worry that your head and beard are trying to catch up with me."

The men laughed heartily.

"Tea, Nguni? Drink some tea with me," David insisted, immediately bounding into the kitchen before the big man could respond and returned moments later with a matching china cup and saucer and a large plate of shortbread biscuits that Hanna had recently made. David invited Nguni to sit on one of the Morris chairs beside him. After pouring two cups of tea, he laced his friend's beverage with sugar – four teaspoons of the white crystals – remembering precisely how Nguni enjoyed his tea. Some memories of good friends were never lost to time.

Their reunion was electric, and all David's concerns and worries evaporated. He felt rejuvenated, alive and filled with the spirit of youth.

David took his seat in the other chair beside Nguni. "What brings you so far, all the way from your village near Port Elizabeth?" David asked curiously as he carefully placed a teacup of hot liquid beside Nguni. "It is a very long way."

"I came to see you, Boss David," Nguni smiled warmly. "Is it not right that two old bulls meet to remember the days when they were boys? We are both old now and I was tired of talking to my six wives. I am in need of remembering the times we had."

A laugh exploded from David's throat. "Indeed, we did have some good times when we were young buffalos. We are old *dugga boys* now," David said, referring to old buffalo bulls, caked in mud and covered in battle scars.

"Much has changed in this time," Nguni said, a look of deep reflection clouding his face.

"Yes, it has," David likewise became pensive, "but surely the days of our youth were very kind to us."

The banter flowed smoothly between the two friends, eager to catch up with the many years that had passed between them.

"What about your father?" Nguni asked although he was sure he knew the answer.

"He died many years ago, my friend. When he was 73 years of age; he was an old man, but he had a good life."

"What of my friend, your brother, Boss Morris?" Nguni leant back in his chair, obviously relishing the comradeship.

"He is well," David replied, "but he still gives people a difficult time, me included. He was married for many years and had five children, but then he got divorced. He married another woman. She was very young, and her eye was looking mostly at shiny stones that she could wear with her expensive clothes and shoes. After five years, that marriage ended rather badly. My brother does not trust many people now, sadly."

"He is a good chief. He will look after your family very well."

"He does, Nguni, he does," David mulled. "He cares for people in ways that surprises even me. There is a side to him that feels deeply for people. But, as you know, he can be tough. Morris can be very confusing at times," David reflected with a cocky smile. "He did not like the children from my father's second marriage, yet he wanted to help them. Morris is very sharp, and he knows exactly what he wants to do all the time, but when it came to our half-brothers, the children from the second wife, he was a very confused person in many respects.

"There were two of these brothers in particular," David paused briefly to chuckle, "Paddy and Archie. I liked them both. Paddy was a bit like me, and Archie a bit like Morris, but my word, they gave Morris a lot of trouble; well, Archie did!"

Nguni took another satisfying gulp of his tea, draining his teacup. David noticed the vaguely annoyed look Nguni had cast into the bottom of the dainty porcelain cup.

"Let me make us some proper tea," David offered as he stood again. "But first, I must fetch some bigger cups."

"Your culture has a strange way to drink tea," Nguni frowned and waved a dismissive hand at his delicate china teacup, but then allowed a soft chuckle to reverberate along the veranda.

"Come with me," David placed his hand on Nguni's shoulder and gave it a reassuring squeeze. "Let's go to the kitchen and make some *real* tea. I still have those enamel mugs and the teapot we used on the wagon treks."

Nguni smiled as he lifted his bulk out of the wooden chair and followed David, who carried the tea tray in with him. In the kitchen, David filled the kettle and set it to boil as he rummaged at the back of a cupboard, emerging, all smiles, with a dull mustard-coloured enamel teapot. It had a few dents, and chips of enamel the size of thumbnails were missing in places exposing the blackened metal beneath.

Nguni laughed, and his eyes lit up. "I remember this teapot. It has served us well."

"Yes," David chuckled. "We enjoyed many cups of tea in the bush with this teapot. But my wife does not like this one. She wants me to throw it away, but I refuse. I knew there was a reason I wanted to keep it, and now that reason is here." David hoisted the teapot in a pseudo salute, then pointed to a dent in the spout. "Do you remember when that happened?"

Nguni's low rumble of laughter surfaced like a distant thunderstorm. "Yes, I remember. We were all about to drink some tea when the rhinoceros decided to join us." Nguni's laugh erupted uncontrolled as he recalled the events. David couldn't help but join in.

David reflected on that day. They had just inspanned the oxen, and a fire was made to boil some water for tea. Eight men, including Nguni and David, were sitting silently in a circle watching the pot start to bubble. As wisps of steam began to waft from the spout, David took the pot off the fire, holding the handle with a folded rag to avoid being burnt. Just then, a massive rhinoceros walked into the clearing, standing motionless in confusion as its myopic eyes tried to interpret what it could smell in the air.

The men with their backs to the beast froze; they did not need to ask what their comrades in front of them had seen as the horror on their faces said it all. Time stood eerily still for man and beast. However, for David, a new dilemma was unfolding.

Desperately conscious of not making a sound, nor twitching a muscle for fear of startling the giant horned creature only a few yards from them, the heat from the pot's handle, which had stood over the fire for some time, rapidly began to seep through the cloth in his hand. Reflexes overtook all abilities to endure the now blazing hot handle, and with a startled scream, David dropped the pot into the fire. Steam, ash and smoke exploded and hissed from the burning logs as David involuntarily leapt to his feet, turned and ran. The laager was only ten yards away, but even before he reached the safety of the enclosure, two men had overtaken him.

Startled by the sudden commotion, the rhinoceros likewise

turned and, with much apparent disgust, crashed its way through the bush, never to be seen again. Gingerly, and with great hesitation, the men returned to the fireside and rebuilt the fire that had so unceremoniously, albeit unintentionally, been extinguished by David. The men of the drive went to sleep laughing and joking that night.

"I have thought of that day many times," Nguni commented through his laughter.

"Two men ran past me," David reminded his friend, "but you ran over the top of me."

"You were too slow, Boss David," Nguni complained jokingly as he wiped a tear from his cheek. "And you were in my way!"

"This," David pointed to the dented spout, "is from that day."

David retrieved a large tin from a cupboard while the men chatted casually. The container had prominent pale blue and white stripes printed horizontally around the entire can, and, on opening the lid, he retrieved a scoop that he filled with sugar and then shovelled into the teapot. David then opened a lightly waxed paper packet with 'Tanganda Tea' printed boldly upon it. An old, discoloured silver teaspoon resided within the packet, which David removed. Instead of spooning in the dried black leaves, he widened the opening and simply poured a generous helping into the enamel teapot.

Peering into the blackened interior of the pot, David nodded his approval of the small mountain of tea and sugar piled within. The teapot was filled with boiling water from the kettle on the stove, and a few glugs of milk added. The concoction was then stirred vigorously. Tilting the teapot towards Nguni, David waited for his friend's nod of approval at the dark brown colour; several loose pieces of tea leaves floated on the surface, spinning gently as they kept up with the after-effects of David's rough stirring.

This method of making tea while on the march in the African bush, surrounded by oxen, wagons, dust and grime, had become a tradition. Sometimes David made the tea, sometimes Nguni, Daluxolo or a wagon driver, but always some of the men were required to give their approval before it was served. It was not necessary, but someone, nobody remembered who, had started this tradition, and it had been adopted.

Nguni nodded his approval and smiled. "This is good. I do not know why you people drink weak tea in small cups, then put in the sugar later."

"I know." David agreed. "It is a strange custom they have, but for sure, this way is better. Come, let us sit outside."

The two old friends returned to the back veranda and took their seats in the old wooden chairs. David had placed the re-set tea tray on the small round table between them and left the tea to brew for a few minutes before filling their respective enamel mugs. He offered Nguni a piece of Hanna's shortbread.

Nguni carefully chose a rectangle of the buttery-sweet biscuit with a frown of concentration on his brow. Popping the entire portion in his mouth, he raised his eyebrows and nodded in satisfied approval. David followed suit, dropping a few crumbs on the paving.

"This is nice," Nguni mumbled as he munched, savouring the flavour. "Boss Morris would be happy."

David almost coughed a laugh, quickly covering his mouth with his hand before more crumbs escaped. "You remember him well. My wife made these for him whenever we were in London. She was not allowed to return to Africa until she had made Morris a batch of shortbread."

Nguni chuckled softly. "Do you remember Nkosazana used to make these cakes for Boss Morris when he was young, in Bulawayo, when she worked for him?"

"I remember," David laughed easily now that he had dispatched his shortbread slice. "It made him fat."

This time it was Nguni who lost a few crumbs of shortbread from a short laugh. "You were telling me about the brothers from your father's second wife?"

"Paddy and Archie?" David gazed into the garden with a faraway look. "They were characters, those two."

CHAPTER TWO
Ireland 1913

Archie pedalled hard down the winding dirt farm road, his bicycle shuddering in violent objection to the corrugations. The weather around Dublin had been marvellous over the last fortnight, but recent rains had caused puddles in the road, forcing Archie to lift his feet high off the pedals as he sped through them.

A scrawny young Irishman with an almost permanent scowl on his brow, Archie had handsome features when he deigned to smile, but being just 13 years old, it would take a few years yet to fill out his adolescent body. He was running late; he had been enjoying the afternoon with a friend in the next village and had not been watching the time. Dinner would be served soon, and his mother, Helena, would be angry if he were late.

Rounding a gentle bend in the road, Archie saw three young girls in a field on the farm to his right. He knew his older half-brothers, Morris, David, Louis and Harry owned the farm, but he had never set foot upon it. It didn't bother him, however, as he had no interest in agriculture, and even less interest in his half-brothers, who were, in his opinion, all stuck-up old codgers.

Archie noticed the girls seemed a little confused, glancing at the ground, then back to the farmhouse, taking a couple of paces towards the farmhouse, then returning at once to where they had been standing. Archie stopped peddling and coasted for a moment, watching them intently. When one of the girls caught sight of him, she waved to catch his attention.

Archie's heart skipped a beat. He had seen one of these girls before and had always wanted to meet her, but hadn't the courage to cycle through the farm gates and strike up an awkward conversation; it just wasn't proper. He was suddenly at an age where girls were becoming curiously attractive for some inexplicable reason.

Now the girl was signalling urgently to him. He immediately struck out on his pedals and turned sharply through the farm gates. Archie was forced to move off the dirt driveway to get closer to the damsels, but the grass was too thick, so, in a fluid movement, he alighted, rested his cycle on the ground and approached them, a rare smile beaming from his face.

"Hello," one of the young ladies smiled openly. She looked about a year or two older than the second girl, who seemed utterly flustered. "Thank you for coming over; we need some help if you would be so kind?"

Archie's heart melted on the spot. "Of course," he readily agreed.

"That is my friend, Amanda O'Grady," the beautiful girl smiled at her shy friend. "And that's Paula Cassin, a good friend who lives on the farm next-door. Amanda's parents manage this farm. Her father started digging a well over here yesterday," she hurriedly pointed to where Amanda stood, just a few yards away. "He hasn't finished, so it's not too deep, but one of her lambs fell in, and it's a bit too deep for us to climb down there and rescue it."

"Let me have a look," Archie squared his shoulders and tried to sound as masculine as he could and strode over to the offending hole.

Archie greeted Amanda politely. "Good afternoon, Amanda. Let's see how we can get your poor lamb out."

"Oh, thank you so much," Amanda's voice sounded almost pitiful. "I'm so worried about the poor thing."

"Stop fussing, Amanda," Paula scolded her friend. "The lamb's fine, and this young gentleman will solve the dilemma, no doubt."

Archie acknowledged Paula's comments with a reassuring smile. The well was only about four or five feet deep, just enough to keep the hapless creature out of his reach, and perhaps not deep enough to need a ladder. However, it was muddy and sufficiently wet to ensure he would be going home a very dirty lad. There was no water in the bottom of the shallow hole, but the damp mud was glistening pure black. Archie understood the situation immediately, and for these three beautiful young ladies, he was prepared to accept any punishment his mother would mete out to him when he got home filthy dirty.

"This will be easy, and will only take a moment," Archie said confidently.

"Oh, do be careful," Amanda implored.

Archie removed his threadbare jacket, a hand-me-down from his several older brothers. This he handed to Amanda's beautiful friend, then crouched at the edge of the dark hole, peering at the muddied young lamb that gave a mournful bleat.

"She doesn't bite, does she?" Archie asked with a mocking grin.

"Of course not," Amanda giggled sheepishly, obviously enjoying the humour and the gallant young man who had rushed to her rescue.

Archie turned slightly and let his legs drop into the depths and, while holding tufts of grass, allowed himself to sink lower, knowing full well that all manner of clothing was now horribly smeared with black mud. As his grip began to fail, he realised with a small amount of panic that he was going to drop, and may even land on the poor creature. Suddenly, sliding down the last foot, Archie landed in the sodden earth with a squelch, then overbalancing, wedged his back against the far wall. He knew his clothing was now all but completely ruined, but he didn't care.

"Are you alright?" Paula asked with urgency and concern in her voice.

When Archie stood straight, his head was just above the rim of the well, and, giving a very pleasing smile, confirmed all was well and going exactly to plan. He reached down, held the lamb firmly, and hoisted it up and over the edge. He could tell Amanda was relieved to see her lamb rescued and free once more, almost giving it a passionate hug, but stopped short when she saw how filthy it was.

"Thank you so much," she almost squealed.

Paula started laughing. "Now how are you going to get out?"

"Very easy," Archie grinned, trying to act more masculine than his years, but at his first attempt to clamber out the hole, he realised the walls were so slippery he couldn't get any purchase with his feet. Try as he might, he realised he was in a somewhat awkward predicament.

"Ahh..." Archie mused, concealing a growing realisation he was stuck like a cork in a wine bottle and needed some assistance. "I think this mud is more slippery than I imagined."

"Here, hold my hand, and I'll try and pull you out," Amanda's beautiful friend offered.

"You'll be sorry," Archie laughed. "You will get covered in mud."

"Not as much as you," she laughed heartily. "You should look at yourself right now, you should," she said in a thick Irish accent and laughed even harder.

Archie was enjoying the banter and laughed along with her, knowing full well that he must look an absolute sight. "What's your name?" Archie enquired.

"Kate," she said with a twinkle in her eye. "Kate Hart."

"I must apologise, I haven't introduced myself to you. I'm Archie. Pleased to meet you, Kate," Archie smiled back at her sheepishly.

"Kate is visiting us from a small town called Shannon, all the way from the west of this fine country of Ireland," Amanda proudly added to her best friend's introduction.

"Here," Kate lent forward and extended her hands to grip Archie's.

As Archie began to pull himself out of the pit, Kate leant back to take the weight. Suddenly her feet slipped on the damp grass, and in one fluid motion, she landed on her posterior, the frills on her pale blue skirt flying in every direction, before sliding into the hole to join Archie.

For Kate, this seemed to be the funniest thing ever, and for Archie, although laughing along with her, he wasn't quite sure if he should be pleased or concerned to be in a hole in the ground with a most delightfully attractive young lass.

"Looks like we both have a problem," Kate said while catching her breath. "Heavens, just look at the state of me now."

"Both of us," Archie confirmed. "Come along; we need to get you out of here."

With Amanda and Paula carefully hoisting Kate from above, and Archie pushing from below using his cupped hands as a step-up for Kate, she was quickly out of the muddy confines. Then, with two girls bracing themselves and each holding one of Archie's hands, he was propelled out of the hole without difficulty.

With the situation now resolved, much to Amanda's delight, she thanked Archie profusely.

Archie cleared his throat. "I believe you are the daughter of Elaine and Adam O'Grady?"

"You know them?" Amanda's eyes revealed an element of surprise.

"Well, in a sense. My brothers own this farm, and I sometimes hear them talking about Mr and Mrs O'Grady, who run the farm for them."

"You must be a Langbourne then?"

"Yes," Archie replied meekly, and cast a glance at Kate, hoping to keep her in the conversation.

"Well, I'll be," Amanda smiled copiously. "Pleased to make your acquaintance Mr Archie Langbourne. My parents speak very fondly of your brothers. I have only met two of them, but they are much older than you. They are adults, in fact."

"Yes, I know," Archie sighed resignedly. "They are my half-brothers. My father remarried and had a second family; I come from the second marriage, so am much younger than them. Your mother brings groceries from this farm to our home every so often. I have met her."

"Indeed, she does, Mr Archie Langbourne," Amanda grinned. "I have been given the delight to help her pick those delicious vegetables myself."

"Well, I thank you," Archie said with a very slight bow of appreciation, "but I'm sorry you didn't come with your mother to deliver them. I would have met you years ago. And by the way, I'm not anything like my half-brothers," Archie quickly added in an attempt to disassociate himself from them.

"If you are like your brothers, you must be a very nice man, and therefore I am pleased we have met, even if it is in a muddy hole. Do come in and meet my parents, and maybe clean up a little."

"No, I thank you, but certainly not in this state," Archie declined. "I'll meet them when I am more presentable. As it is, I am terribly late for dinner."

"As you wish, Archie," Amanda grinned mischievously.

Kate suddenly joined the discussion. "You will come and visit us again, will you?"

Archie's heart skipped a beat. "Of course, without a doubt. Without a doubt," he repeated and smiled broadly.

"Do make it soon, won't you? I return to Shannon town two days hence."

"Tomorrow?" Archie asked, hopefully.

"Tomorrow then," Kate smiled coyly and quickly glanced at Amanda seeking confirmation.

"Right oh," Archie responded before Amanda could say anything. His day had turned out so well, and he certainly wanted to see the delightful Kate again. "Tomorrow then," he confirmed, his eyes twinkling at Kate.

As Archie walked back to his bicycle, he turned several times to look back at Kate, who never took her gaze off him, and, as he cycled out of view, he waved back, hoping to receive a wave in return, which he did. He didn't stop smiling until he got home. His life had suddenly become fascinating and far more exciting than anything he had experienced before.

Dirt roads became cobbled streets as Archie pushed into the outer suburbs of Dublin, and then, turning into St Kevin's Parade, pulled up at the front door of the family home, dumping his cycle on the pavement without due regard for pedestrians passing by. Although his father, Jacob, had scolded him repeatedly for doing this, the joy of the busy afternoon just spent had a magical effect on curbing

Archie's ability to remember the reprimands. He was mindful enough, though, to remove his mud-encrusted shoes before he stepped inside.

When Helena saw Archie walk nonchalantly into the lounge, she shrieked. "Archie! Don't you dare come in here with that mud! What in the world happened to you?"

"I was rescuing a lamb from..." Archie attempted to explain before being abruptly cut off by Helena.

"Out! Out! Take yourself outside Archie Langbourne, immediately!" Helena shouted as she stood and pointed a threatening finger at the door. "Jacob! Where are you? For Heaven's sake, look at your son."

Jacob appeared from a side room looking very flustered. When he saw Archie standing in the entrance to the lounge, coated in thick black mud and grinning sheepishly, all he could do was cover his mouth with his hand to hide the instinctive laugh about to erupt like a volcano.

"Paddy!" Helena called in desperation, "take your brother outside and help him clean up. Immediately. Out, out!" she demanded.

Paddy, emerging right behind his father, took one look at his younger brother and began to laugh. Sensing his mother's distress, though, he checked himself and walked over to the bemused Archie, leading him outside by the shoulder.

"Come on, Brother," he encouraged calmly, trying to soothe the situation, "let's get you cleaned up. What happened?"

Paddy, some five years Archie's senior, had a gentle and warm way about him. Blessed with good looks and eyes that always seemed to be smiling, Paddy was Helena's favourite son; dependable, conscientious, loving and always willing to help. His sisters, of whom he now had three, adored him.

Of his three brothers, only one was a daily problem, and that was Archie. It fell to Paddy to look after and manage Archie; often Helena would throw her hands up in frustration, with Jacob burying himself in his study to ponder his vast array of Jewish literature and prayer books. Paddy was the only person Archie would listen to and obey willingly, and this was not lost on his parents.

Late the previous night, as the home fell silent and Jacob was about to blow out the candle, he heard his wife sigh heavily.

"What troubles you, my lovely?" Jacob asked.

"Archie troubles me," Helena replied bluntly. "What is the matter with that child? He always seems to be getting up to some sort of mischief."

"He is young, Helena," Jacob defended his son. "In time he will settle and prosper."

"I can only thank our good Lord that he respects Paddy. We'd be floundering without him."

Jacob chuckled softly. "When I look back on Esther's children, I see many similarities with ours. We had Morris, who was like Archie, and we also had David, who was like Paddy. David and Morris are very close, and it is David who somehow managed to keep Morris at bay. Of the seven older children, Morris was by far the most complicated – and still is," Jacob smiled.

"I think Archie is more difficult than Morris ever was," Helena retorted.

"Well, perhaps. But look at how Morris and David turned out. I have great faith in Paddy and Archie," Jacob replied.

"I know," Helena said resignedly. "Of all our children I find Archie the most trying."

"He will turn out alright, my lovely. Believe me. Morris was just like him when he was but a child. Have faith in our Lord."

Helena rolled over in the bed. "Well, let's see what new adventures tomorrow brings. Good night, Jacob," she sighed.

That conversation was not quite one day old, and already Helena was reflecting on what was said. She sighed in resignation. Back on the street, screened by Paddy with a towel, Archie had changed into clean clothes. At the same time, his soiled attire was unceremoniously plunged into a bucket of water by a very indignant Helena. When the household had returned to some semblance of normality, the family gathered for dinner, and Archie excitedly expounded his rescue efforts twice over.

Jacob finally cleared his throat and took on an authoritative air as he dabbed at his lips with a serviette.

"Archie, we have something important to tell you," he declared.

Archie looked at his father, inquisitively. He had seen that look before and understood the tone of voice. "What is it, Father?"

"Your brother, Morris, wishes for you and Paddy to travel to London in the morning. He wants you to help him with his business. It continues to prosper, and they need to expand."

"With respect, Father, tomorrow will not do," Archie responded forcefully and cast a glance in Paddy's direction for support. "In any case, I don't want to help Uncle Morris. He's such a grouch."

Jacob raised a hand to silence his son. "Calm your tongue, young man. He will employ you, pay you money, and what's more, he will pay for your journey to London. We are very blessed to have Morris and his brothers in our family, and you should not be complacent now that they are offering you gainful employment."

Archie immediately thought about meeting Kate that afternoon, and his promise to return the next day. "Well, I'm not going," Archie replied shortly and folded his arms in defiance.

"I have already made the arrangement with Morris," Jacob continued, his voice a steady monotone. "I have discussed this with your mother, and with Paddy, and we all agree it will be a fitting opportunity for both of you." Jacob cast his eyes at Paddy, looking for support.

"It is an excellent opportunity, Archie," Paddy quickly spoke to his younger brother. "I'm rather excited to go to London. I have always wanted to go there, and to be paid to go, I think, is a tremendous advantage."

"I have plans tomorrow," Archie stubbornly objected, "it simply won't do."

"What plans?" Helena asked, almost condescendingly.

Archie opened his mouth to tell her precisely what he had intended but the embarrassment of revealing he was going to see a pretty young lady, made him change his mind abruptly.

"I have already procured the tickets," Jacob finalised the discussion. "You and Paddy will depart at 8 o'clock in the morning.

You will still have to travel to the station; therefore, it will be a very early start for you boys. Your mother has already packed your clothes, Archie."

Outraged at how his parents had planned his life without consulting him, Archie abruptly scraped his chair away from the table and stormed off without asking permission to be excused, a blatant insult of which he was well aware. Helena was about to scold him, but Jacob raised his hand slightly to silence her.

"Go talk to your brother," Jacob spoke to Paddy in a soft tone and nodded his approval for him to leave the table. "Don't forget you need to leave the house at six o'clock in the morning if you are going to make that train."

As the train pulled out of the Dublin railway station, Archie pressed himself deep into his seat, arms folded across his chest and his face thunderous. Paddy, sitting directly across from him, looked at his younger brother inquisitively, then began to laugh.

Archie stared hard at his brother. "It's not funny," he almost growled in frustration.

There was more to his anger than just being commanded to London by his eldest half-brother or the fact that he didn't like Morris; there was something else. It was the sudden end to his secret hope of fraternising with a beautiful young girl for the very first time. What made it even more annoying was that Kate seemed equally eager to spend time with him. Morris' summons had abruptly ripped this joy from his heart. Not only that, but he was also denied a chance to explain to her why he could not fulfill the promised rendezvous.

Archie had made his mother promise she would tell Elaine O'Grady, the manager of the farm, that he had been sent unexpectedly to London when she next saw her. Sadly, he knew this would not happen for at least a month, by which time Helena would surely have forgotten. Furthermore, Kate would have long since returned to her hometown of Shannon. Kate would be leaving Dublin the next day, and that would be the end of that – forever. Archie was livid.

"I will never forgive Uncle Morris for doing this to me," Archie grumbled aloud. "Or Father."

"Relax, Archie," Paddy sighed and looked out the window as the blackened brickwork of the surrounding homes slipped past. "You should see this as an adventure. You always wanted to visit London, and now Uncle Morris is paying you to visit. This could be fun."

"Never," Archie shrugged defiantly, his arms remaining tightly folded. "I had plans for my life, and being forced to go to London against my will without notice is... is..."

"Never mind," Paddy calmly interrupted him. He understood how Archie felt, but as far as he was concerned, there wasn't much he could do about it either.

For Paddy, this was indeed an adventure. At 18 years old, he was ready for some excitement. His current job at a small shoe factory on the outskirts of Dublin, keeping their books of account, was unexciting. It also suggested that he would not progress up the corporate ladder with much alacrity, so the call from his older half-brother was a godsend to him. He knew Morris could be difficult at times, but he could deal with that; he was not overly concerned.

Everyone in the family, except Helena, regarded Morris as the head of their household, and what he said, happened – like it or not. It was only because of his generosity in supporting their rather large family that they were dressed in fine clothes, ate well, and in good health. Coupled with Morris' massive wealth and business empire, it went without saying that he was respected as an important member of the family.

However, this came at a personal cost for all the siblings, as Morris was notoriously complex; his abrupt mannerisms and demands always had the family on edge. It was apparent to Jacob that Morris did not approve of his second family with Helena, who was also Morris' cousin. Because of that fact, Jacob had insisted Helena's children show respect to their older half-brothers by addressing them as uncles.

Paddy, though, had a very tolerant and obliging demeanour, and the issue of dealing with Morris was a minimal one for him. As a result, Morris was quite accepting of Paddy. It was the reason family members would liken his character to that of David, the second eldest son of the first family.

David was loved by all the extended family and highly regarded by anyone who had any dealings with him. He was calm, very kind, and a delight to be around. He had married a beautiful lady, Hanna, whom everyone adored. The two of them made a perfect pair.

A frown crossed Paddy's forehead as he stared blankly out at the blur of passing buildings and sank deeper into his thoughts. He now had the unenviable task of looking after Archie without the backup and support of his father. Knowing this would likely be a difficult task, he resigned himself to the fact that all he could do would be to take one day at a time. If that was all it took, he could make his peace with that.

"He had better pay me well," Archie interrupted his brother's thoughts.

Paddy stared at Archie with a frown. "Uncle Morris will pay you fairly," he said exasperated.

"He had better, after destroying my life," Archie huffed.

"What life?" Paddy spread his arms in confusion. "Let me give you some sound advice, young brother," his tone changed as he pulled himself up in his seat. "If you want to get along with Uncle Morris, you had better work extremely hard, and as sure as I'm sitting in front of your face, he will pay you a fair wage. Your wage will increase with your efforts, as will your promotion up the company ladder, and as it is the family ladder, your prospects are much better than most people's. Furthermore, don't argue with him. It's not worth it; you will never win an argument with Uncle Morris. Trust me."

Archie shrugged and looked at his shoes forlornly.

"I said, don't argue with him; I'm not coming to your rescue. I've heard stories about Uncle Morris," Paddy continued, driving his point home. "Now sit back and try and enjoy what's coming. You may even enjoy London. I hear it's a magnificent city."

"Uncle Morris is an old man," Archie mumbled. "How can he even be my brother? He's 40 years old."

"Morris is 38," Paddy retorted, frustration evident in his voice, "therefore he is your senior, and very successful. It would help if you respected that. Learn from him. He is doing you a favour, so snap out of your mood and act like an adult!"

Archie, arms still folded, gave his brother an icy stare, then looked out the window. Nothing more was said. As far as Archie was concerned, Morris and his business were only half the problem – the other half was that he had just lost a fascinating interlude with a beautiful young lady who seemed to have an attraction to him, clearly, all because of Morris!

The remainder of the journey was fraught with delays. After disembarking from a ferry at Liverpool, Paddy decided they would overnight in a lodging and catch a train to London the next morning. Boarding the train the following day, Paddy's spirits lifted slightly. He noticed Archie had begun to accept his fate and was a little more talkative as he watched the changing landscape with keen interest. When they entered the inner city of London, the two brothers became quite animated despite the drab buildings and the equally drab people walking the grey streets. As dull as everything looked, London seemed far more exciting than Dublin, and with a lot more people. The acrid aroma of burning coal added to the impression that this was a progressive city.

Baggage in hand, the brothers alighted from the train. Paddy, holding a hand-drawn map, began navigating through the throngs to the mysterious Langbourne Coetzee warehouse, the company that would be employing them.

It didn't take long to find the establishment, despite the lengthy walk, with both eager brothers somewhat disappointed at the outside appearance of the building. It was in desperate need of maintenance and a coat of fresh paint, and almost all the overhead skylight windows needed replacing.

"Not particularly inviting," Archie mumbled.

"No," Paddy agreed despondently. "One wonders if anyone actually works in there, or if it is just a warehouse?"

"Well hopefully this won't be our place of work," Archie sighed. "What exactly does Uncle Morris want us to do here?"

"I have no idea," Paddy shrugged. "Come on, let's see what awaits us."

After knocking on the large wooden door, showing its age by the several peeling layers of paint and raw wood splinters at the edges, they were greeted by silence. They upscaled their knocking to banging with fists, which finally elicited a muffled response from an irritated voice within, curtly demanding the boys walk around to the rear of the building.

Looking at each other in surprise, Paddy and Archie picked up their belongings and trudged around the block. The alleyway behind the row of buildings was even more foreboding. Dustbins lay upturned or on their sides, the contents of which were strewn haphazardly in every direction, evoking a distinctly abandoned atmosphere. Stray cats casually roamed the area, seemingly well-fed on the numerous rats that scurried away as the boys approached.

"This is disgusting," Archie winced as a giant rodent scampered just in front of his path. "I thought Uncle Morris was a wealthy businessman. I did not expect to find his warehouse in this dump."

"Me too," Paddy looked over his shoulder cautiously. "It's not quite what I expected."

As they approached a door that they believed might lead to the correct warehouse, it flung open violently, and a short stumpy man glared at them. He had garters just above his elbows made from what looked like steel springs; they held his lengthy sleeves in check.

"Yes?" the man demanded curtly.

"Good morning, Sir," Paddy replied politely, "we are looking for Mr Morris Langbourne."

"You won't find 'im 'ere," he replied abruptly in a thick cockney accent. "Ooh are ye?"

"Paddy and Archie Langbourne," Paddy replied nervously.

"Right oh, come in then," the surly man invited, and promptly turned on his heel, disappearing into the gloom of the warehouse. "Lock the door behind ye," he yelled as a parting shot.

Paddy and Archie stared at each other with a mixture of amusement and confusion, then followed the man inside.

Mr Witherspoon, the warehouse manager, was a grumpy man, blunt in responses laced with copious sarcasm. Being a heavy smoker, his index finger and thumb were stained dull yellow from nicotine. The Langbourne boys didn't take to him very well, but, under the circumstances, had little choice but to tolerate his unpleasantness. Each time Witherspoon cast his attention elsewhere than at the newcomers, Paddy and Archie would exchange disapproving stares.

Witherspoon told them that Morris would arrive shortly, and true to his word, they only had to wait another 20 minutes before their attention was suddenly drawn to a rough clattering at the back door. When the door clattered angrily open, Morris appeared in a dark suit and bowler hat, a significant air of importance exuding from every pore.

"Paddy, Archie. Welcome," Morris beamed as he attended to the faulty lock on the door.

The younger brothers smiled as they stood to greet their eldest brother and break free of Witherspoon's incessant ramblings. A familiar face and the unexpectedly warm welcome raised their drooping spirits almost instantly. They noticed that Morris had gained a bit of weight since they last saw him, which had been some years earlier. When he removed his hat, they saw the hairline above his temples had begun to recede slightly, enhancing his sophisticated, almost authoritative look.

Paddy immediately walked over to greet Morris with a firm handshake. Archie followed obediently and did likewise. He still regarded Morris with reservation, so didn't contribute to the exchanges of conversation, which mostly consisted of news of their Irish family. In typical style, however, Morris kept the idle chit-chat to a minimum, quickly ending the conversation to instruct Witherspoon on business matters before shepherding the young brothers out of the warehouse, onto the street, and into a hostel not far down the road.

"I have booked a room for you two for one month," Morris said proudly. "You will be quite comfortable here. Breakfast is included. I have covered the board and lodging for the month, but after that, it is for your account."

Archie puffed out his chest, the first of many questions desperately waiting to burst forth. "You require us for an entire month?"

Morris smiled broadly. "At least a month, maybe more. There is much I require you to do, and my brother... Uncle David," Morris corrected himself, "suggested I employ you two rather than pay a wage to a couple of strangers who will probably, like all the rest of them, leave me after a fortnight."

That last comment raised eyebrows. Archie was about to ask a question that suddenly came to mind, which had something to do with why employees left after only two weeks, when Paddy, sensing Archie's prickly mood swing, smartly changed the subject.

"It is very kind of you to give us paid work, Uncle Morris, and to provide this comfortable accommodation. We are very grateful, not so, Archie?"

Archie muttered an agreement.

"Right oh lads," Morris spun on his heel and entered the hostel as he continued to talk, "let's sign you in and drop off your bags, then we will hire a buggy and go back to my home for dinner. Rose Bertha is expecting you."

And that was precisely what happened. Morris and Rose Bertha had bought a flat on Castletown Road in Fulham. The buggy ride took well over half an hour to get there, during which time Morris relaxed a little and asked for more details of the family. Paddy did all the talking and soon noticed that Morris took particular interest in their eldest sister, Bloomy, and their father, Jacob. When Morris asked if the manager of his farm, Elaine O'Grady, was sending farm produce to the family, Archie finally spoke up.

"I was there the day before yesterday."

"Oh, really," Morris' eyebrow arched in curiosity. "What took you there?"

"I didn't intend to go there, but as I cycled past the farm, Mrs O'Grady's daughter and a friend summoned me because a lamb had fallen into a well, and they needed some help to retrieve it."

"And did you save it?"

"Oh yes, it was no problem. A little messy, but no harm done."

Paddy snorted. "A little messy? Archie almost brought the entire paddock back to the house with him."

Morris laughed at that joke. "Well, good for you. So, how was the farm looking?"

"Same as always, I suppose," Archie shrugged dismissively and stared out at the passing suburb.

Morris stared at Archie for a moment, then rolled his eyes skywards; he expected definitive answers. Giving up on the conversation, he also turned his attention to the suburbia that passed by, leaving Paddy feeling somewhat awkward.

Castletown Road consisted of identical four-story flats abutting each other. Every entrance had a grand portico, held up by three Grecian-style concrete pillars, half of each porch shared between two neighbours. The facade, just like every other building in the entire street, was painted in a light sandstone colour. Each side of the road was identical to the other, right down to the latticed wrought ironwork bannisters that led down to an unseen level below the street.

"Goodness," Archie exclaimed as they turned into Castletown Street, "just look at the length of this building."

Morris chuckled when he saw the amazement on Archie's face. "Yes, it does seem that way, but they are individual buildings, just joined together. I live at number 30, about half-way down on the right."

If the outside of the buildings weren't impressive enough, both Paddy and Archie were dumbfounded at the opulence and magnificent grandeur evident inside the home of Rose Bertha and Morris Langbourne. The carpets were plush and absorbed any hint of an echo, while dark, brooding paintings of important-looking men and women adorned the hallway. Deeper inside their home, the artwork lightened up with landscapes and floral arrangements. Selected paintings were of semi-naked young women frolicking in gardens with distant looks on their faces. Archie especially admired these paintings, while trying desperately to keep his interest in the revealing ladies unnoticed. The home was electrified, so the crystal chandeliers twinkled as the bare light globes burned brightly, easily reflecting the hues of blue and red sparkles from the crystals. Paddy and Archie feasted their eyes on all the visual delights.

"Paddy, Archie! Welcome," came a woman's voice from behind them.

They spun around to see Rose Bertha gliding towards them. She was wearing a black, pleated full-length skirt; her white frilled blouse buttoned up to her neck.

"Hello, Aunt Rosie," they said in unison.

Although they knew her correct name was Rose Bertha, Jacob had instructed them that it was a bit of a mouthful and so 'Aunt Rosie' would be both a polite and acceptable way to address her. Jacob later admitted that he had discussed this with Morris by letter to ensure there would be no uncomfortable issues when the boys finally arrived. Because Jacob was conscious of the sensitivities Morris held with regards to his second family, he felt it best to clear up all possible contentions sooner, rather than later, to prevent small problems evolving into family disasters.

He was right, as usual, and Morris had replied to his letter in a very mature and understanding manner. Morris was a good 25 years their senior, and even though he was their half-brother, Paddy and Archie were too young, according to the dictates of society, to call him and his wife by their first names; it would be disrespectful and improper. Hence the titles Uncle Morris and Aunt Rosie were suitably appropriate to all concerned.

"My, you have grown!" Rose Bertha exclaimed, looking the boys up and down. "Last I saw you was at our wedding. I think, Paddy, you were just seven years old, and Archie, you were but a toddler of two."

"I remember being at your wedding," Paddy smiled. "You haven't changed a bit."

"Why thank you, young man," Rose Bertha said as she closed the gap and gave the boys a motherly hug.

"I think I was too young to remember any of that," Archie said through a smile as he endured the maternal greeting.

"I'm not surprised," Rose Bertha giggled. "Come upstairs and meet your nephews and niece, then let's have some dinner."

Paddy noticed that almost from the moment they entered the flat, Morris had disappeared somewhere, and they were left in the care of Aunt Rosie. The first level of the flat was designated the children's area. A nanny tended to the children's needs, but kept a low profile, standing quietly and not engaging at all with the new arrivals during the introductions.

The eldest son, Cecil, was ten years old. He was dressed in formal clothing and spoke impeccably; his manners were surprisingly adult-like and caught the boys a little off guard. Leslie, one year Cecil's junior, talked and dressed almost like his brother, both seeming a little shy and reserved at meeting these strangers. Harry, at six years old, didn't seem to have the inhibitions of his older brothers, and engaged with Paddy and Archie readily, proudly showing them his favourite toy and inviting them to play with him. Eunice, the youngest of the four, was just three years old, and shyly hid behind her nanny's skirts.

Rose Bertha then ushered all the boys downstairs for dinner, leaving the nanny to tend to Eunice. The dining table was decked out elaborately, with silver cutlery and elegant crockery. Paddy and Archie concentrated hard on employing their best etiquette and table manners, as they felt under sudden pressure to make a stylish impression on their obviously very well-to-do relatives.

"Where's Uncle Morris?" Paddy suddenly noticed Morris' absence soon after they started eating.

"Oh," Rose Bertha looked up coyly, "he is a very busy man and works almost every spare moment he has. He will be in his study upstairs. I will take him his dinner later this evening."

Although Archie was almost relieved that Morris was not around, and he could relax a little, it was a bit awkward to be eating at his table without him being at the dinner table with them. Still, Rose Bertha readily held the conversation the entire evening. After the meal, a definite sense of discomfort began to set in, causing Paddy to feel that he and Archie might be in the way of family time. The dynamics of the household were very different from what he was used to in Jacob and Helena's home, where everyone was relaxed, and there were no airs and graces. Casual conversations were constant, with a little calling between the rooms on occasion, the odd shriek of laughter, or an unsolicited and mighty sneeze.

Fortunately, Rose Bertha once again took the lead as hostess and, after excusing herself to take a plate of food up to Morris, she returned to inform them that Morris would be down shortly to explain what the next day had in store for them, and to bid them good night.

True to her word, Morris appeared after only ten minutes, apologised that he had not been able to join them for dinner, and thrust a piece of paper and a one-pound note into Paddy's hand.

"That's the address of your hostel," Morris explained to Paddy. "Walk up to the top of the street and hail a coach. This money will more than cover the fare. I will meet you both at the warehouse at eight o'clock in the morning."

The boys thanked Uncle Morris and Aunt Rosie for the meal, and, in seemingly no time at all, they found themselves on the pavement outside. It was not that their expulsion from the flat was rude or overly rushed, their welcome had felt genuine and warm, but somehow Morris seemed to have mastered the art of dealing with social etiquette in a very truncated way.

"Well, that was interesting," Paddy mulled as he looked down the long row of identical and expensive homes.

"So, you will be working with Uncle Morris doing his accounts, and I'll be stacking boxes in the warehouse?" Archie looked at his older brother, quizzically.

"Seems so," Paddy answered without looking at Archie.

"For how long?"

Paddy shrugged. "I don't know. I get the feeling it will be for a month."

"Better not be more," Archie grumbled. "I have things I have to do in... in Dublin." He had almost said Shannon Town as his mind was still on the beautiful Kate Hart.

"Come on," Paddy began to stride out. "Let's work out how to hail a coach. It's very late."

"A month. That's all," Archie grumbled loudly.

It would be more than 20 years before Archie would set foot on Irish soil again.

Nguni looked at David and raised his eyebrows in confusion. "I thought you said Boss Paddy and Boss Archie gave Boss Morris a lot of trouble? To me, they were happy."

David laughed. "Oh, they were fine, for a couple of months, but then Archie began to get difficult with Morris. Paddy was alright, he seemed happy, but Archie? I have never known anyone to trouble Morris as much as Archie. He was like the honey badger after someone stole his food!" David laughed again but shook his head at the memories of those problematic incidents.

"It troubles me to hear when brothers fight," Nguni's shoulders slumped.

"Yes, me too. Morris would write and tell me how much trouble Archie caused. They were doing wonderful work, actually, so Morris needed them, but I think Archie was too much like Morris, and they would argue all the time. So, one day I had a solution," David grinned as he reached for his tea.

Nguni also took his mug and sipped noisily, looking at David sideways through slit eyes. "How did you fix this problem?"

"I suggested Morris send Archie to me, here in Rhodesia. Archie would be very far from him and still be able to work in the business."

Nguni chuckled. "You are very smart, Boss David. And did Boss Archie show you respect?"

"Oh yes, very much so, and I liked Archie. I have great respect for him too."

"I wonder why Boss Archie and Boss Morris were fighting all the time?" Nguni mumbled as he put his mug down.

"I know why," David sighed. "They both were bosses."

CHAPTER THREE
London 1913

"What is it with you and Uncle Morris?" Paddy stormed into the room he shared with Archie at the lodging. He slammed the door behind him, instantly regretting it as the noise echoed down the narrow corridor.

"Uncle Morris has completely hijacked and destroyed my life," Archie spoke through gritted teeth.

"No, he hasn't," Paddy pinched his eyes in exasperation. He pulled up the only chair in the room and sat on it, back-rest forward, resting his forearms on the seat-back. "Uncle Morris gave us an opportunity; I am grateful for this opportunity. You have such an attitude. What is your problem? You need to sort it out. This is family we are dealing with, and you know what Father says about family."

Archie simply glared at Paddy, the anger in him so great that his eyes were bloodshot. He sat down heavily on the edge of his bed.

Paddy softened his tone. "What's the matter, Archie? First, you wanted to go back to Ireland, then when Uncle Morris offered to send you home, you refused. Now you are giving him such a hard time it is reflecting on me. It's making me very unhappy, stressed and miserable. What's going on, Brother?"

Archie looked down at the floor. He took a deep sigh, and when he looked back at Paddy, his expression had calmed. He reached under his pillow and retrieved a letter he had received some time ago.

Archie steadied himself. "The day before we left Ireland, I met this lovely lady. Kate Hart was her name. Do you remember that day I came home covered in mud?"

"Oh, yes!" Paddy cringed at the memory. He composed himself. "That was rather hard to forget," he smiled kindly at Archie hoping to build on this moment of restraint.

"Well, I had arranged to meet Kate again the next day, but of course, Uncle Morris and his inconsiderate machinations dragged us here, to London, so I couldn't. I couldn't even tell her why I didn't show up the next day."

Paddy played this over in his mind, trying to piece the puzzle together. What was immediately evident to him was that Archie had been bowled over by this fair lass, and had fallen in love at first sight. He could sympathise with him, he knew the feeling, but what he couldn't understand was Archie's almost all-out war with Morris over this.

"Archie," Paddy began, empathy evident in his voice, "It's not really Uncle Morris' fault; he had no idea. When he offered to send you back to Ireland, why didn't you go?"

"Kate was not from Dublin; she lived in Shannon. She was visiting Amanda's farm for just that week. I got this letter from Amanda, the farmer's daughter," Archie waved the envelope at Paddy, "to say thanks for helping her get the lamb out the hole, and in it, she said Kate's family had all left to go to America. There's no point of going back; I'll never see her again."

Paddy stared at his younger brother, sympathetically. He understood the situation now, and thought, perhaps armed with this information, he might be able to steer relations within the family back to some form of normality. How, exactly, he wasn't quite sure.

"I feel for you. I was in your position once," Paddy confessed. "I was madly in love with a beautiful lady, but sadly, she was not in love with me. It wasn't meant to be. I know how hard it can be. You're only 13, Archie, there is so much opportunity out there for you, and I know one day you will make the girl of your dreams very happy."

"There'll never be anyone like Kate," Archie mumbled.

"You don't know that Archie. Believe me you don't. Besides, you only knew her for what, ten minutes? Now please, for my sake, turn a new page. Start afresh and stop blaming Uncle Morris for this. We are young, and our lives are ahead of us. Come on, Brother," Paddy implored passionately.

Archie took a deep sigh and shuddered slightly, almost as if he was accepting his fate. "Alright, I will. I fear that Uncle Morris likes me less than I like him now."

"Yes," Paddy agreed, "that is quite obvious, and really, your fault entirely. But change your attitude, and things will get better. Will you do this for me?"

Archie nodded his agreement and stared at his shoes. The brothers sat in silence, contemplating the moment. Some truths had been aired at last, and there was a hint of change. A flutter of reconciliation settled in the room.

Suddenly, footsteps were pounding the wooden floor in the corridor, and then they stopped at their door. Paddy and Archie both looked up, finding it strange. They had not had visitors to their room as yet, but they could tell that someone was definitely standing outside their door.

There was a sharp knock and Paddy leapt to his feet, opening it promptly. Before him stood Morris.

"Uncle Morris!" Paddy greeted him in surprise.

"Paddy," Morris said through a frown. "Archie," he nodded a stern greeting.

Archie stood quickly. "Good evening, Uncle Morris."

Paddy stepped slightly aside. "We didn't expect to see you here. I'd offer you a seat, but our furniture is a little meagre."

"No need," Morris declined the invitation, "I'll be brief."

"Is everything alright?" Paddy asked anxiously. Morris had never been to their lodgings, so he had a strong feeling this visit could only bring ominous tidings.

"I have some important news for the two of you," Morris scowled. "Your Uncle David in Rhodesia urgently requires help down there. I have taken the liberty of offering your services to him. You are plainly not happy in London."

"Rhodesia?" Paddy exclaimed.

Morris looked Archie in the eye. "You would be doing your Uncle David a great service if you…"

"When?" Archie interrupted.

Morris caught himself. It was not the interruption that checked him, but Archie's beaming smile. It was the first time he had ever seen him smile.

"There's a ship leaving Southampton tomorrow night," Morris spoke with suspicion. "If you catch the train tomorrow morning, you will make it in time."

Paddy stammered briefly, "I, well, certainly, Uncle Morris, but what about the accounts and…"

"I'll deal with that. You need to get to Rhodesia as soon as possible."

"I must write to Father and explain…"

"Not necessary, Paddy, I have already telegrammed him. He gives his blessings. Here is some money for your tickets and meals, and some brief instructions on how to find your way. You will need to catch a train when you disembark from Cape Town."

"Thank you, Uncle Morris," Archie was grinning broadly. "We will do our best for you."

This comment took Morris by complete surprise. He looked at Archie with some confusion but just saw a smiling, genuinely happy face.

"Have you boys had dinner yet?" Morris inquired cautiously.

Paddy and Archie shook their heads.

"Hmm…," Morris looked at Archie, suspicion still evident on his face. "Alright, get your coats; there's a tavern on the corner. Join me for dinner. I'd like to talk with you both, and besides, I need to explain a few things about what to expect in Africa."

CHAPTER FOUR
Cape Town 1913

Paddy and Archie stood on the bow of the Union-Castle Line ship and watched as the flat top of the majestic Table Mountain loomed ever closer. They had never seen a mountain so high, and already a sense of adventure began to overwhelm them. As they drew even closer, the settlement at the foot of the mountain started to take on signs of life as microscopic movements were discernible.

Suddenly, both boys saw a puff of smoke eject from the top of a single, rather prominent hill beside the flat-topped mountain. A second or two later, the deep boom from a cannon thumped their eardrums.

"What was that?" Paddy exclaimed.

An elderly gentleman in a grey day suit next to Paddy smiled. "That was the *Noon Gun*. They fire it every day without fail at exactly twelve noon."

"Heavens," Archie put a protective hand on his chest, "I thought they were firing at us."

The stranger laughed heartily. "Not at all. They do it so that ships can adjust their timepieces to the exact time. It is primarily so that they can work out their exact location when they are out at sea. It is essential for a navigator to have an accurate time indicator when he is charting his course."

"My word," Paddy said with some relief, shaking his head in awe. "I was starting to wonder about the hostilities of Africa."

The passenger tousled Archie's hair and laughed. "First time to Africa, I hazard a guess?"

"Yes," both Archie and Paddy said through chuckles.

"You'll enjoy it there," he said, pointing towards the land. "Great continent, great people. Just stay away from the lions, buffaloes and elephants. Also, the snakes and spiders," he burst out laughing.

The brothers laughed along with the stranger, albeit nervously.

Disembarking from the ship, the boys began to make their way out of the harbour area. As they were about to exit, Paddy suddenly put his hand on Archie's shoulder and turned him to face the direction they had come. He waved a hand at the pier they had walked along.

"Do you remember Father telling us a story about our brothers buying old army boots for virtually nothing and selling them for a huge profit?"

"Yes," Archie nodded, looking a little curious. "What about it?"

"I wonder if this is the wharf where it all happened?"

They both stood in silence for a moment, watching the hustle and bustle as people of all races busied themselves with their daily routines.

"I suppose so," Archie nodded his acceptance of what likely was correct. "There are a lot of dark coloured people here. It is the first time I have ever seen a dark man."

"Me too," Paddy said vaguely. "I was told we would see darker skinned people, but this isn't what I expected. Look there," Paddy suddenly pointed to three short men walking hurriedly up a gangway. "They are neither dark nor light like you and me."

"Huh," Archie exclaimed as he watched the men disappear into an opening in the ship. "I think we have a lot to learn about this continent."

Leaving the docks, they went in search of the train station. On finding it, the task of working out departure times and destinations was a relatively straightforward affair. The train to Kimberley was departing within the hour, so with tickets purchased, and their luggage safely ensconced in their shared compartment, the boys excitedly explored the other carriages. They stopped in the dining car for a pot of tea served by a tall African man in a starched white uniform. It was a very novel thing to be served tea by such a well-presented and friendly gentleman, so much so that the boys couldn't wipe the grins off their faces. Archie, in particular, was fascinated by the dark skin-tone of the waiter and couldn't keep his eyes off the man's beaming face. The waiter's smile was infectious, and Archie would marvel later how white and perfect his teeth were, contrasting sharply against his ebony face.

For most of the passengers on the train that day, the journey was boring and monotonous, but for Paddy and Archie, it was an adventure of epic proportions. They constantly marvelled at the passing landscape, which every now and again, was punctuated by antelope that either stood grazing nonchalantly or went bounding off in a seemingly joyous and playful sprint. Some would spring with majestic leaps in the air, their backs arched high, before falling gracefully back to earth in slow motion.

There were bigger animals too, large antelope as big as cows, with intimidating, lethal-looking horns. They saw several creatures that looked like dogs, and animals as tall as trees, but not knowing what these species were, they simply soaked in the steam-driven safari.

What caught their attention in no small measure was the warmth of the African day, the clear blue sky dotted with pristine puffs of white cloud. The air was fresh and carried with it a myriad of new and exciting smells that tingled at their nostrils; not a hint of acrid coalsmoke in the air – that was unless the engine of the train was directly upwind of them.

As the day drew to a close, and the sky turned to mesmerising hues of blood-orange, mauve and indigo, the brothers proceeded to the dining car for a delicious meal. On returning to their compartment, their plush benches had miraculously turned into narrow beds, festooned with starched white sheets, a blanket and pillow.

"This country is incredible," Archie marvelled as he carefully caressed the soft blanket on his bed.

"This is all rather overwhelming," Paddy admitted. "I could

easily live on this train; what more could a man want?"

"When do we disembark?" Archie asked. He knew the answer but was in no hurry to get to Bulawayo.

"A few more days," Paddy replied as he looked out the window into the blackness. He cupped his hands around his eyes to hide the reflections. "Look at those stars!"

Archie pulled a window down, letting the outside air roar into their compartment. Both boys peered into the night sky in awe before a blast of coal smoke suddenly billowed into the room. Paddy quickly shut the window.

"I can't wait for tomorrow," Archie grinned. "Hopefully we break down and can spend a week on this train!"

"Yes," Paddy agreed through a contented sigh, "that would be a welcome delay."

Despite the excitement and wonder of their journey, the monotonous, soporific clunking of the wheels on the joints of the iron track caused the boys to fall asleep very quickly.

There were stops along the way, of course; four hours in Kimberley, and another six in Mafeking, and many others that were far briefer. Those were at sidings that seemed to be in the middle of nowhere and appeared to serve no discernible purpose whatsoever. Finally, after two and a half days of travelling, the boys arrived at the Bulawayo Railway Station where they disembarked. A quick enquiry with a pompous conductor as to the whereabouts of Langbourne Brothers had them walking down a road until they found Fife Street. A left turn, and a few blocks further they would find the business they were after.

On entering the Fife Street store, the brothers stood in fascination as they gawked at the vast variety of stock on the shelves and long display tables. The store was bustling with customers selecting goods, inspecting them and cashing up at the till. All the while, there was a low hum of conversation over the occasional clink of glass, a clang of metalware, or the sound of fabric being ripped from a bolt of material. For Paddy, these were the sounds of commerce.

"May I help you, Gentlemen?" A voice suddenly snapped the brothers out of their bewildered trance.

"Oh, good morning, Sir," Paddy looked up at the tall man beside him. "We are looking for Mr David Langbourne."

"He's not here at the moment I'm afraid, he is up at the warehouse on Abercorn Street, but Mr Louis Langbourne is here."

Paddy felt a wave of relief sweep over him. To hear his family name on the other side of the world, so far from home, had a certain comfort and reassuring tone to it. "Mr Louis Langbourne would be perfect. He is expecting us."

"One moment, I'll get him for you," the gentleman said as he strode off. He had a very welcoming smile, and this helped to relieve Paddy's mild anxiety.

A moment later, a tall man in a dark suit tailored perfectly to fit his lanky frame appeared from a doorway and walked over to the new arrivals. There was a rather blank and curious expression on his face.

Paddy whispered to Archie without looking at him. "That's Uncle Louis, I recognise him."

"I'm glad you do," Archie mumbled through a smile.

Louis stopped in front of the brothers. "Good morning, Gents. How may I be of assistance?"

"Good morning Uncle Louis," Paddy extended his hand. "I'm Paddy, and this is Archie."

"Goodness me!" Louis exclaimed and shook their hands vigorously. "I had forgotten you were due to arrive. I would never have recognised either of you."

"Well, I was about five or six years old when I last saw you, and Archie was just an infant."

"My word, how time has flown. Come on, let's go to my office and talk. Mr Loxton," Louis called to the tall store manager, "please do me a favour and send a message up to the warehouse. Ask Mr David to join us? Oh, and please arrange for a tray of tea to be brought to my office."

"Certainly, Mr Louis," Brian Loxton replied with a broad smile. "Right away."

"Thank you, Mr Loxton," Louis said as he ushered the young men into his office. "Tell me, how is the family? How is Father?"

Louis asked.

David joined the brothers barely 20 minutes later, sporting a smart grey day suit and his signature Derby hat, which he hung on a coat stand by the door. As he had visited Ireland only two years prior, he recognised the younger brothers immediately, and they likewise knew him. With broad smiles and hearty handshakes, Paddy and Archie felt very welcome in their new country.

"Welcome to Bulawayo," David grinned as he poured himself a cup of tea and took a seat. "We have plenty of work for you and lots to teach. Where shall we put them?" David directed his question at Louis.

Louis raised a curious eyebrow at Paddy. "I believe you are accounts orientated?"

"Yes," Paddy agreed, "I had a job as a bookkeeper in Ireland, and since working for Uncle Morris in London, I have also tended to the company books."

"Splendid," Louis smiled. "I think we will put you under Mrs Collier for the time being. She keeps our finances under strict control. You do know our secret *black rhino* code, do you not?"

"Yes, of course," Paddy concurred.

"What about you, Archie?" David asked the youngest of the two. "What have you been doing in London?"

"I have been working in the warehouse, Uncle David. I know the codes too."

"Excellent, then I think we can place you under Mr Michael Johnson on Abercorn Street. We have a huge and busy warehouse there," David looked pleased and took a sip of his tea.

"Actually," Archie said slowly, drawing everyone's attention, "I was hoping to move out of the warehouse and progress up the ranks a little. In London, I had been managing the Langbourne Coetzee warehouse quite competently for some time now."

David and Louis flashed a look at each other, then at Paddy, who looked slightly embarrassed.

"I think we will start you in the warehouse," David told Archie, firmly, "and then we will evaluate your performance. Things in Africa don't work the same way as they do in London. You see,

Morris uses different systems because his is not simply a warehouse, but a purchasing office as well. Here in Bulawayo, we are a wholesaler and retailer. Quite different, actually."

"I see," Archie looked uncertain.

"That goes for you too, Paddy," David placed his cup and saucer down and crossed one leg over the other. "You will find the books of accounts quite different too. You will need to adjust your methodology and thinking."

Louis cleared his throat and leant his elbows on his desk. "You two will have an advantage over most if you think about it. Nobody in Rhodesia has had the experience of a larger international purchasing office. Once you learn our ways, you will be very experienced in many sectors that others are not."

Paddy shot a look at his younger brother. "I never thought of it that way."

Archie's face lit up. "When can we start?"

Louis nodded knowingly at David, then beamed at the new arrivals. "First, let's sort out your living arrangements. Tomorrow your new adventure begins."

"The young one," Nguni's deep voice pulled David back from his thoughts. He shook his head sadly. "He sounds like a difficult child."

"Oh yes, he certainly was," David chuckled. "Archie gave us all a hard time, but none more so than Morris. Archie and Morris clashed at every opportunity, even when they wrote letters to each other."

"So," Nguni raised an eyebrow as he looked at David, "your two brothers are here, in Bulawayo?"

"They were here, for a time," David sighed. He picked up a little square of shortbread and knocked some loose crumbs off against the side of the plate. "Much has happened since then."

Nguni didn't respond; he sensed some sadness in David's voice.

"Archie and Paddy had been in Bulawayo for about a year, and then, in 1914, a big war started in Europe. They called it 'The Great War'. It spread to Africa, just north of Rhodesia, to a country called Tanganyika, which was known as German East Africa."

"I've heard of it," Nguni said forlornly and reached for his cup of tea.

"The British were worried that the Germans would advance into Rhodesia, so they sent people up there to fight. Archie was too young to fight; he was only 13 or 14, so he stayed here in Bulawayo, but Paddy was old enough, and he went to fight. He didn't want to, but he did."

"What happened to Boss Paddy?" Nguni asked tentatively.

"Eeee..." David trailed off, shaking his head sadly from side to side. "It was a brutal place, Tanganyika."

CHAPTER FIVE
Tanganyika 1914

The old military vehicle came to a noisy, grinding halt. Paddy looked across at a fellow soldier in the Southern Rhodesia Volunteers (SRV), a division of the British South Africa Police. A blade of sunlight cut through the canvas covering and into the dim interior of the rear of the vehicle; it was thick with dust drifting aimlessly through the fetid air. The man had a look of desperation and sadness, a look that Paddy was sure he exuded too. The motion sickness that was welling up from his stomach did not bode well either.

"De-bus!" a drill sergeant shouted abruptly from somewhere outside. All the soldiers mumbled indiscernible words, portraying their consummate relief at being freed from the uncomfortable transport and the arrival, at last, of this portion of the journey's end.

As the men tumbled out of the troop carriers, continuing to mutter surreptitiously, the sergeant's voice bellowed again: "Fall in! On the double. Move it, move it! You shower of rabble!"

Members of the SRV grumbled and groaned as they found their allotted positions within their squads, straightening their uniforms, stretching their necks or attending to wayward belts, webbing and uniforms. Paddy shouldered his rifle and joined his fellow volunteers holding his right arm rigid and straight out to his right side, touching the man to his right on the top of his left arm with a clenched fist. With his head turned to the right to ensure a perfectly straight line was forming, he felt the man to his left touch his left shoulder in the same way. A well-drilled outfit, everyone shuffled with tiny steps until the squad was in perfect formation before dropping their arms and coming to attention.

Once they were stood 'at ease,' the sergeant bellowed loudly enough for all three squads to hear him without difficulty. They were all told, in no uncertain terms, that they had travelled as far as mechanical transport could take them, and from this point on their journey would be on foot, mostly in single file. Almost all the assembled soldiers seemed relieved to hear this news, but an underlying premonition warned them that they should not be so pleased with this state of affairs.

They were proved right. Conditions from that moment on were about to become almost intolerable in every conceivable respect. On being dismissed, the ranks had one hour to prepare some nourishment, which consisted of cans of pressed meat, or bully beef as they sometimes called it, or, if they were so inclined, an opportunity to light a fire and boil some rice. With the time constraint, they saved rice for a rainy day. Little did the men know that almost every day for the next three months, it would be a rainy day, and copious amounts of it too.

After devouring his tin of bully beef, Paddy, like most of his unit, found some shade and lay in the long grass, lighting a cigarette before catching forty winks. The trek ahead of them that afternoon was uncertain, so whatever sleep was permitted, they took.

Right on cue, after the lapse of precisely one hour to the minute, they were ordered to form up in single file and start marching through the bush. The troops went north, following a narrow winding path, a vibrant orangey-red slash of bare soil that sliced through the dense green foliage. To Paddy, it looked like some celestial body had swung a razor-sharp blade through the jungle creating a stark gash in the thick green foliage of the forest. The wound it created almost appeared to bleed when it rained.

And rain it did. Incessantly. The raindrops were so large they slapped at the brim of the soldiers' hats with such force they could not hear a comrade in front or behind. They dejectedly trudged on, one foot in front of the other, slipping and recovering, wasting precious energy. On the morning of the third day, after only five hours of broken sleep, the sun came out, tantalisingly warm and comforting on the bare backs of the soldiers who hung their clothing on bushes and shrubs to dry. Then, barely an hour later, the rain came again, and the path once again started to bleed its earthly colour.

On the fifth day, the sun came out, heralding a heat that made the men boil under their wet clothing. This time the sun remained and made the soldiers wish for the rain again. The humidity was so dense that their clothes couldn't dry, wouldn't dry, and the health of the men rapidly began to deteriorate.

Rashes set in, painful boils erupted, and the skin between the men's toes began to split. In hours a small cut could turn into a festering wound, and that was just the beginning. Parasites were everywhere. Mosquitoes abounded in their millions, and with them came the dreaded malaria; ticks causing terrible fevers and hitherto unknown microscopic parasites that lived in still water and slowly infected a man's internal organs.

Streams became rivers, and the ground was oozing slippery mud. The bush was so thick it was difficult to see more than a few yards ahead at any given time. Scorpions, centipedes, snakes and spiders ruled the jungle; these were creatures that even a rifle and a .303 bullet could not offer any defence against. They attacked silently when one was not watching. A large mammal, such as an elephant, lion or leopard, was not a threat when a man held a modern rifle. Even a German soldier with a similar weapon could be engaged on a level playing field. Still, a snakebite, the sting of a scorpion, or an infected mosquito bite could do a lot of damage, and there seemed to be nothing available to prevent it.

There were other hidden foes that no soldier could prepare for, more dangerous and debilitating than a bullet – bacterial and viral diseases. If not carried by a mosquito, it was borne in the water and food. Dysentery, cholera, dehydration and fever could put a man in hospital, rendering him utterly useless in support of his comrades, and, if not summarily treated, death was sure to follow swiftly and inexorably. So it was that after only six days on the march, men began to drop from sickness, even before a rifle was fired in anger.

Finally, reconnaissance scouts reported a German outpost was half a day's walk ahead, and by that afternoon, the men experienced their first action of the Great War. Hospital tents at the rear base began to receive their first war-wounded, and the wounds were not minor.

Paddy had fallen ill in the early part of the skirmishes. Fighting for his life, and for his comrades and country, he kept up the assault while his guts turned to liquid, and his strength sapped away. Cracking hideously around his head, bullets came from hidden places, and Paddy fired blindly in the shooters' direction. Standing up to advance just two or three paces in the mud became a strength-sapping task. Disobeying his body, but obeying officers' commands, he pushed ahead.

After only three days of engaging German outposts, Paddy's strength gave out, and he became delirious. He was not the only one. He had been moved to the rear and hospitalised. As the war intensified, the infirm were desperately required at the battlefront. As soon as a man was reported to have turned the corner of recovery, he was prematurely ordered to leave the hospital before being well enough to take up arms at the front line once again. And so, Paddy obediently returned to the action, unwell, weak and feeling ghastly beyond imagination.

Courageously, the exhausted soldiers pushed on. The balance of the war eventually tipped, and the Germans began their retreat, fighting a very effective rear-guard action. The Rhodesian soldiers pursued the Germans over hills, down into valleys and through torrents of rivers. One evening, after an exhausting trek of over six miles, involving two skirmishes, Paddy and his men arrived in a fortified camp held by a South African contingent.

No sooner had all the men – muddied, sick and utterly fatigued – dumped their haversacks on the ground and undone their webbing, a message was handed to their leader with instructions to return to their base camp some 10 miles away, immediately.

Paddy groaned. "You have got to be joking, man," he

complained.

"What are they thinking?" another added.

"That's impossible!" someone else exclaimed from within the group of prostrate bodies lying in the mud. "It will be dark soon. We can't walk in the dark."

"Sorry lads," the sergeant sighed. "Orders are orders. Grab something to eat; we march in 30 minutes."

Despite intense complaints, the soldiers obeyed their orders and, within half an hour, melted into the bush in single file.

A fortnight later Paddy's platoon was operating like a well-oiled machine. They had begun to understand the terrain, the bush and some of the German military tactics. They advanced upon a heavily defended outpost held by the enemy and waited to launch their assault. Instructions were rapidly and silently distributed using hand signals. Just as the attack was readied, the German platoon saw them and attacked first – with a cannon.

Bullets began flying from a variety of machine guns, the green leaves of trees fluttering around the men as the bullets shred and tore vegetation from their branches while the enemy cannon reloaded. Paddy received a signal to join in the planned taking of a small hill to his right, with laid down cover. Crouching as low as he was able, Paddy headed off without hesitation. He had only run about 20 yards when a shell from the German cannon exploded against the trunk of a tree barely ten yards in front of him.

The percussion was so intense it stunned him, and he spun around, trying feverishly to regain his bearings, to keep his balance and re-orientate himself. Just then he felt what he was sure was a punch from a clenched fist in his hip, and he fell hard.

Pain seared through his body like a ferocious fire, and then the world went eerily silent and black.

"Where am I?" Paddy croaked as he opened his eyes.

He was in a tent, and a man with a stethoscope around his neck stood over him.

"Good morning, Soldier," the doctor smiled sympathetically. "Welcome back."

"What happened? Where am I?" Paddy looked about in total confusion. He tried to sit up, but the doctor gently put his hand on his chest and pushed him down. The pain that seared through his body convinced him that lying down was a better option after all.

"You were shot, in your hip. You were fortunate, but sadly, the bullet is still in there."

"The hip?" Paddy repeated, racking his brains to remember what happened before he blacked out. The pain began to flood his entire body.

"We don't have the facilities to perform an x-ray, and we won't risk any surgery out here. You will just have to grin and bear it until we can transport you to a proper hospital."

"This is a field hospital? Where am I?" Paddy asked, gingerly reaching up and rubbing his forehead. It pained him immensely, just doing that small movement.

"Yes, a field hospital near Kanga. Still in German East Africa, but away from the action. We will wait for you to stabilise before we attempt to transport you to Neu Langenberg. It's about an eight-hour drive from here, and the road is rough. They have an x-ray machine there, and will surgically remove the bullet."

"Do you have any pain killers, Doctor?" Paddy asked. "I'm in a lot of pain right now."

"Certainly. That much I can do for you. The good news is your fighting days are over."

"Well, that's one consolation," Paddy managed to grumble before he closed his eyes and slipped into unconsciousness again.

Paddy had been in the field hospital for four days before the doctor came with good news.

"Your progress has been encouraging, as far as the wound is concerned. I'm confident it will not affect your ability to walk."

"If they could take this bullet out of my back and relieve the pain, I might try and stand up," Paddy complained.

"I understand," the doctor said with some compassion in his voice. "I have managed to arrange an ambulance vehicle to get you to Neu Langenberg tomorrow. They will operate there."

"What I would do to be able to sit on a toilet again. This dysentery won't let up, and you have no idea…"

"I know, I know," the doctor sympathised. "I'm going to try a different drug."

"Thanks, Doctor," Paddy sighed. "I've had enough of this war."

"I'm sure we all have," the doctor grinned. "Here, I've found you that paper and pencil you were after." He handed Paddy a simple pad of coarse paper and a pencil that had been sharpened down to barely an inch.

"Thank you." Paddy took the items from him gingerly as a flash of pain seared through his abdomen. "I'm a little overdue with my correspondence. If I don't write to my Aunt Gerty, I fear my reunion with her will be worse than fighting in this swamp."

The doctor enjoyed his joke and laughed heartily. "If you'll excuse me, Private, I must tend to that Australian soldier they brought in yesterday. Tea will be here shortly, and," the doctor's face broke into a beaming smile, "the cook has made a delicious cake today."

Paddy smiled his appreciation, then closed his eyes. The exertion of talking to the doctor had exhausted him, but the thought of finally being able to put pencil to paper renewed some energy from deep within. Anything to take his mind off his predicament was a godsend. He opened his eyes and stared at the blank paper. Wriggling the tiny pencil in his fingers, he began to write.

Base Hospital
Kanga, GEA
Saturday 21st Oct. 1916

Dear Aunt Gerty,
    I must really apologise for not writing sooner, it's my own laziness entirely and my dislike for letter writing, and if I did not think somebody would be worrying over me, I really don't think I'd ever write. My last letter I wrote to you was at a place called Masai on the 26th August, but it was never posted owing to my going out on Patrol, and leaving the letter behind in my spare kit. Unfortunately my spare kit has not yet caught me up.
    I suppose you already know all about me being wounded, so that's not worth worrying about here. The pain at present is very little, but I'm going down to 'near Langenburg' to go under their X-ray and have the bullet extracted, so I'm pretty sure of getting some pain there. This wound (I think) won't interfere with my walking in any way, as soon as it's healed up, I'll be fit again, and at present I'm having the first decent holiday since I've been on this Campaign, and 'by Jove' I need it. I was absolutely run down. Just a week previous to me being wounded I had a very

bad dose of Fever and was laid up for six days, and it took it right out of me.

There is plenty of Fever just round this part of G.E.A.. It's one tremendous big 'Swamp' and we are camped in about the centre. The heat both during day & night is oppressive. Worst I've yet been in, and as for the mosquitoes, they're a real treat. When on Patrol one night I sat under a tree with one blanket over my knees all night playing with the mosquitoes. There are also plenty of Tsetse & Horse Fly around here and they sting in the day time. It's a fine country. The rains will be on shortly here, and I don't envy our chaps in the least. In some parts of this swampy country the surface of the land is under water (about 2 feet) from the middle of the rainy season till long after the rains are over, and the natives all travel or visit in canoes. There are plenty of big rivers, some of them 10-12 feet deep in the centre and we have to cross in punts. Crocs and buck here in abundance. Also elephant and buffalo.

I suppose you heard all about the (B.S.A.P's & S.R.V's) 6 day's fighting amongst the Iringa Mountains. Well, we had a real rough time there. The Germans fought a 'Rear Guard Action' that is just enough men to hold us up during the day and running away every night, and holding us up again next day. This went on for six days & nights and for three of those nights running I had no sleep. First night we dug in, next day we scraped them, 2nd night we followed them up through real African Jungle, walking about 1 mile per hour. Rested 2nd day. Tried to cut them off 3rd night. Fought all day 3rd day and on Picquet 4th night, when I got 4 hours sleep. Not bad. For two solid weeks I never as much as washed my hands, so you can imagine the state we were in. Food, we had very little, and excitement more than is good for one's health. I'm sorry to say I did not enjoy myself then, and wished the Germans anywhere but where they were. One day they ran leaving a lot of kit behind. No, we poor B. Coy did not get the loot, but we got the pleasure of running after them. No exaggeration, running and plenty of bullets whizzing around. Lovely, and when we had driven the Germans from those hills and followed them down 'B' Coy were detailed to go back west for the Big Guns which were 20 miles away and our Capt. Hendries picked out all the men he thought were fit enough to go, and yours truly was one. Fed up. Fed up was not the word, but like a penny hero back we went, and caught the guns up about 15 miles back, and started off for our camp. Work. I never worked so hard in my life. We were pulling the guns up these tremendous mountains, and holding them back when they were going down. From 7am to 6pm that day we travelled 6 miles and

when we arrived in camp a note was awaiting us that we (the Spent), had to come back to camp immediately, and we did, arriving there at 10:30pm and leaving the following day at 6am. Swear. I never stopped swearing. Nobody could talk to me I was so disgusted.
(PS: excuse scribbling and mistakes as I can't sit up)
When I even think of it now I get wild, poor Paddy. I'm in every dammed thing, they seem to think I'm unbeatable but now I've got a rest, and I'm not in the least bit sorry. I needed it, and don't mind admitting so.

    As for the war here, I have not the slightest idea when it's going to be over, and I should not be surprised if it goes halfway through the rainy season.

    Best love to you all and hoping that this letter will reach you in the best of health and also family.
Your loving nephew
Paddy

Ptk Paddy Langbourne 236
B.Coy   S R V

A look of horror was frozen on Nguni's face as he sat in silence, staring at David.

"That fighting was terrible," Nguni shook his head in disbelief. "Did Boss Paddy get better?"

David's shoulders slumped as he stared into the garden. "Yes and no. The operation was successful, and he walked with a limp, but the bullet was not the biggest problem."

"How is that so?" Nguni looked confused.

"It was the disease that was the worst. It never left Paddy. When he returned to Bulawayo, he never fought in a war again. He worked for Langbourne Brothers and did a tremendous job, but he was a sick man. He never complained, but you could tell. He was the only one of us brothers that never argued with Morris, or any of us come to think of it."

Nguni grunted and shook his head again.

"Mind you," David lightened up as he reached for his cup, "we all would argue with Morris at one time or another, but we were brothers, and we respected each other as such. Our arguments wouldn't go on for too long. I think Louis' argument was the longest," David laughed.

"Boss Rooi?" Nguni said in surprise. "But I remember him being a very nice man, I did not think he would fight with Boss Morris."

"Oh no," David chuckled, "it was not a fight, more of an argument that Louis refused to lose. It went on for a very long time, and he won the argument for a change."

"Ghaw!" Nguni exclaimed. "Tell me how that is so."

CHAPTER SIX
London 1926

Louis sighed in exasperation. "Morris, it would be an enormous mistake if we pulled out of Samuel Cohen's business. You can't agree to lend someone money and then suddenly pull out for no good reason when Samuel calls for it. You certainly can't tell me to agree to a deal I negotiated in good faith and then put me in the firing line when you pull the rug out from under everyone."

"There is a good reason to pull out, and that is because of what happened after I agreed to the deal. Cohen is now locating his store on the wrong side of Eloff Street. That was not the understanding," Morris waved the back of his hand at Louis in disgust. "That's madness! It's too risky; he will fail. I don't like the risks, and we are pulling out!" Morris tossed his pen on the table in an act of defiance.

"David?" Louis looked at his older brother in desperation.

The four brothers sat in Morris' study, an ostentatious room in his home on Castletown Road. A threatening cloud hung over the mens' heads as they carefully negotiated the familiar minefield of aggression that Morris threw at them whenever they needed to discuss a difference in business policies.

Shooting a glance at Harry, David leant forward in his chair to emphasise what he was about to say. "You might be right, Morris, it may be a little too risky, and yes, I agree that the money is substantial. But because you initially agreed, and some time ago at that, Louis shook hands on the deal with Cohen on our family's honour. It would be wrong to go back on a commitment just because you suddenly feel uncomfortable with it."

"That's before you told me they are occupying the premises of the old Store Brothers, on the corner of Eloff and President Streets. Why am I upset?" Morris theatrically threw his hands up in the air, "I'll tell you why, because Store Brothers have gone bankrupt! The building is too big, the rent's too high, and above all, nobody in Johannesburg shops on that side of the street. No, I have good reason to pull out. Additionally, there was no contract signed between us," Morris argued.

"There is no logical reason why people would not cross a road to buy what they want. Besides, there was a handshake," David immediately countered, concern seeping into his voice, "so it is also our business reputation at stake; our honour."

"*My* honour," Louis added, thumping his index finger on his chest.

"Morris," Harry quietly entered the conversation, "Samuel Cohen needs our help. He will succeed; we are quite sure of that. I have had a good look at the site. It's not that bad, really. Talk of the town says nobody shops on that side of the road, but I have to disagree. I stood on the corner for two hours, and I found that not to be the case. If we pull out, he will be unfunded and fail and lose a lot of money. He has fully committed himself, primarily because of Langbourne Brothers' promise to finance him. I don't want to be blamed for someone else's financial demise, especially because we listened to town gossip."

"In any case," Louis added, "we have a written guarantee that, if he fails, we will be the first company to be repaid, in full, before any other creditor. He is an honourable man, and that stands for something, does it not?"

Morris looked up at the ceiling as if asking for divine help. He could already see that he was going to lose this particular argument against his brothers. "That was before he took over the Store Brothers' lease. And don't forget, Cohen went into competition with us in Kimberley. He became our enemy. Isn't he supposed to be our friend?"

"Yes, he is a friend, and in this venture, he is not a competitor; it is not a wholesale operation but a retail store," Louis objected. "Furthermore, he has agreed to buy 50% of his stock from us. It is a win-win situation all round; extra sales for us *and* interest on the loan."

Morris paused, directing his glare at Louis. "Alright," he suddenly capitulated, "I'll agree to the loan, on the strict proviso that one of us brothers sit on their Board of Directors, and be present at every directors' meeting."

Morris' three younger brothers leaned back in their seats, relief evident in their postures. It was always challenging, and very rare, to swing Morris across to their way of reasoning.

"Samuel will agree to that," Louis nodded his acceptance to his brother's demand. "I'll make sure he does."

"One more thing," Morris continued, "if a Langbourne can't sit on a board meeting, then that meeting does not take place. Cohen must be absolutely clear on that. Understood?"

"Understood, Brother," Louis nodded carefully.

"One of us needs to sit on the Board to protect our money. When the loan is paid back in full, with interest, we shake hands and walk away." Morris sat back and looked out the window. Frustration clouded his face. "What are they going to call this... this shop?" Morris asked, a little too casually.

"It's not a shop, but a departmental store modelled on a new concept in America, with a centre island where the cashiers are situated," Louis explained to his brother for the umpteenth time. "Never been seen before in Africa. They are calling it OK Bazaars."

"What? OK Bazaars!" Morris ranted. "What kind of name is that? Who thought that stupid name up, Cohen or Miller? How ridiculous."

"I think it was Miller's wife," Louis ventured.

"What was she thinking?" Morris threw his hands in the air again. "Did Miller say *'Oh, we need to think up a name for this shop?'* and his wife said *'Okay'*?"

Louis chuckled. "I believe that's just about exactly how it happened."

"Heaven help us," Morris sighed heavily and rolled his eyes. "That is the very reason I insist one of us sits in on every one of their board meetings. Heaven help us."

CHAPTER SEVEN
Johannesburg 1927

Louis stood on Eloff Street, looking across the busy roadway at the multi-storied structure. It was magnificent; four floors high with dozens of massive Grecian pillars gracing the length and breadth of the entire building. Between each pillar, and on every floor, were ornate balconies. The ground-floor windows were pasted over with old sheets of newspaper, effectively impeding any curious bystanders' view of the mysterious activities inside. However, there was not a soul on the pavement at this particular time.

Louis smiled; it was not that long ago that he remembered Eloff Street being a quiet road, affording sedate passage to the upper class of Johannesburg in horse-drawn coaches. Now, in a short space of time, the street accommodated some noisy automobiles that bumbled about at dangerous, though somewhat convenient speeds with loud modern engines fuelled by a petroleum product. As he watched one of these automobiles splutter past him, annoyingly close to a rickety buggy, Louis knew horse-drawn vehicles would soon disappear from the streets entirely; progress seemed unstoppable.

Gracing the street at regular intervals were trees that grew from carefully constructed circular gaps in the concreted pavements. They were young, taller than a man, yet a little short of the awnings that overhung the walkways of the brick and stone buildings, which had rapidly sprung up in the centre of Johannesburg.

Waiting for a chunky British-made vehicle to pass, Louis stepped off the pavement and strode over to the wood-and-glass door of the old Store Brothers building. He held a cane in his right hand that he swung in time to his stride. It was not that he needed a cane to walk; far from it. Louis was in reasonably good health, but it gave him an air of importance, and he liked that. It became his hallmark feature, almost his fashion, or 'trademark', in much the same way as Harry wore suspenders instead of a belt, and David always sported a Derby hat.

Knocking hard on one of the wooden door frames with the handle of his cane Louis waited for a response. He didn't have to wait long; he heard a chain rattle, and the door swung open. A short man with a fierce scowl guarded the entrance, a darkened interior sulked behind him.

"Good morning Samuel," Louis greeted the gentleman.

Samuel Cohen beamed profusely when he recognised the tallest of the Langbourne brothers.

"Louis Langbourne!" Samuel exclaimed, extending his hand in greeting. "Come on in. Have you come to check on our progress?"

"Indeed," Louis grinned as he entered the cavernous interior. "You've been busy it seems. Show me around."

Samuel locked the door behind them before excitedly taking Louis for a walk about the showroom. Gesticulating freely, and his voice traversing several octaves, he was obviously excited, and proud to have the opportunity to show off his new venture. To Louis, it was as expected, possibly better. There was a tremendous amount of stock that had been carefully displayed in a departmentalised fashion, but more curiously, a large rectangular shaped counter in the centre of the store. Tellers would stand inside the fortress, which boasted four cash registers to conduct sales.

Louis tapped his knuckles on the countertop. "Interesting, but how do your cashiers get in and out of this... counter?"

Samuel lifted a flap beside Louis that revealed craftily hidden hinges. "Through this," he grinned. "Michael Miller got the idea of a central cashiers' station when he was in New York, in America."

"My concern," Louis turned to face the businessman square on, "is that customers could easily walk out the door without paying because the cashiers will be too busy to notice."

"Fear not, Mr Langbourne," Samuel said with a flourish, "we will have assistants constantly monitoring the doors. In fact, their primary station is at the door, so they can greet the customer as merrily as possible when they arrive, offering assistance, and then bid them a farewell as they leave. It's all about customer service, making them feel welcome when they arrive and that they need to come back when they leave. It is a big thing now, customer service. But as you can see from the layout of the store, assistance is hardly a necessity as OK Bazaars is, in reality, a cash-and-carry store. Customers help themselves."

"But what if you have an influx of customers all at one time, surely..."

Samuel quickly cut Louis off with the wave of a dismissive hand. "That would be a very rare occurrence, Mr Louis. Sadly, projections are that it will take at least a year before we would be lucky enough to face that dilemma, and when we do, we will increase our staff complement to suit. Perhaps on the opening day, and through the opening week, people will be curious to see what innovations we are bringing to Johannesburg. Still, Miller believes we will only get to optimum sales in one year. He anticipates we will become profitable in three years."

Louis looked about him with an intense frown. Something bothered him. "Samuel, I don't want to sound pessimistic, but you have an awful lot of stock here. Certainly, enough to keep you fully supplied for two or three years. It can't be good for your cash flow. You are a retail store, not a storage facility."

"Over 50% of this merchandise came from your warehouse, so you should be pleased with my purchases," Samuel countered pleasantly.

"On credit," Louis scowled.

"Well, yes," Samuel reluctantly agreed, shrugging his shoulders in embarrassment. "That is true, and for which we are eternally grateful. If it eases your mind, I have sent a telegram to Miller in America asking him to stop buying until I report on how sales are going."

"Miller is still buying stock?" Louis raised his eyebrows in surprise. "Please, Samuel, you need to control your spending."

"I know, I know!" Samuel held up his hands to make his point. "That is why I told him to stop. We will open on Monday, four days from now. Let us gauge how Johannesburg treats us then."

"Alright," Louis said slowly, "I'll be here on Monday to see for myself. Morris has requested a report on your opening day."

Louis could see a faint ripple of fear cross Samuel's face when Morris' name surfaced. He could understand why. Samuel Cohen and Michael Miller had had three meetings with Morris in London, and after each encounter they had left the building in a cold sweat. Louis smiled inwardly as he recounted the last meeting. Morris could be very blunt, sarcastic and even condescending at times, and on that day, he had been on top form.

Samuel quickly took Louis by the elbow to distract them both. "Come with me, Mr Langbourne. I want to show you something on the top floor. We have a Tea Lounge for our customers. You will love it."

After a hearty breakfast on the veranda, Louis gathered his coat by the front door and looked himself over in the mirror. He thought he looked quite dapper in his trendy attire, and fussily straightened his tie, which really didn't need any adjustment at all.

"Leah? Herbert?" Louis called for his family, "we need to leave now. Hurry up; it's an important day in Johannesburg."

Leah, his lovely wife of 21 years, appeared gracefully from one of the bedrooms, dressed in a dark grey dress that draped loosely around her ankles. An elegant pair of narrow patent leather shoes peeked from under the generous folds.

Leah smiled lovingly at her husband. "What time will Mr Cohen open his doors?"

"Nine o'clock precisely, but I want to be there at least half an hour before to look around, and then to count how many people come in during the first hour. Besides, it will give you a chance to look at the merchandise before the public has access to it. Herbert, where are you? We will be late!"

"Here, Father," Herbert called as he trotted down the passage, still munching on a piece of toast.

Herbert was 20 years old, and unlike his father, was not tall. It was only Louis who seemed to buck against that trend, and hence his family codename, 'Giraffe'.

"Good show, shake a leg," Louis bustled his family out the door. "Herbert, I want you to watch everything that Mr Cohen does this morning. It is an excellent opportunity for you to learn how a new business opens its doors on the first day."

Louis was not going to let the opportunity pass by for his son to benefit from such a valuable commercial lesson as the opening of Johannesburg's newest store. Over the weekend, Louis had seen a large advertisement in the newspaper pronouncing the grand opening of OK Bazaars and the bargains on offer. He had to admit the advertisement was catchy and grinned to himself at Samuel's gall at announcing the latest, best and 'never-to-be-missed' grand opening with very Americanised terminology. Louis just hoped it would work; he would like to report back to Morris that the store got off to a good start. After all, this was personal – his judgement was at stake.

The drive from Louis' home in the suburbs to Eloff Street was a mere 20 minutes. Bundling Leah and Herbert into his 1923 black and maroon automobile, Louis grated the gears and took off for the centre of Johannesburg. The vehicle purred gently as it rattled along the rough suburban roads. On approaching Eloff Street, the traffic became so congested that progress was slower than walking speed.

"This is madness," Louis grumbled in frustration. "We never had this problem when we had horse drawn carts and buggies. What is this world coming too?"

"An accident up ahead, perhaps?" Leah suggested.

"We only have about half a mile to get there and we will be late for the opening. Then we have to look for a parking space," Louis sighed in resignation.

"Park over there," Leah suddenly pointed off to her left. "There's a parking space there, and we can walk the rest of the way."

"Are you sure?"

"Yes, it's not far. Quickly before someone else takes that parking space."

Louis pulled heavily at the steering wheel and manoeuvred his vehicle to a stop. Alighting, Louis, Leah and Herbert strode off for Eloff Street, and the closer they got to their destination, the worse the traffic problem became. Weaving between the stationary vehicles, Louis noticed the delay was caused, not by an accident, but rather by a throng of people, standing and waiting – somewhat impatiently.

The crowd became denser, slowing his progress until he was forced to stop. He was only one block from the old Store Brothers building and could see a gigantic red sign claiming the site of 'OK Bazaars'. Louis guessed Samuel had mounted that sign the previous night. His first concern was that it detracted from the look and feel of Eloff Street, a classy part of town. He feared someone from one of the hundreds of committees that existed in Johannesburg, or a council member, would vehemently protest the affront the sign was causing the character of the street.

Louis was standing next to a beautiful lady; she didn't appear to be involved in conversation with anyone. He leaned close to her ear.

"Excuse me, Madam," Louis politely interrupted her musings as Herbert jostled against his shoulder, "do you know why there is such a crowd here this morning?"

"Of course," she smiled sweetly, "we are all waiting for the 'OK Bazaars' to open its doors. Have you not read about it in the papers?"

A look of both astonishment and horror crossed Louis' face as he stared out at the mass of people blocking the main thoroughfare of Johannesburg. There were hundreds upon hundreds of people standing patiently on the street and pavements. Not a car was visible as the road was so congested with pedestrians.

Louis turned again to the lady, a look of confusion replacing his shock. "Why is it…? Why do you…? What is so special about the opening of this store?" he stuttered.

"Well," the young lady smiled broadly, "according to the

newspapers, and all the gossip around town, this store is based on an American concept, with exciting new things to buy, and at unbelievably cheap prices. I've heard," she shielded her mouth with the back of her hand and dropped her voice to a whisper, "that all the retailers in Johannesburg and Pretoria are petrified of this store."

"Petrified?" Louis asked, somewhat bemused.

"My father said he has seen trucks loaded with goodies arriving for two weeks. Even the railway station has been abuzz. I have a friend who works at the station, and she said crates have been arriving for the OK Bazaars for weeks. I'm not going to miss my bargain today!"

"Thank you," Louis politely tipped his hat as he turned to leave. "Good luck, I hope you manage to find a worthy bargain."

Louis surveyed the scene for a moment and a hollow sickening feeling settled in his stomach. "Leah, I'm going to find the rear door. Will you wait here and come in when they open the doors?"

"Certainly, darling. I'll see you inside later."

"Herbert, follow me," Louis demanded as he turned to his right.

Louis pushed his way through the crowd, begging their pardon, excusing himself, and offering several apologies as he inadvertently stood on toes. As he turned down a side street, the mass of humanity thinned, and finally ended when he turned into the alleyway behind Samuel's store. With Herbert grinning broadly behind him, Louis knocked sharply on the delivery door with his cane.

A moment later, Samuel opened the door, a look of sheer terror cemented firmly on his face.

"Have you seen...?" Louis began in earnest.

"Come in, come in!" Samuel almost pulled Louis inside. Herbert duly followed.

"They're all waiting for you to open your doors, Samuel," Louis hissed. "What have you done?"

"I'm scared," Samuel Cohen confessed. Despite the cool of the morning, he had a sheen of sweat on his brow. "I've called the police. These people will mob my shop. How can I control a crowd like that? We can't open today; we can't."

"What did you say in your advertisement?" Louis demanded as he walked from the storeroom to the central part of the store, stopping in his tracks as he saw the sea of faces in the windows; the newspaper covering had been removed, and the windows thoroughly cleaned. Cupped hands accompanied hundreds of faces behind the clear glass as the would-be customers peered anxiously into the shop. The sight was like a jolt of electricity, and Louis backtracked rapidly, bumping into Samuel, who in turn knocked Herbert clean off his feet.

Samuel helped Herbert up and dusted him off with his open hand, apologising profusely. "I used the suggestions of Miller," Samuel turned back to Louis, "the terminology the Americans use. You've read the advertisements, haven't you?"

"Yes, they were good, but not *that* good." Louis snapped as he again poked his head around the door in disbelief. "I can't believe this."

Just then there was another knock on the rear door.

"That must be the police," Samuel sounded relieved as he rushed for the door.

The sergeant, a tall and imposing man with a manicured moustache, entered the storeroom with six other uniformed police officers and spoke to Samuel and Louis in low tones. He seemed rather condescending, appearing annoyed that the debacle on the main street of Johannesburg was causing a dreadful inconvenience to not only the police force but to the entire city of Johannesburg. The officer appeared flustered, bemused and overwhelmed all at the same time by the situation, especially after he poked his nose around the corner and saw the sea of faces on the other side of the window. A strange human hum filtered into the showroom, adding an ominous air to the interior.

It became clear to Louis that the sergeant probably lacked training in keeping order in large gatherings; it had not been a common problem in the past, but certainly would be essential on this day. Realising the situation was dire, Louis took control as best he could and made suggestions, that he hoped would be taken as instructions.

Three police officers were posted at the front door, with orders to allow customers into the store in single file. When Samuel deemed the store was at capacity, he would signal them to close the doors and from that time on only permit as many people in as those that left. Another two police officers were stationed at the centre counter, near the tills, to maintain a civil order at the checkouts. The sergeant and the remainder of his men exited the rear doors and made their way to the front of the new store. Their instructions were to form the crowd into an organised queue that wrapped around the block, and thus clear the street so traffic could flow again. At this moment, the crowd was simply a disorganised mob.

Giving a long sigh, and forcing a nervous smile, Samuel strode through the empty store towards the main door. He nodded pleasantly to the staff he passed, offering token words of encouragement as he went. The low hum from outside changed its tone ominously as Samuel placed his hand on the door handle. Louis was sure he saw his partner take a deep breath. Samuel opened the doors to the new OK Bazaars at nine o'clock that morning and allowed a very excited mob of Johannesburg's citizens to stream in and flood his new venture. Louis and Herbert stood on upturned wooden crates in a far back corner of the store and observed.

At a quarter past two that afternoon, the flustered image of the shopkeeper in his shirtsleeves was seen exiting the rear door of OK Bazaars and running, post-haste, for the Post Office. He was not wearing a jacket, and the tail of his untucked shirt flapped gaily in the wind. Barely five minutes later the man returned as quickly as he had left and hurriedly let himself back into the store. Samuel Cohen had sent an urgent telegram to his partner, Michael Miller in America, and it contained only three words; *'BUY LIKE HELL'*.

It was reported in the papers the next day that an opening this grand had never been witnessed before, and that the likes of it would probably never be seen in the city of Johannesburg again.

Nguni nodded his approval at David's story. "So, did Boss Samuel pay the money back to Boss Morris?"

David reclined in his chair with a coy smile. "Yes. It took several years, and Louis sat in on many of their board meetings. Even some of my sons, at one time or another, attended their meetings. They were excellent lessons for my sons. When Samuel was ready, he paid us back all the money he had borrowed, we shook hands, and our deal with him ended.

"It was a good deal, and the first we ever did without a written contract. We gave our word and shook hands at the beginning and the end. Throughout my life, loyalty and honour have always been an essential part of our family's principals."

The two old friends allowed the silence to settle on them as they stared quietly into the distance and reminisced.

"Drink some tea, Nguni," David suddenly said as he reached for his cup.

Again, the men went quiet as they slurped noisily at their sickly sweet tea. Usually, David would drink his tea quietly and politely, but when he was in the bush with Nguni, social etiquette was not necessary. Besides, the noisy slurping of the hot beverage seemed to give the tea more flavour. It showed appreciation and enjoyment, and it was more gratifying to the tongue.

Nguni put his mug down carefully. "That was a good story," Nguni sounded pleased.

"Yes." David smiled contentedly as he likewise returned his cup to the table, "Louis wanted to buy shares in OK Bazars for our company," David continued. "Samuel offered Morris half the shares in the business after he paid back the loan, but Morris was not interested. We all tried to convince Morris to buy these shares, but he would have none of it. Much to Louis' dismay, Morris had other ideas and wanted the money for other businesses.

"Perhaps it was a mistake; perhaps Morris should have bought shares in the business because Cohen and Miller were brilliant people, and they made OK Bazaars an incredibly successful business. It still is a big business."

"I know it. We have seen the OK Bazaars in Port Elizabeth."

David smiled at this statement. "Anyhow, Morris is the chief of our family, and we could not convince him."

"Did Boss Morris not like Boss Rooi?" Nguni asked.

"Oh, yes. Just because they would argue it did not mean they didn't like each other. Quite the opposite, Morris is very close to all the brothers, as we are to him. Archie was simply problematic. He gave us all a difficult time, but particularly Morris. We had to find a way to fix this problem with Archie; it was becoming unbearable," David frowned.

"How did you fix that?" Nguni cocked an inquisitive eyebrow.

David chuckled as he leant back in his chair. "We found a way."

CHAPTER EIGHT
Bulawayo 1928

It had been ten years since the Great War had ended. Life in Rhodesia was good, and business prosperous. Paddy recovered from his ordeal in German East Africa, which later became known as Tanganyika, and threw himself into the Langbourne business with great enthusiasm. However, he was constantly beset by bouts of nausea, illness and recurrent malaria, which regularly laid him up for several days at a time, much to his irritation.

Archie, meanwhile, also threw himself into the business with cracking zest and exuberance. David and his brothers were pleased with Archie's performance, but it came at a cost. Boardroom meetings were fraught with arguments, opinions, counter arguments and generally disruptive discussions. Many meetings were deliberately held at times the brothers knew Archie would not be available to attend.

Despite Archie's dedication to work, he also enjoyed socialising, especially with the fairer sex, and made sure he capitalised on such engagements whenever he could. Owing to his handsome looks, he was quite successful with the single ladies of Bulawayo, and developed the reputation of being a 'ladies' man'. It did not concern him one iota; in fact, he relished the salutation.

After a week of particularly stormy confrontations between Harry and Archie, David conspired with Paddy to send Archie to Johannesburg to spend a week under Louis' supervision at the

Langbourne Coetzee warehouse.

"I think we just need a break from him," David told Paddy, exasperated.

"I agree, David," Paddy smiled softly. "He has been a little cantankerous this last week."

"What is it with Archie? He always thinks he knows best. I think he is worse than Morris, and that's saying something," David scratched his head.

"He's young, and he's stubborn. Some of his suggestions are good; we have to admit that," Paddy defended his younger brother.

"Yes, they are, but his suggestions involve spending a lot of company money. I don't think he realises what budget constraints Morris puts on us."

"True," Paddy agreed. "I'll talk to him about that again, but meanwhile I'll tell him his presence is required in the Johannesburg office for a week."

"Thank you, Paddy," David smiled and gave his young brother a grateful squeeze on the shoulder.

"I don't think he will be too happy about it; he is looking forward to taking Reverend Fall's daughter out for dinner tomorrow night."

"Oh heaven's above," David looked distraught, "not *'our'* Reverend Fall?"

"Yes," Paddy grinned.

David shook his head in despair. "We really should create a policy that our staff, Archie in particular, should never fraternise with our customers' daughters. The last disgruntled father who came in here was too much for me to bear. Please, get Archie on that train tonight."

Paddy laughed heartily. "Will do, David."

Archie gathered his tweed coat, Fedora hat and duffle bag before stepping off the train onto the Johannesburg platform. Once the steam and passengers had cleared, he found himself to be the last man standing.

"Just perfect, nobody here to greet me," Archie thought to himself. Nudging his hat to a more rakish angle, he strode off to find the

Langbourne Coetzee premises, where, he assumed and hoped, Louis would be waiting to greet him.

The building was not difficult to find, and a man at the entrance invited Archie to take a seat while he informed Mr Louis that he had a visitor. Louis wasted no time in coming through to greet Archie with a hearty handshake.

"Welcome to Johannesburg, Archie. Your first time?"

"Hello, Uncle Louis," Archie returned the warm greeting. "Indeed, my first time here. It's a big town."

"A city," Louis corrected him. "Come through and put your things down in my office. You have arrived just in time for lunch. We will be dining at the Johannesburg Club with Danie Coetzee and some of our customers. Have you met Mr Coetzee yet?"

"No," Archie replied, somewhat bewildered by the speed at which his day was suddenly progressing. "We have corresponded, but never met in person."

"Good. Well, you will meet him shortly. You know he is a silent partner of our business? Let's go, or we shall be late."

"Yes, err, no..." Archie tried to respond but gave up as they marched out the door. He struggled to keep pace with Louis' lengthy strides.

Lunch at the Johannesburg Club was a grand affair, and Archie feared he was a little underdressed. However, as he was wearing a jacket and tie, along with the fact that Louis didn't seem perturbed by his attire, he put the concern behind him.

Danie Coetzee was much taller than Archie. He had a natural ability to ooze authority, and unintentionally demanded absolute respect, which Archie was surprisingly quick to give. Danie gave the impression that he should be feared, but his gentle and kind nature seemed to draw people to him. Louis appeared quite at ease in Danie's company, and Archie's respect for Louis grew.

"Aah... Here he is," Louis motioned with his whiskey glass to a rotund man who entered the club.

"My apologies, gentlemen," the man said as he mopped his brow with a handkerchief in one hand while he shook hands with Louis and Danie with his free hand. "Traffic is ghastly outside."

"No apologies necessary, Mr Hart," Louis smiled easily. "We too have just arrived. My young brother," Louis turned to Archie, "Archie Langbourne. Archie, meet Mr Hart, an important customer of Langbourne Brothers."

"How do you do, Sir," Archie shook the big man's hand.

"Likewise, Mr Archie," John Hart returned the greeting with a solid handshake that completely smothered Archie's thin hand.

Louis gripped Archie on his shoulder to stress what he was saying. "Mr Hart manufactures and imports cooking utensils. He has the largest factory of its kind in the southern hemisphere, and, I am pleased to say, we are one of his biggest customers. When you visit any hotel in Bulawayo, chances are the crockery and cutlery you eat off came from Mr Hart's establishment."

"And I value the Langbourne business," John Hart's entire body wobbled when he laughed.

Lunch was a decadent affair, and Archie sat mostly in silence, absorbing the conversation that bounced between the three older men at the round table.

"I'm very pleased with the performance of world economies throughout the 1920s, especially here in Africa," Mr Hart commented as he placed his knife and fork together, having enjoyed his rather large portion of steak immensely. "I believe it may be time for me to venture into a new industry."

Danie carefully laid his cutlery down and dabbed at his lips with a pristine white serviette. "I would advise some measure of caution," Danie said softly, as was his way, immediately drawing everyone's attention.

"Why so?" Mr Hart stifled a burp.

Archie noticed a concerned crease appear on Louis' forehead, and quickly became more interested in the unfolding conversation.

"Well," Danie continued as he sat straight in his chair, "we have seen many years of prosperity since the Great War, and although I cannot put a finger on the reasons for my concerns, I am not entirely sure this can go on forever. There will have to be a downturn somewhere along the way. I urge you, Louis," Danie suddenly directed his attention to his friend, "to also consider pulling your horns in, as it were. For now, anyway."

There was absolute quiet at their table as Danie's warning was digested. Archie's eyes darted between his luncheon companions.

"Well," Louis broke the brief pause, "this is not something I would have considered, and certainly the first time I have heard such concerns. I am only accustomed to improving business, not slowing down. Have you discussed this with Morris yet?"

"Not in detail, but I have touched on the matter," Danie said as he carefully folded his serviette and gently placed it on the table. "As I said, I have no solid basis for this opinion. It is simply my gut feel. Not something I should bother your brother with just at the moment, simply alert him to my sentiments."

Mr Hart shifted his bulky weight uncomfortably. "Although I regard what you say with much respect, I believe we should make hay while the sun shines, and it is certainly shining right now," he chuckled at his joke.

"That it is," Danie said pleasantly, nodding his head in agreement with Mr Hart's statement. "Certain international news broadcasts I have read, though, are somewhat disturbing; well, to me, anyhow. I merely suggest some caution at this stage, that is all."

Hart dabbed his forehead with his handkerchief. "I have a brother in America, on the east coast. Like me, he is an industrialist and is very successful in that country. Far more so than when he lived in Ireland. He tells me that industry is booming over there, and he intends to expand to the west coast before the year is out."

"He is to be congratulated," Danie smiled. "As I said, I have no firm basis upon which to offer this cautionary advice yet, but there is concern evident within the circles with which I associate."

Archie, who had been listening intently to this conversation, suddenly found himself sidetracked. His mind began to swim in wild circles.

"Excuse me, Mr Hart," Archie abruptly spoke for the first time. "You say your brother used to live in Ireland?"

"Indeed," Hart responded with a smile. "So did I before I came here."

Archie felt a slight flush rush his cheeks. "I met a young lady before I came to Africa called Kate Hart. She was from Shannon, in Ireland. Any relation?"

Mr Hart raised his eyebrows in surprise. "Indeed, my niece, my brother's daughter. They were from Shannon."

"How about that?" Archie smiled broadly. "I heard she is in America now?"

"Yes, and no. Kate does indeed live in America," Hart smiled broadly, "however right now she is here in Johannesburg. Kate is visiting my family at present."

Archie's heart skipped several beats. He could not believe what he was hearing. "Oh, my word. How about that? Is there any possibility I could meet her while I am in Johannesburg?" Archie almost pleaded.

"Of course, Mr Archie. I'm sure she would be delighted."

Archie wasn't quite sure how to structure his next question, so spoke carefully. "Is she married?" he asked with a somewhat shy smile, then quickly added, "Any children?"

"No," Mr Hart chortled, "she is not spoken for. Tomorrow night? Come for dinner and meet my family."

"That would be wonderful. Thank you, Mr Hart."

Archie was thereafter unable to concentrate on Louis' instructions for the remainder of the day and certainly struggled to fall asleep that night.

Having come to a stop outside a red-brick double-storey home in the leafy suburb of Rosebank, Archie alighted from the taxicab and paid the driver. He carried a bouquet of red Transvaal daisies as he bounded up the steps leading to the front door. He knocked, and then waited in nervous anticipation.

Kate opened the door a moment later. Her beauty made him catch his breath. He had first met her 16 years previously when they were both barely teenagers, and here she stood, a strikingly beautiful young lady. Archie had not expected to see such a shapely and attractive woman, and even though he had rehearsed what he would say, the words vanished into thin air.

Archie suddenly realised Kate had said something to him, and he had completely missed it. "Excuse me?"

"I said, are those for me?"

Archie blushed. "Oh, yes, I'm sorry. I, umm... Kate, I... Ahh... the reason I didn't come the next day is because my brother sent me to England the following morning."

"I wondered why," Kate said softly without showing much emotion or concern. "Come in, let me introduce you to the family."

Archie sensed that Kate wasn't interested in his excuses, but he felt it was vital that he cleared the air with her.

"Kate, please wait," Archie stood his ground. "I'm being honest; when I got home that evening, I found that I had been summoned to London by my eldest brother. My parents had already packed my bags and bought a ticket on the eight o'clock train for the following morning. I didn't know how to get a message to you, although I did try. Then I heard you had left Ireland, and I truly had no way of finding you."

Kate smiled sweetly at Archie. "I believe you, Archie. Perhaps it was destined that after I went to America, and you to England, that we should meet in South Africa. I knew you would find me somehow, and I am pleased you did."

Those words ricocheted around Archie's head, and his heart began to pound.

They were married exactly one year later.

CHAPTER NINE
Cape Town 1933

Louis locked the door of his room at the Mount Nelson Hotel in Cape Town and made his way to the courtyard. He was not feeling well at all; in fact, he was feeling decidedly poorly, but he needed to meet his brother before he boarded the ship to England for medical treatment.

As the spring days in 1933 had been delightful, Louis had arranged to meet David in the hotel courtyard on the afternoon of his arrival. Louis knew his older brother had disembarked the ship from Southampton that morning, and so had earlier left a note at reception for David for when he arrived.

Louis was only 52 years old, but he now needed his cane to help him walk. The yellowing of his skin and greying of his hair made him look much older than he was. On entering the leafy courtyard, Louis saw huddles of men, some in earnest conversation, some sharing a joke, and all in good quality day suits. There was a group of ladies beautifully adorned in flowing summery dresses off to the right, enjoying a high tea in the spring afternoon.

Louis scanned the area for David but, as he was not yet to be seen, chose a vacant bench nearby and gingerly walked over to it. He hoped that David would arrive soon as he was feeling frail and unstable. As soon as Louis was seated a waiter in a fresh, crisp uniform offered his services, and Louis ordered a black tea; it was about all he could stomach that afternoon.

Before the tea arrived, David, smartly dressed in a grey suit and his customary Derby hat, entered the courtyard and scanned the patrons. Louis noticed that David looked in his direction fleetingly, but his eyes searched further. When David's gaze came back to him, he raised his hand to catch David's attention. David was unable to hide his shock at the state in which he found his younger brother, and Louis did not miss David's look of horror.

"Louis!" David almost hissed when he neared his younger brother, "You look terrible. I didn't recognise you at first!"

"Hello, Brother. Indeed, I am much the worse for wear. It's my liver, you know. Too much of the good life, they say." He forced a smile. "How was your trip?"

"It was fine, thanks," David replied, then abruptly changed the subject. "You can't sit here in this state. Let me help you to your room."

"No, it's fine, thanks. I've ordered some tea. I feel like some tea and a little sun on my shoulders. Tell me, how was London? Morris?"

"Good, busy as ever," David said as he sat on the bench beside Louis. "Morris will meet you at the harbour in Southampton and take you to his home. He has booked you in to see a top specialist in Harley Street the day after the ship docks."

Louis nodded with a faint smile. "They don't think they can fix me, you know. It seems as if my days are numbered."

"Nonsense!" David exclaimed. "Medical treatment has come a long way in the last few years."

The two brothers sat in silence, contemplating the unhappy discussion. It was an awkward silence as they both knew Louis was probably quite correct. They stared at the happy people mingling around the courtyard, all oblivious to the two brothers and the heavy emotions that flowed between them.

David suddenly stiffened.

"What's wrong, David?" Louis asked nervously as he tracked David's stare to a small group of businessmen.

"That man there, about to sip his tea."

"Yes, I see him. What about him?" Louis asked quietly.

"That's the commander who was in charge of the group of Boers who captured me."

"Him?" Louis exclaimed and shot a look at David. "Are you sure?"

"Yes, that's him! Reitz, Commander Deneys Reitz."

Just as the man put his teacup to his lips, his eyes locked with David's and he froze; time stood still for both men. After just a brief moment, the ex-Boer commander smiled and lowered his teacup onto his saucer, placed them on a small table by his side and walked over to David. David stood to greet him and extended his hand.

"Commander Reitz," David addressed him. Their handshakes were very firm.

"It's just Mister Reitz now. It is good to see you, Mister David Langbourne from Rhodesia," the man said with a broad smile.

David wanted to laugh but just shook his head in awe. He realised they were still shaking hands, so released his grip. "My brother, Louis Langbourne," David suddenly remembered to introduce Louis.

Louis did not stand, but they shook hands all the same.

"Once we stood as enemies, and now we are friends," Deneys beamed. "How strange is war?"

"I was never your enemy, Mr Reitz," David corrected him. "Perhaps your captive, but never your enemy."

"That is true," Deneys said. "You were as good as your word and did not tell the British where we were."

"That is so," David smiled.

"We did chase you, but those Xhosa men who helped you outsmarted us. They were very clever."

"I will tell them that one day, Sir."

"Please do. I have never come across such ingenuity and cunning as those men exhibited. My men were rather embarrassed by the entire affair."

"I'm pleased to see you survived the war," David said, changing the subject.

"Yes, we capitulated, regretfully, and I didn't wish to accept British rule, nor did I want to remain in this country after that, so I was exiled to Madagascar. Yet, here I am today. How strange is life?"

"Are you in business?" David enquired.

"No, politics," he said with a wry smile.

"Well, I'll be," David marvelled. "That's a radical career change, is it not?"

"It was inevitable, I suppose. My father was a politician through and through. He was the President of the Orange Free State at one time, and then the State Secretary of the South African Republic. He signed the Declaration of War between the British and the Boers. Did you know that?"

"I did, actually. I can't recall who told me. So, after going into exile, you returned. That would make for an interesting story."

"Indeed. A long story. I will write a book about it one day, perhaps. But now I must return to my colleagues, if you will excuse me," Deneys extended his hand once more. "No hard feelings Mr Langbourne from Rhodesia?"

David chuckled as he gripped the man's hand firmly. "No hard feelings Mr Reitz from South Africa."

One simple solid shake confirmed the sentiments and Deneys turned to leave. David watched him walk away but suddenly called to him urgently.

"Mr Reitz, what of Piet van Tonder? Do you know what happened to him?"

Reitz turned slightly to face David. "He farms in Hankey, near Patensie. Go see him one day. It will do him good. Pass my regards to him when you do."

As he walked back to his cup of tea, David took his seat next to Louis. The brothers sat in silence for a minute.

Louis eventually broke the silence. "You will go to see him one day? Piet van Tonder?"

David shook his head slowly. "No," he said wearily, "I don't think I could do it. We said our last goodbyes a long time ago, in a different world. It would be too difficult for both of us. There is nothing left to say."

Louis sighed and looked up at Table Mountain, which loomed

ever-present above him. A deep sense of sadness overcame him. Louis knew that when he said his farewell to David the next day, it too would be their last goodbye.

The journey to England on the modern steamship was comfortable enough for Louis. The 1934 New Year was celebrated on the ship, but Louis confined himself to his cabin and didn't attend any celebrations. The weather was generally good, and often he found himself lounging on a deck under a light. Despite the plentiful food on offer, he had little appetite, and he was unable to garner any enthusiasm for shore excursions.

Morris met Louis at Southampton Harbour and escorted him to London by rail. Like David, Morris had been horrified by Louis' appearance and state of health.

"You will see a specialist tomorrow in Harley Street," Morris told his ailing brother as they settled into their coach. "I know him. He is the best gastroenterologist in England and specialises in diseases of the liver."

"I don't think I have long left, Morris," Louis said matter-of-factly.

"Nonsense!" Morris exclaimed dismissively.

"Seriously, I don't think there is much they can do for me. I've seen some of the best doctors in Johannesburg and Cape Town, and their prognosis is much the same."

"Let's see what Dr Fraser says tomorrow," Morris said as he slid back into the seat and stared out of the window. He didn't want to discuss this topic any further because he had a strong feeling Louis was almost certainly right.

"Where do you live now?" Louis changed the subject.

"I have a flat in Marylebone, in the middle of London. Lovely place. You will love it there. I have prepared the guest room for you. It has a magnificent view over the east of London."

"I look forward to meeting your fiancée," Louis said, to break the uncomfortable silence.

"Evelyn? Yes, indeed. She is keen to meet you too," Morris beamed.

"I'm sorry it didn't work out with Rose Bertha," Louis kept the conversation steered away from his health. "Do you hear much from her these days?"

"No," Morris replied somewhat abruptly. "Our divorce was not favourable, and I want nothing more to do with her. I have employed Freddy to administer the London office. He also handles my financial obligations in the divorce settlement. I think this arrangement suits us both."

"Very sad," Louis sighed, "but that is how life is, I suppose."

By the time the brothers arrived in Marylebone, Louis' strength had deteriorated dramatically, so he was immediately tucked into bed, and a doctor summoned. Dispensing some drugs from his well-used leather bag, the doctor departed with strict instructions to Morris on dosages and care until they could see the specialist the following day.

Twice in the night Morris stole a visit into Louis' room to check on him and found him sleeping peacefully. When he checked on him again at six o'clock the following morning, Louis was awake.

"Good morning, Louis. How are you feeling today?"

"Dreadful," Louis mumbled.

"Some tea, Brother?" Morris asked.

"That would be nice, thank you. No milk, please," Louis responded softly. "Tell me, before you go, how old is Evelyn?"

Morris raised his eyebrows at the question. "She's 26. Why?"

"A bit of a catch for you, dear Brother? I didn't expect her to be so young. Over 30 years difference in age between the two of you."

"Keeps me young, Brother. Keeps me on my toes," Morris smiled sheepishly.

"Please do me a favour," Louis said as he attempted to shift into a sitting position, but promptly gave up. "When I'm gone, please keep Herbert involved in the business. He's a good lad."

"You're not going anywhere," Morris objected harshly. "In any case, I like Herbert, and he will always be involved in the family business. Now relax, and I'll get you some tea."

When Morris returned a short time later carrying a tray of freshly made tea, he found Louis had closed his eyes for the last time.

* * *

Nguni feigned rubbing his nose, but he was, in reality, wiping a small tear from his cheek. "That is very sad, my friend. I liked Boss Rooi."

"Yes, I miss him dearly," David said, his voice faltering slightly.

"Where is my friend, Boss Morris?" Nguni suddenly changed the subject.

"He lives a very long way away," David replied with a smile, grateful to move off the topic, "in a country called America."

"Why does he live there? Does he not like Africa?"

David gave an exasperated sigh. "His fiancé, Evelyn? She wanted to live there. She was much younger than Morris and very beautiful. When Evelyn said she wanted to live in America, Morris found it very difficult to say no. But it now seems she was like the crafty jackal; she had a special reason to go there, which she did not tell Morris about. When he found out, it was too late and caused a big problem for him."

"Boss Morris is a clever man. How could he…"

David interrupted the burly man. "She was very beautiful, my friend. Very beautiful and young."

"Ahh…" Nguni nodded; he understood.

"It cost him dearly. Evelyn liked diamonds, lots of diamonds," David said cryptically as he reached once more for the teapot.

CHAPTER TEN
London 1933

"Good morning, Mr Langbourne," the sales assistant greeted Morris as he walked through the regally etched glass doors. The man was wearing an expensive tailored suit and silk tie, as befitted one employed in a high-end jewellery store.

"Morning," Morris replied curtly. He did not miss the fact that the young man had remembered his name. He had bought a fortune in jewellery from this establishment, after all, and was therefore not surprised the salesman remembered who he was. "I'd like to see the owner, please."

"Certainly, Mr Langbourne. Mr Merdjan will be right with you." The assistant gave a shallow bow and immediately backed away to find his employer.

Morris browsed the display cabinets and admired the array of expensive gold, silver and diamond craftsmanship that adorned black velvet or white satin cloth. He had to admit that Robert Merdjan knew how to show off his merchandise. Morris was trying to imagine a delightful diamond necklace draped around his fiancée's neck when his thoughts were suddenly interrupted.

"Mr Langbourne, Mr Langbourne, how wonderful to see you again," Mr Merdjan enthused, genuinely happy to see Morris. Robert Merdjan was a tall man with sharp features. His total baldness enhanced his facial lines and genuine smile.

"Morning Mr Merdjan," Morris responded, looking pleased. He

liked the jeweller because, as far as Morris was concerned, Robert was the best jeweller in the business, and was a master of his trade. Robert also treated Morris exceptionally well, almost like a long-lost friend, and gave him very acceptable discounts.

After a few pleasantries, Morris got down to business. He wanted a truly exceptional necklace for Evelyn. She was, to him, the epitome of beauty, and therefore only the best diamonds, in his mind, could justify her stunning looks. Anything less would pale into insignificance.

For Robert Merdjan, seeing Morris walk into his store was like throwing on the electric switch in a circus on a dark night; all the incandescent coloured light globes would light up at once in a majestic display of splendour, the music would burst into life, and suddenly everyone was laughing; excitement in the air. For Robert, Morris was a customer who truly appreciated fine jewellery, and he was an absolute delight to have in his store. He could tell Morris was smitten with his fiancée.

Morris selected a magnificent necklace and had Robert gushing his praises at Morris' exceptional taste, as he always did. After concluding the deal, the jeweller struck up some trivial conversation, which he planned to steer towards the economic woes of the day, hoping to get another perspective from one who seemed to be in the know.

"I saw you and your lovely fiancée at the theatre last Friday," Robert smiled broadly. "She was absolutely magnificent on your arm; a real head-turner."

"Indeed, she is," Morris freely admitted. "Did you notice that she was wearing those Cartier emerald earrings you sold me earlier this year?"

"How could I miss them?" Merdjan embellished his response with raised arms. "*Everybody* noticed them."

"It's the first time she has worn them," Morris looked somewhat disappointed. "She asserts that she will only wear diamonds. She only wore those earrings that night because she was wearing peacock green shoes."

"I noticed the shoes, I noticed the shoes," Robert sang joyfully, although, in reality, he hadn't. "Only diamonds? She is a lady of high taste. Have you set a date for the wedding, Morris?" Merdjan moved onto a polite first name basis.

"No, Robert, not yet," Morris sighed resignedly. "She is a very complicated lady. She wants me to commit to moving to America before she will agree to a date."

"America?" Robert exclaimed. This time there was genuine concern in his voice. He well knew that the Great Depression, as they were now calling it, was at its worst in America, but what was more of a concern to him was that he would be losing a vital customer, and perhaps a friend. "Heaven forbid, Morris! America? There is no employment there; food queues, shortages, hardships, crime. Please, I implore you, do not go there."

"I understand that well, Robert, but she puts a strong case forward for us to go," Morris shrugged. "As you are aware, she is a most beautiful lady, most beautiful," Morris reiterated, "and she wants to become a movie actress. It's all the rage now – movies, cinema, fame... The film industry, believe it or not, is still surviving in these tough times, and the place to go is California. Hollywood is the place she has set her mind upon."

"I beseech you, Morris, don't do it. Don't go. I have a good friend in Hollywood, a fellow jeweller in a high-end store. He writes that times are extremely tough there."

"Of course they are," Morris retorted, beginning to take offence at the direction the conversation was going, "a jeweller, of all things, during the Great Depression, and in America, will certainly be having a hard time, make no error. No, if I go to America, I will only invest in businesses that make sense."

"Such as?" Robert asked curiously.

"Property, of course. Property prices are at ridiculously low prices now. And maybe the movies. Tell your friend to sell his jewellery business and buy property. What's his name?"

"Martin Cohen," Merdjan replied somewhat startled. "He dropped Cohen and took on another surname; I'm not sure what it is now."

"Why would he do that?" Morris asked quizzically.

"Cohen is a very Jewish name, and it seems Jews are not particularly welcome in California. He has had to Anglicise his name to stay in business."

"Really?"

"Martin tells me it is challenging for the Jews there. In fact, any minority group. You've visited America. Did you not notice the Jews are very marginalised? I would think seriously about going there, Morris."

"In America? Yes, I have been there, but only the east coast; New York. But I haven't heard this," Morris objected gruffly. He was not enjoying the way the conversation was heading. Morris suddenly patted the box containing his diamond purchase and scooped it up. "No, if I give this magnificent diamond necklace to Evelyn and commit to going to the USA, I know she will relent and set a date for the wedding. Thank you, Robert, your service and advice have been of great value as always," Morris smiled as he strode out of the shop.

Morris was correct in his thinking; the extravagant diamond necklace and a commitment to migrate to America secured a wedding date. Thus, in 1933, Morris, at 58 years of age, married for the second time to Evelyn, who was a mere 26 years old.

Evelyn, a divorcee, already had a son called John, whom Morris readily accepted. He rented an executive penthouse in Marylebone, in London, pending their departure for America. Although Morris had every intention to uplift his business and lifestyle for the 'land of the free', personal events hampered these objectives.

The first crisis was Louis' health. It was a devastating blow to Morris, who took it very hard. Later that year, once all Louis' arrangements had been taken care of, and his son, Herbert had assumed Louis' role in the business, he married Evelyn. Evelyn fell pregnant very soon after that, and therefore the sea voyage to America had to be postponed yet again. Three months after Annie was born, the new family of four boarded a cruise liner and crossed the Atlantic Ocean.

As the ship entered New York harbour, slowly slipping past the imposing Statue of Liberty, Morris once again marvelled at the massive structure that he and Rose Bertha had silently sailed past when they visited on their honeymoon 33 years previously. The copper green statue, donated to the American people by the French government, and designed by Gustave Eiffel, the same man who designed the Eiffel Tower in Paris, was distinctly symbolic to all those who emigrated to this new country.

On disembarking, Morris became temporarily confused with the paperwork at the immigration desk. He noticed the interrogation that the couple in front of them was going through, and quickly realised they might have a problem with the arrogant official tending to them.

Morris lent down to John's ear and whispered to him urgently. "If anyone asks you what your name is, just say it is John Langbourne. Don't worry about your previous name; from now on and forevermore it is John Langbourne. Do you understand?"

"Yes, Mr Langbourne," John said politely.

Morris cast a furtive glance at the immigration officer just a few feet ahead of him. "And call me 'father' from now on."

"Yes, Father," John said politely.

Morris turned to Evelyn. "John's name is now Langbourne. From now on he must be known as John Langbourne."

It escaped Morris that this exact scenario had played itself out between his father, Jacob, and himself back in 1889. When they left for Ireland, and he changed his name from Breitstein to Langbourne. He told his children never to utter the name Breitstein again. And that is precisely what happened.

"And Annie?" Evelyn snapped back. She was tired, and in a foul mood, and the infant in her arms was beginning to get very heavy. "We have no paperwork for her, either. She is only three months old. You should have thought about this before we left. What if they send us back?"

"They won't," Morris hissed in aggravation. He too was in a very irritable mood.

The immigration official had dealt with thousands of people who had come to the American shores, most of whom were usually tired, stressed or both, so dealing with all these stressful people was not unusual. However, dealing with Morris was a very different kettle of fish altogether. The encounter began quite civilly but rapidly descended into a battle of wits. A shouting match ensued, and when three-month-old Annie started to exercise her new-found lungs and voice, and John pulled on everyone's clothing, playing with items on the officer's desk, things became very heated and uncomfortable. It was when John tipped an ink bottle over the officer's paperwork and on his tunic that he rapidly processed the Langbourne family and sent them on their way.

They booked into the Pierre Hotel for a few weeks while Morris visited his contacts and explored various opportunities, opening a bank account and sorting out other trivial, but necessary matters. It was also a time for the family to settle after the voyage and acclimatise to the culture. The strange twang of the population's accents was always of particular intrigue. The next step of the journey was again by ship to California, via the Panama Canal, where they checked into the Beverly Wilshire Hotel in Los Angeles.

Once settled for the second time, they moved to the Ravenswood Apartments on Rossmore Avenue. This accommodation, although perfectly adequate and comfortable for Morris, did not please Evelyn one bit, and after some very robust discussions, Morris reluctantly relented and moved his family to El Royal Apartments on the same street, just a few blocks along. It infuriated Morris no end that he had been subjected to yet another move for such little benefit, and was the subsequent cause for many a heated argument. Not far from the new apartment could be seen a monstrous higgledy-piggledy sign on top of a range of hills spelling the word 'Hollywoodland'.

It was from El Royal, during an impromptu taxicab ride to escape the chaos, noise and constant arguing of his young family, that Morris saw a sign above a store called 'Arthur's Jewelry'. He asked the cab driver to pull over, paid the amount due, and then entered the store.

His suppressed love for fine jewellery came roaring back, and for the first time since he left England, he suddenly felt grounded.

Morris loved jewellery for four reasons: he had a fascination for gemstones, they looked magnificent, they were a tremendous investment, and they looked delightful when worn delicately on a lady. There was another unspoken reason why Morris enjoyed diamond jewellery; whenever he gave Evelyn a gift of diamonds, she doted on him a little more, showering him with love and affection. He didn't admit to this publicly, but he certainly enjoyed the attention.

The sight of a jewellery store reminded him of the recent lack of affection within his household so he decided the purchase of an exquisite necklace or set of earrings might be just the ticket to restore normality onto his domestic circle. It did not escape Morris' attention that ever since they set foot on American soil, Evelyn's character had changed significantly. Still, he put that down to a new environment, a young child and the unsettled situation she was experiencing. Indeed, an elegant and fashionable diamond-encrusted accessory should, according to Morris' way of thinking, go a long way to restoring the status quo in the Langbourne household.

Entering the store, Morris was immediately approached by a very handsome middle-aged man, the broad and welcoming smile causing Morris to warm to the gent very smartly. Slender, and wearing a tailored grey suit, Mr Arthur introduced himself to Morris with a firm handshake and invited him to browse his store. Despite the rather decrepit state of the exterior of the building, Morris was quickly taken with the interior displays and fit-out of the store itself. The presentations of jewellery were magnificent, and there was not a display counter that did not catch Morris' eye.

Mr Arthur knew his jewellery intimately and took great delight in fielding Morris' incessant questions and intense scrutiny, so much so that Morris began to relax in his company, thoroughly enjoying the attention he was receiving. Although Morris quickly decided on a diamond-encrusted bracelet, he did not let the jeweller know, preferring, instead to spend as much time as possible in the store, and, secretly, away from his home.

The conversation soon moved to a more personal level with

Morris, in his usual way, throwing out the questions, and learning more about this intriguing salesman and the city to which he had now migrated. It turned out that Mr Arthur had worked for his father in the jewellery business, but had recently broken away to go on his own.

"My timing," he admitted, "was horrendous. No sooner had I opened my doors for business, the country went into recession. We've been in a recession for six years now, and no sign of it ending."

"I'm aware of your recession," Morris nodded sympathetically, "it's pretty much worldwide. They are feeling it in England too. They are calling it the 'Great Depression'. I have just left England."

"I can tell," Martin nodded with a knowing smile. "Your accent is not from here. But you must have done alright in England. Not many people come in to buy high-end jewellery from me, and I can see what interests you. You have a very discerning taste, Sir."

Morris smiled inwardly; he realised that Mr Arthur was very sharp and didn't miss a trick. "Yes," Morris conceded, "I did well there, but I believe I can do better here."

"What? You are looking to invest in a country that is fraught with food queues, massive unemployment and a collapsing economy?" Mr Arthur exclaimed. He unintentionally flashed a look at the bracelet that Morris was interested in, and immediately regretted doing that.

Morris noticed his glance at the diamond bracelet and knew what he was thinking. "Yes," Morris said slowly, "the time is right for my investment intentions. Property, mainly."

"Ahh," Martin quickly recovered himself, "indeed, property is almost being given away right now. Those with money would do well to purchase real estate. May I introduce you to a good friend of mine, Kramer is his name. He is respected in the realty business?"

Morris accepted the introduction; he didn't have any contacts in Los Angeles, but he knew he would be testing out several other realtors before he decided on anyone in particular. Mr Arthur also suggested a lawyer, a good friend of his father's, called Jerry Giesler.

"Mr Giesler is reputed to be the lawyer for the movie stars," Mr

Arthur said as he wrote some details on a piece of paper. "He's not cheap, but one of the best."

Morris was very grateful that he had come into the jewellery store that day. Mr Arthur was a wealth of information, and happy to share it, easy to talk to, and seemed to know just about everybody in Los Angeles who was worth knowing. Morris didn't purchase anything, but promised to return the following week; he found Mr Arthur more impressive than his jewellery!

CHAPTER ELEVEN
Los Angeles 1935

For two weeks, three Los Angeles realtors took the brunt of Morris Langbourne's antics and business pressure. His demands were fierce, his negotiating almost impossible to deal with, and his energy seemed boundless. Desperate to secure what might be the single biggest property sale in several years, the realtors sweated, stressed, pandered to and fought for Morris' favourable attention. He chose, in the end, Mr Arthur's suggested contact, Mr Howard Kramer, who was about the same age as himself. When the deal was done, Morris returned to Arthur's Jewelry to thank Martin for the contact.

Martin Arthur, with his generous smile and warm welcome, led Morris to his office and poured him a cup of fresh coffee. They chatted convivially before Morris thanked him for pointing him in the direction of his realtor friend, and the famed lawyer, Jerry Geisler, who would be handling all his affairs from then on.

"I had heard from Mr Kramer that you purchased some property. My congratulations," Martin saluted with his coffee cup.

"Yes, he did well for me, thank you," Morris grinned. He knew he had put all the agents through the wringer and was sure none of them, including Mr Kramer, thought much of him, but Morris didn't care. "I bought several properties in Beverley Hills as investments, which I will develop over time, and another beautiful property in Holmby Hills, which I will develop for myself, sooner rather than later."

"Holmby Hills? That's a very nice area," Martin mused. He knew that only the very wealthy bought there, and he had secretly questioned Morris' wealth. It also occurred to him that he had no idea how Morris had made his money, or where he had come from; he had just arrived in town and begun scooping up property left, right and centre.

"Yes, I want to build a large house; at least a dozen rooms. I also bought a multi-storey commercial building downtown. It was a steal. The owner had gone bankrupt and was in big trouble."

Martin's eyebrows lifted even further. "A dozen rooms! That will be a pretty large home, I must say. Where did you buy your commercial property, if I may ask?"

"Mmm… Two of them," Morris mumbled as he put his coffee cup down on the desk, "Beverly Drive, not far from here, and Canon Drive. Have you heard of them?"

"Beverly Drive!" Martin raised his eyebrows even further in surprise. "Well, yes, of course."

"I also got some bargains in Liemert Park in the Crenshaw district, and in Burbank. And a building that houses a lovely departmental store called Nancy's, right in the heart of Hollywood."

Martin was dumbstruck. The conversation ebbed and flowed for a while, Morris enjoying Martin's company, and Martin pleased to tell Morris all about his life and career, quietly hoping that Morris would turn the subject to jewellery so that he could make a sale.

"I like Los Angeles," Morris said abruptly. "Sunny, neat, and the people are very accommodating."

"It is," Martin agreed, "but it comes with its dark side too."

"How so?" Morris questioned, his curiosity aroused by the unexpected remark.

"It's not so welcoming for minority groups; those of African descent, Jews, Hispanics…"

"Really?" Morris unconsciously sat straight in his chair. "I'm Jewish, and I've not had a problem here."

Martin looked at Morris, his head tilted slightly. "It may be different for you. Your name doesn't sound Jewish, and you are not trying to run a business. Above all, if you will forgive the assumption, you have a lot of money. If you want to buy property, mark my words, they will want your money, Jew or not. It's different for me; I want people's cash. I don't have money so if people want jewellery, which is a luxury, and if they know I'm a Jew, they won't come into the store."

"You're a Jew?" Morris asked.

"Yes, my real name is Martin Arthur Cohen. I dropped my surname to survive in business. I now call myself Martin C Arthur. It's worse for the community with darker skins. They can't hide who they are."

"I've met a friend of yours in London, a jeweller," Morris leant forward in thought and tapped the desk with his fingernail. "He told me you had dropped your surname, now that I remember it."

"Ahh... That would be Robert Merdjan. How is the good man?"

"He is well. You ought to write him as he doesn't know what your new name is," Morris suggested.

"I will most certainly do that," Martin agreed with a smile.

Morris found himself thinking back to when he was a young boy, and his father had changed the family name from Brietstein to Langbourne, for very similar reasons. Morris quietly thanked his father for his foresight.

"I can't believe people with darker skins are not accepted here." Morris shook his head in awe. "What is wrong with these people, for heaven's sake? I lived in Africa for many years, and if it were not for the generous help of the people there, I would not be where I am today. Some of my family's most loyal friends are African people. And what's the problem with Jews?"

Martin now understood why he couldn't place Morris' accent, a mixture of Irish, English and African. "It looks like you have a lot to learn about California, Mr Langbourne," Martin said sadly. "I recently went to a function one evening, and the people there were openly hostile towards Jews. I swear I was petrified they would find out I was a Jew; couldn't wait to leave that gathering. Best you keep your religion to yourself."

"I'm a Jew, and I'm proud of it," Morris said defiantly, but silent alarm bells were beginning to ring in his head. "Let's change the subject. I'm going to need an architect to design my new home in Holmby Hills," Morris stated. "You seem to know a lot of people in town, Mr Arthur. Whom do you suggest?"

Martin reached for a small leather-bound book on his desk and began flicking through the pages. "I have a good friend who has just qualified as an architect, or I can suggest a couple of bigger firms, going by the enormous house you have indicated that you want to build. A prominent Jewish man in town owns one of them."

"What about an architect from a minority group? I want to give them a chance. I was given a break once; I want to return the favour."

Martin stopped paging abruptly and stared at Morris, a look of disbelief on his face. "I don't know that there are many mainstream architects in minority groups; certainly none qualified to build mansions."

Morris thumped his finger on the desk. "See what you can find for me, Mr Arthur," Morris suddenly stood to leave, a look of determination briefly flashed across his face. "I'll be back tomorrow. Thank you for the coffee."

When Morris left, Martin Arthur remained seated at his desk. He shook his head in dismay, then gently closed his leather booklet and sighed. Once again, he had failed to make a sale to his mysterious and rather flamboyant potential client. Worse still, he had been tasked with the almost impossible.

"Come in, Mr Langbourne," Mr Williams ushered Morris into his office. "Thank you for stopping by."

Paul Revere Williams, a good-looking man in his early 40s, welcomed his potential client cordially. Tall, with a very open and friendly face, he sported a small, neatly manicured moustache. His smile was warm and genuine, and, in an instant, Morris knew he liked the man.

Mr Williams wore a tailored mustard-coloured suit that highlighted his light brown skin. He presented himself well and spoke with a soothing and authoritative voice. His soft outbursts of laughter during their introductory niceties seemed to come from the back of his throat. Coffee was offered, but Morris declined, preferring to get straight down to business so as not to waste the architect's time.

The men sat at a plush office desk, devoid of any decoration or stationery, apart from four brass ornaments. Mr Williams sat opposite Morris, listening intently to what his potential client's wishes were. Then, once Morris had finished talking, Mr Williams reached behind his chair and produced a large scroll of paper. He rolled it open on the desk and promptly weighted the corners down with the four metal ornaments. Morris immediately realised that they were placed on the desk specifically for that task.

"Fourteen or fifteen rooms?" Mr Williams asked. "Just so I understand correctly, is that number to include all rooms?"

"I'll leave that to you, Mr Williams," Morris asserted, "but a minimum of ten bedrooms. You have 10,000 square feet to work with. There is a lot of land too, and I want to keep the gardens as natural as possible. The house must work with the landscape and vegetation."

"You've come to the right man, Mr Langbourne," Williams chuckled as he stared at his blank canvas in deep thought. "I always believe a garden and the landscape should be an integral part of a building's design."

Then, without a word, Williams pulled a pencil from his drawer and began sketching furiously as he worked on the sheet of paper. He mumbled a few times, but Morris didn't interrupt; he watched in awe as the sketch developed.

It wasn't so much that the simple pencil lines were evolving into a three-dimensional depiction of a Georgian style house that had Morris scratching his head in fascination, but that the image was the right side up from where Morris sat.

"How can you draw upside down?" Morris could no longer contain his fascination.

Mr Williams stopped sketching and looked at Morris with an amused smile. "I've taught myself to draught this way. Some folks here are uncomfortable with me standing on the same side of the table as them."

"Surely not?" Morris said softly, dumbfounded by that comment. "For heaven's sake, why?"

"Mr Langbourne, where are you from, if I may ask?"

"All over. Ireland, South Africa, Rhodesia, England," Morris replied, but tactfully omitted Poland after what Martin Arthur had recently told him.

"It seems clear to me you haven't been in California long," Mr Williams said ominously.

"Indeed," Morris looked at the strange expression on Mr William's face. "I am beginning to feel I have lots to learn."

Williams nodded carefully. "I would say so. Yes, I would say so. But I'm sure you will in good time. Forgive my being forward, Mr Langbourne, but what line of business are you in?"

"Oh, a bit of everything, sales, exports, shipping, that sort of thing."

Mr Williams realised Morris was not willing to share much information, so he returned to his drawing. "Is this the sort of home you were envisaging?"

"Yes, it is. It is," Morris repeated, "I do believe I have come to the right person. Mr Williams, I think we need to agree to our contract more formally."

And so it was that Mr Paul Revere Williams was engaged to build a 10 000 square foot, 14-roomed mansion for Morris Langbourne in Holmby Hills. The commission was so substantial that it made the local newspapers. Morris, as was his way, didn't divulge much about himself or his business career. As much as a pesky reporter tried to find out some juicy information about Morris, he always came up short.

During the building stage of the home, Evelyn ran off to a neighbouring state and sued Morris for divorce, claiming mental and physical cruelty. Because of Morris' unintended high profile, due in part to his massive mansion and his wife's extravagant jewellery and fashion sense, the press followed him everywhere. Not only was Morris of interest to the tabloids, but Evelyn and her children were too. They followed Evelyn to Reno, snapping photos of her looking very content with life and dripping in diamonds, infuriating Morris. He now realised she had hoodwinked him into moving to California because of the lenient property laws. He engaged his new high profile lawyer, Jerry Giesler, who negotiated a settlement.

Morris was a single man when he moved into his Holmby Hills home. He rattled around his mansion during the day and entertained the Los Angeles elite at night. He found himself, however, to be in his element.

Nguni looked at David pitifully. "My heart is sad that Boss Morris is alone. A man needs a woman – many women in my culture."

David smiled as he picked up his teacup. He swirled the brew unconsciously before taking a sip. Nguni followed suit, and carefully agitated the sweet tea, causing the liquid to spin gently.

"One wife is plenty enough in our culture, Nguni," David shot his friend a mischievous smile. "Morris can be a very kind and generous person. As much as he can be hard in some ways, he can be very considerate and thoughtful in others. He has made sure that all his children got the best education possible. Then, when the grandchildren came along, he paid for their education too."

"That is good," Nguni smiled approvingly. "Daluxolo and me, we know that Boss Morris is a hard man, but we also know he has a good spirit."

David smiled contentedly and placed his cup on the small table between them. "We have a sister. Her name is Bloomy; she is the firstborn."

"My eyes have not seen her," Nguni looked at David curiously.

"No, she has never been to Africa. She married a man in Ireland and had many children, eight children, but then the husband went to America, a very long way from her, to start his business. Then he told her to join him, and to bring all the children. She did this, but after some years, the husband left to find another business and never came back."

"Ghaw!" Nguni hawked in astonishment.

"He left her in a town called Pittsburgh. She was abandoned with all her children. But Morris sent her money, and he looked after her so they didn't go hungry. He also helped with their accommodation. He is a generous man underneath."

"It is good," Nguni rumbled. "Boss Morris is a man of men."

"Oh, that he is," David looked up at Nguni, a broad smile spreading across his face. "Morris is saving the lives of many hundreds of people, maybe thousands, yet they will never know. We will never know exactly. Only one man outside our brothers knows this story."

Nguni flashed a startled look at David.

"You are my brother, Nguni," David reached over and squeezed the big man's shoulder. "I will tell you this story, but this story is for you only. But first, the tea has gone cold. Come, we need more, and then I will tell you."

CHAPTER TWELVE
Salisbury - 1940

"I told you, I am not going to die as an employee of Langbourne Brothers," Archie fumed. "I am a brother, I am a part of this family, and I want to be a *part* of this business."

"A half-brother," Harry said coldly.

"Half-brother, quarter-brother, full brother; I don't care; I *am* a brother. We have the same father!" Archie thumped his fist on the boardroom table.

"Now, now, Gentlemen," David said calmly, "a little order and decorum if you please."

David, Harry, Paddy and Archie sat around a simple wooden table in a room in the Bulawayo warehouse that doubled as both a boardroom and staff room. Its primary use was a place where employees would steal a few quiet moments to eat a cold lunch or drink a cup of tea, but when meetings or group decisions were required, it fulfilled the function of a boardroom quite adequately.

David glanced at Paddy, an unspoken request for some assistance in this squabble. It had been surfacing on and off for several months now.

Paddy understood the look David imparted and joined the conversation. "Archie, perhaps you should tell us why you have such a need to be a shareholder of Langbourne Brothers?"

"I've told you before..." Archie began.

"No," Paddy gently interrupted, "we know you want to be a

shareholder, but why is it so *important* to you?"

Archie sighed and slumped back in his chair. David smiled inwardly; he knew that if anyone could talk sense to Archie, it was Paddy and Paddy alone.

"Alright," Archie composed himself. "There is always this 'us and them' attitude between you brothers," he pointed a menacing finger at the eldest three in the room, "and us brothers. Whatever decision I propose I am automatically overruled. I believe we have lost a lot of income and business because I simply won't be heard."

"We listen to you," David responded.

"Yes, you do, but only out of courtesy, but then you go and outvote me – every time. If you or David, or Harry for that matter, propose something, and I don't, you outvote me again. It's as if I am only here on your board as a token to... to what? To our father, perhaps? To show him that you respect his second family?"

"That's not the case," David stopped Archie there, his face flushed with anger. "There are two families, we cannot deny that, but we are all Langbournes, and we should work and behave as such."

Archie threw his hands up in defeat. "With the utmost respect, I believe all of us in this room understand this to be the case, but the problem is with Morris. He will not accept Father's second family and treats us younger brothers as separate from the family. I'll bet Morris tells you lot how to vote. Am I right?"

There was an uncomfortable silence in the boardroom, and in essence, Archie had hit the nail on the head.

All eyes turned to David. He sighed, shook his head slowly, and then stood up to buy time to think. He stood behind his chair and leaned on it heavily.

"You are right, Archie. Morris does have a problem with you and Paddy being equal shareholders in the company. It is not because of this... this 'us and them' attitude you suggest. You have to remember, it was the original four brothers – Morris, Louis, Harry and myself – who took all the financial risks, even laid our lives on the line, to get this company to where it is today. You weren't even born then."

"I understand that," Archie shot back. "I understand. But, be that as it may, I am one of the family, not by choice, mind you," he threw in a little sarcasm for good measure. "If I had been around when you formed the business, I too would have willingly put in the same risks and hard work you did. You've seen my commitment. I want to be respected as a part of the family, and I want a fair share of the profits of the company, not just a wage. I remind you, David, that I have already put in my all for this company. I have tried really hard for you and the family, and whether I get paid dividends or a wage, I will still give my all. As I have repeatedly said, I am prepared to pay for my share in the company."

David looked at Harry, who raised his eyebrows, acknowledging Archie's argument. Harry stared at his hands, not wishing to further the discussion. David looked back at Archie.

"Archie, we appreciate what you say, and I know Morris is aware of the effort you put into this company. It will not be easy to change his policy regarding the business. He has always maintained that Langbourne Brothers is for the original Langbourne brothers who formed the company back in the late 1800s." David paused. "May I make a suggestion?"

With that, David drew the full attention of all the brothers.

"Go ahead," Archie said blandly.

"Our branch in Salisbury is not operating to its fullest potential. We have been considering closing that branch. We own the property it's located on – what's the name of those streets?"

"Speke Avenue and Inez Terrace," Harry grunted.

"What would you say if we sold the property and the business to you? You would be completely independent to make your own trading decisions, profits and losses."

"I see no benefit in that suggestion to me," Archie retorted. "I may as well find my own premises and open my own store. I might even negotiate a cheaper sale than you would offer me."

David sighed with exasperation. "That's true; you could do that. I also doubt that would solve your dilemma. Correct?" David asked rhetorically.

"No, it would not, because then I would be even less a part of this family."

Harry looked up sharply. "You *really* want to be a part of our family business?"

"Yes," Archie leant forward in his seat to stress his point.

"Alright, I have a suggestion then," Harry slouched back slightly, causing everyone to stare at him now. Even David took his seat in anticipation.

"Suppose we formed a new company and put the Salisbury property and business into it. Say we call it 'Langbourne Trading', as opposed to Langbourne Brothers. You have 51% of the new Langbourne Trading, and 'Langbourne Brothers' holds 49% of the shares. That way, you are a part of the family business, and we are a part of your business, but you have the majority vote on all decisions. The only stipulation I would have is that we insist you purchase all your stock from 'Langbourne Coetzee' in Johannesburg, just as we, here in Bulawayo, do. That way, you will purchase your products at the same price we do, thereby keeping all the terms and conditions fair and equal."

A stunned silence followed as the various brothers contemplated Harry's proposal. David looked at Paddy and saw his right eyebrow raise briefly, his head giving the slightest nod; he understood straight away that Paddy liked the suggestion. Harry showed no emotion whatsoever.

Archie then returned his stare at Harry. "I disagree with a 51/49 split in shares. In the spirit of family, it must be 50/50. However, I have 100% of the management rights. In other words, I am the sole decisionmaker. Nobody gets to outvote me. The responsibility of success or failure rests entirely on me."

Another silence followed.

"Alright," David broke the temporary tranquillity, "would that be a workable solution for you all?"

Everyone in the room nodded.

"In that case, I will refer this proposal to Morris in London and see if he agrees, because, as you are aware, all three senior brothers have to agree to any motion. I must say, though, I see no reason why Morris would object."

David looked at Harry who gave a curt nod.

"Right oh then," David continued, "my thanks are expressed to Harry for finding a possible solution to Archie's concerns. Now, moving along, I received a telegram from Morris yesterday. He wants one of us to travel to Japan and meet with some of his agents and suppliers. Their prices are starting to increase, and Morris is not entirely sure these suppliers are playing a fair game. One of us must go to Japan and negotiate hard, but in a diplomatic and convivial nature. Furthermore, he wants us to find new suppliers to lessen our dependence on those we currently have. Any takers?"

A stillness settled over the room as the brothers contemplated what David said.

Harry cleared his throat. "I'd love to visit Japan, but this trip will take a good two to three months, and I'm not in a position to do that right now."

"I've just got back from a very long journey, and I'm exhausted," David said. "Count me out of this one. Paddy?" David asked his younger half-brother, but he already knew the answer.

"I'm sorry, Uncle David," Paddy replied humbly. "Sadly, I'm not well enough to travel so far for so long. I still have a great deal of pain in my back and legs."

All eyes turned to Archie.

"Well, Archie," David grinned, "looks like you're our man. You think you can do it?"

A wave of nervousness washed over Archie. Not only was the task daunting, but as it was an instruction from Morris, woe betide him if he failed. The chances of failure, Archie was acutely aware, were very high.

David noticed his look of apprehension. "Go on, give it a go. You'll be alright, I'm sure. It will be a great experience for you."

Archie understood that this could be a big break for him, but even so, he baulked at accepting the invitation for a little while before finally agreeing.

When the meeting ended, Harry and David were the last to walk out of the room. When they reached the door, Harry turned and leant close to David's ear.

"So, Archie will be relocating to Salisbury?" he whispered, a wry smile spreading across his mouth.
"Yes, it seems so," David stifled a smile.
"I told you my plan would work," Harry grinned.

Archie's trip to Japan was a resounding success. The journey by sea was, for Archie, most enjoyable, and he was greeted, wined, dined and entertained like royalty when he set foot in the fascinating city of Tokyo. He had never experienced such lavish attention, and he loved it. He struck up exceptionally long-lasting relationships with their agents. Negotiations were stiff but lucrative, and the 28-day journey home had him smiling from ear to ear, every single day of the voyage.

On his return to Bulawayo and into the arms of Kate, he reported back to his brothers, and was thrilled to receive an unexpected congratulatory telegram from Morris. It put Archie's confidence on an entirely new level.

Then, with the permission of his four older half-brothers, Archie approached the Standard Bank in Salisbury and negotiated several loans. Langbourne Brothers in Bulawayo would guarantee these loans. Based on this guarantee and the reputation of the Langbourne brothers, the bank did not hesitate to grant Archie his request for credit.

Archie was a little suspicious of the willingness of his brothers to offer their guarantee, but it never occurred to him that it was part of their secret plan to put some distance between him and themselves. Nevertheless, grand ambitions in his sights at last, Archie accepted the bank's terms and borrowed the large sum of money. That done, he visited a Building Society and negotiated a mortgage to build a home in the now trendy suburb of Belgravia, a stone's throw from the area known as The Avenues. Once the mortgage was secured, he purchased a plot of land he had his eye on, known as 11 Philips Avenue, right on the corner of the main road into town called Second Street.

Commuting between Salisbury and Bulawayo, Archie simultaneously began supervising the construction of his home and his business. The land on the corner of Inez Terrace and Speke Avenue housed the existing Langbourne Brother's Salisbury warehouse. It was more a dilapidated wrought iron shed than a functioning warehouse. The building, a simple single-story shack, was unhesitatingly demolished. Plans were drawn up by a local architect, and an excellent builder was engaged.

Construction of the two-story brick building that covered a quarter of a city block began in earnest. Not sure whether he should locate the main door of the building on Inez Terrace or Speke Avenue, Archie instructed the architect to place the main entrance on the corner of the building, thereby having the access on both streets. Archie insisted a flagpole be erected on the roof above the main door to fly the national flag once trading commenced.

The double-storey family home, with Kate's input, was architecturally designed to incorporate several internal and external arches. Set back from the street to benefit from a substantial garden, Archie knew Kate would be able to spend many hours pursuing her love of flowers.

Kate gave birth to a son nine months after they were married, whom they named John. Their second son, who came four years later, they named Louis, after Archie's half-brother. The acre block of land on Philips Avenue would, Archie knew, give his boys plenty of room to grow in a healthy and safe environment. Unexpectedly, the new 'Langbourne Trading' building in Salisbury progressed rapidly, forcing Archie and Kate to move there permanently, before their home was complete.

As the date of completion of the Inez Terrace building drew near, Archie took the opportunity to appraise the brothers of his plans to commence business in Salisbury. The meeting was brisk, and Archie placed his initial order of stock. It was a substantial order and would need filling not only from Johannesburg but from Bulawayo and Port Elizabeth too. Harry was quick to remind Archie of his credit terms, which immediately caused tempers to flare.

"Of course I understand your contract, you have told me often enough," Archie exploded. "What will you do if I don't pay you back?"

"We will take the business from you for ourselves," Harry said coolly.

Archie knew he had the brothers over a barrel with his loan structures. "You're going to take over my bank loan and mortgage too?"

Paddy cast a furtive glance at David.

"Now, now, Gentlemen," David quickly moved to quell what he knew was about to become a heated discussion. "Archie, we have agreed to help you, and we will honour our word. It is our family policy, as you know. We know you will honour your side of the agreement too. When do you plan to open for trade?" he quickly changed the subject, hoping Archie would do the same.

Archie shot a menacing glance at Harry before addressing David. "About three months from when we make the final move to Salisbury. I, along with Kate and our boys, will leave for Salisbury on Monday and begin stocking the warehouse."

"How is your home coming along?" David asked pleasantly.

Archie almost grunted in frustration. "It's running behind. I thought we would be able to move in before the business opened, but sadly we will have to find a hotel for about four weeks until we can take up residence."

"Ah!" David exclaimed, "I have a very good friend who owns a lovely hotel in Salisbury. Mr Thomas Meikle. I'll give you a letter of introduction before you go. He will more than likely give you a favourable rate."

"Thank you, Uncle David," Archie beamed. "Which hotel is it?"

"Meikle's Hotel, of course," David grinned. "Right in the middle of town."

"I've heard of it," Archie scratched at his temple. "I believe it's very nice."

David straightened his tie and cleared his throat. "I've stayed there myself — a lovely establishment. Kate will be happy residing there until your home is ready. She may not want to leave. Now, one last thing, if I may?"

The brothers all nodded for David to continue.

"I think, under the circumstances, perhaps, Archie and Paddy, it is time that you drop the title of 'Uncle'. In business circles, it is probably better that you call us by our first names. After all, we are all adults."

"Agreed," Harry nodded his approval with a scowl.

"Thank you kindly," Paddy accepted the gesture, smiling broadly.

"Thank you... David," Archie said, catching the word 'uncle' in his throat. It felt very awkward to call David by his first name without the preceding title. That small difficulty was, however, soon overcome.

Gently closing the door to her hotel room, Kate walked down the long, silent corridor of the Meikle's Hotel. The narrow plush strip of light green carpet, running the length of the highly polished wooden floorboards, dulled her footfalls. She barely noticed the various paintings that were hung on the walls anymore. The family had been living in the hotel for over a month now, and the novelty was wearing thin.

It had become a tradition that she would make her way down to the lobby adjacent to the reception at five o'clock and order a tray of tea. Her two sons, John and Louis, would be left in the care of their nanny, Sally, who would bathe them and then change them into respectable evening clothes, as the establishment demanded, before they would join her half an hour later. Meanwhile, like clockwork, Archie would walk into the hotel reception at five minutes past five and greet Kate with a peck on the cheek and a carefree smile before plonking himself down in a pale green lounger beside her. Five minutes later, a waiter in a crisp white uniform would deliver the tea. Archie would tell his lovely wife about his day, the supervising of the warehouse construction and the progress of their new double-storey home in the suburb of Belgravia. This routine was repeated every weekday evening without fail.

"Archie," Kate said one particular evening, genuine concern evident in her voice, "I heard that the war in Europe has moved into North Africa. Have you heard about this?"

"Yes, I have," Archie shook his head slightly and cast a worried look at the carpet. "I wouldn't concern myself with that too much; it is a very long way away."

"I know," Kate frowned, "but when the Great War began, it also spread down this way, and fairly rapidly. Look what happened to Paddy."

Archie paused for a moment, just long enough for Kate to realise he was indeed perturbed. "It is a worry, my darling. If it does make its way down here, it will surely affect our business."

"I'm not worried about the business," Kate said sharply.

"I'm too old to fight, don't you worry yourself about that," Archie reassured Kate, giving her hand a quick squeeze. "The war office won't be interested in me at all. We will be alright."

"I feel I need to do something for the war effort," Kate said sadly. "So many young men are leaving to join the fight. I have no idea, though, as to what I could possibly do."

Archie was pensive for a while, and Kate sensed something was wrong. She held her tongue, knowing that Archie would pass his concerns onto her as soon as he had ordered his thoughts.

"I heard from David today; he telephoned me from Bulawayo. It seems the Jews are being persecuted in Europe, particularly in Germany, Russia and Poland. He was distraught as all our families are still in Poland. All my cousins, aunts and uncles; everyone."

"Yes, you told me your father was the only family member to leave Poland," Kate commiserated.

"Indeed, he was the only one. That's how and why I met you in Ireland," Archie flashed a smile at Kate trying to lighten the subject. It didn't work.

"Most of my relatives are in Warsaw," Kate eased a deep sigh of grief from her lungs. "Oh, what is this world coming to?"

Archie cleared his throat. "David said he, Morris and Harry are sending money to England for the war effort; I think it's to help rescue Jews who are affected. He asked if I could contribute, but we all know I am in debt up to my eyeballs. It is David, Harry and Morris who are lending me money, so they are aware of my financial situation. I will find other ways to help."

"I can raise money," Kate suggested. "I can do volunteer work at the Salisbury War Office or something."

"Yes, that is an idea," Archie smiled broadly. "We're seeing that young Jewish surgeon and his wife for dinner tomorrow, Kipps and Muriel Rosin. He will be good for some sound advice on how we can help."

"Daddy! Daddy!" John interrupted as he ran into the reception area, his younger brother following just as excitedly.

Both Archie and Kate tried to calm them down as other patrons looked disapprovingly over at the commotion.

"Hush, Hush," Kate fussed over her sons, casting nervous glances at the other guests.

"Louis and I are going to start a business!" John exclaimed. "We are going to be businessmen just like you."

"Oh, that's nice," Archie said through a soft chuckle. "What business are you going to do, may I ask?"

"We were exploring today," Louis piped in, "in the kitchen!"

"No, wait, wait!" John quickly tried to put his hand over Louis' mouth. "I'm telling, I'm telling. We were exploring in the kitchen and…"

"I don't think you're allowed in the kitchen," Kate interrupted John.

"No, we are, we are. Eklem, the waiter, took us there and showed us around. My word, it's big, and they make a lot of food. But there are a lot of cupcakes that get thrown away every day because people don't buy them all, and they have to make fresh ones each day. So, Louis and I are going to collect the thrown-out cupcakes from the bins and sell them outside on the street after school. We will be rich!"

Archie looked at Kate, who simply raised an eyebrow, but she was smiling slightly.

Archie signalled his boys to come closer to him. "Listen, my sons; if you want to become businessmen and make money, you have to learn how to run a business properly. You can't just take leftover cupcakes and sell them on the street. That's not how it's done."

The wind instantly left the young boys' sails, and Kate sensed that John was about to object, painfully.

Kate looked at Archie. "Dad," she addressed him as she

customarily did in front of her boys, "if John and Louis want to be businessmen, why don't you teach them how? Just as your father taught you, and his father before him?"

Archie's face lit up. It was as if a fire ignited in his chest. Suddenly he had a new purpose in his family life, something different to dealing with his business endeavours and his older brothers. It might also take his mind off the ever-depressing conversations that always revolved around the war in Europe, now spreading to Africa. He knew he could teach his sons well, and probably learn some things himself in the process. John was frightfully bright and might even challenge him with his incessant questions.

He recalled his father, Jacob, once telling him how Morris had always tested him. Without doubt, everyone knew the eldest son in Jacob's family was unusually gifted with numbers, but Archie was convinced he could handle John and Louis' curiosities quite capably.

"Splendid idea," Archie smiled broadly at Kate. "Would you boys like to learn how to be businessmen?"

The rapturous agreement from the boys forced Kate to immediately shush the youngsters again as patrons glanced over at them. Some scowled, but many were smiling at the apparent excitement of the youngsters.

"Right oh, Right oh," Archie grinned happily, "but first we need to form a business, and we need a name, and we need a constitution, and some office bearers to chair the meeting and…"

"Archie," Kate stopped him with a solemn shake of her head. "One step at a time, and perhaps start with a club, rather than a company. Let's walk before we run, shall we?"

Archie smiled. "You are right, my darling. Well, boys, let me think on this tonight, and tomorrow we will have our first lesson."

"Good," Kate agreed and pulled her boys close to her for an enveloping hug. "Now, the dining room is open for children, and you boys need to have an early dinner, and then it's off to bed for you both. Shall we?"

The young Langbourne family adjourned from the lobby area, Archie beaming like a proud father, but Kate with a shroud of worry settling on her shoulders. The war in Europe sounded terrible, and she feared desperately for all their relatives.

At precisely five o'clock the following day, Archie closed a folder he had been reading. It had been a tough day supervising the building work in Belgravia, and an even harder afternoon doing much the same at the new Langbourne Trading warehouse on Inez Terrace. Taking one last look at the two-storey frame and cluttered masonry work, he turned his back on it all and made the five-minute walk along Speke Avenue to the Meikle's Hotel.

A symbol of strength and stability, the two large bronze sculptures of muscled lions atop the hotel facade stared unblinkingly at Archie as he entered his temporary accommodation. He was a stickler for punctuality and routine, and so, at precisely five minutes past five, he walked through the large doors of the reception area. He smiled when he saw his beloved Kate waiting patiently for him in her usual chair, a waiter carefully placing a tray of tea on the table in front of her.

"Hello, my lovely," Archie said as he kissed her on the cheek.

"Good to see you, darling. How was your day? How is the house coming along?"

"Not long to go now," Archie said as he took his usual seat beside her. "I would guess they will finish in about three to four months."

"Heavens," Kate sighed. "As lovely as it is staying at the Meikle's, I miss my garden and privacy."

"Not long now," Archie tried to soothe his wife. "How were the children today?"

"They're alright," she sighed. "They are anxious to learn how to become businessmen; you have certainly started something there." Kate suddenly looked slightly uncomfortable. "John and Louis went exploring again. I told them they are never to do that."

"Got into some trouble, did they?" Archie mused as he took a careful sip of his tea. "I trust you disciplined them?"

"Yes, of course, if they were naughty, but they aren't. Children do need space to play, and they desperately need friends their own age."

"There's a park right across the road," Archie waved his hand towards the entrance of the hotel. "Ask Sally to take them there."

"She does, and so do I," Kate complained. "There's only so much you can do with two boys in a park. Today they sneaked off on their own. You should have seen their clothing when they got back. Cobwebs for Africa, dirt, sand, sticks. I'm embarrassed to send their clothing to the laundry tomorrow."

"How did they get that dirty?" Archie asked curiously.

"How would I know?" Kate snapped.

John and Louis had found a wooden trap door in one of the several passages in the hotel that revealed a low cavern under the building. The entire ground floor of the hotel was suspended on short wooden stilts, and this made for a labyrinth of passages and hidden alcoves between the earth and the underside of the timber ground floor.

The brothers had excitedly crawled deep into the foundation of the hotel and almost became lost. Emerging a little while later, covered in dirt and spider webs, they felt that to explore even further, they needed some light. Because Archie was a heavy smoker, John knew there were matches in his bedside drawer, and so retrieved them.

A little later the mischievous boys secretly removed the trap door and scurried back under the floorboards, securing the trap door neatly over their heads once more. Somewhere beneath the library and the main bar, they made a clearing and claimed it as their new 'fort'. Gathering up a discarded brown cement packet, they set a match to it and watched the flames grow. And grow they did. When the bag had almost burnt through, John sent Louis to find another combustible item, and he returned moments later on all fours with yet another discarded cement bag, which they immediately threw on the dwindling flames and revived the small inferno.

It was exhilarating for the two boys, and they watched in fascination as the packet roared with flame and smoke. Just as the fire petered out and left the two scallywags sitting in the smoke-filled darkness, they heard muffled shouts overhead, and the floor above their heads began to vibrate and rumble. It was as if a herd of impala; perhaps even elephants, were dashing across the floor above in all directions. The boys sat cross-legged, staring at the underside of the hotel floor in wonder and intrigue.

"I wonder what's going on up there?" John mused.

"Sounds like a dance party," Louis suggested.

"Wonderful," John exclaimed, "let's go see!"

The brothers crab walked as fast as their arms and legs could carry them. Just as they arrived at their secret trapdoor, they heard a commotion behind them. Looking back, two hitherto unknown trapdoors were wrenched open at the far side of the hotel and light streamed in, coupled with angry voices. Quick as sticks, John and Louis clambered out of their underground fort and closed their trapdoor behind them. They were rather upset that others had discovered their secret hideaway.

Horrified to see the state of her charges, covered head-to-toe in dust, soil and cobwebs, Sally immediately had both boys bathed and changed into fresh clothes. With the sudden fuss their nanny made over them, the boys completely forgot about the dance party.

While Archie and Kate were enjoying their ritual evening cup of tea, Archie noticed that Kate looked somewhat perturbed.

"What else is bothering you, darling?" Archie quizzed.

Kate frowned intently. "I'm not sure. I've been watching the manager over there, and he seems very strange this afternoon, especially towards children."

"Really?" Archie asked. "How so?"

"I can't put my finger on it. Every time he sees a child, he beetles over and greets the child by whispering in their ear. I swear, at one time I thought he was sniffing Mr Thompson's son's hair."

Archie leaned back in his chair and looked over at the pompous manager. He was buried in some paperwork at the reception desk. "I think you imagine it, my dear. Why would he do something like that?"

Kate shrugged and reclined in her seat. "You're right. Maybe I've been in this hotel too long."

Archie suddenly smiled. "I've thought about how I will go about teaching the boys how to run a business. We will form a club, just as you suggested, and have regular meetings and record all that we discuss."

"Go on," Kate reciprocated the smile.

"We'll create rules that shall become our 'constitution', and create a motto and a crest. Our motto should be something to do with helping your fellow man, and this will instil some sense of civic responsibility in the boys. We'll also collect subscriptions, and run a set of accounts so they learn how to manage money; then when we have enough, the money can be donated to charity."

"I like your thinking," Kate commended her husband. "This evening will be a good time to start; Sally has bathed the boys early for a change so we can start dinner sooner and then you boys can have your inaugural meeting. Don't go on for too long. I want them in bed by eight o'clock."

"Oh, you should be a part of it," Archie insisted.

"No, let it be just for you boys. I spend all day with them. It will be good for you."

"Good show," Archie chuckled. "Oh, here they are now."

As John and Louis entered the lobby, smartly dressed in their evening attire, the manager caught sight of them and called them over. Stepping around the counter, he greeted the boys jovially and bent down to whisper something in each of their ears.

"See!" Kate exclaimed, sitting bolt upright.

"How unusual," Archie agreed, frowning at the manager's antics. "Usually, he totally ignores children."

After a brief chat with the lads, he waved them off casually towards their parents.

"What did he say to you?" Kate demanded as soon as John approached her.

"Nothing," John said nonchalantly.

"He was whispering to you. What did he say?" Kate continued.

"He just said hello, and asked what we got up to today," John replied and broke away to greet his father.

"I told him we found some purple flowers in the park today with Sally," Louis added as he hugged his mother. "I'm hungry."

Kate looked at Archie and shrugged, a look of confusion etched across both their brows.

With almost uncontrollable excitement, John and Louis took their seats at the circular writing desk in the hotel room. Archie sat proudly and placed a sheet of white paper in front of him, carefully laying a sharpened pencil upon it.

"Right, boys," Archie began, "today we are going to form a family club, and we are going to be members of that club because we belong to this family."

"Goodie," John said gleefully, hardly able to contain his anticipation for what was coming next.

"So, before we start, we need to find a name for the club, and most importantly, decide on the rules. We will run the club as if it is a business, alright?"

"Yes, Dad," John agreed without hesitation.

"Right oh. For starters, we need a name. Any suggestions?"

"The Elephant Club," Louis exclaimed. "I love elephants."

"No," John almost shouted his condemnation. "The Lion Club, because lions are fearless and strong."

Archie held up his hand to calm his boys down. "No, no. The name must be something to do with what the club is all about. Might I suggest the Langbourne Club?"

"Okay," John said reluctantly.

"Better still," Archie continued, "I think we should call it the Langbourne Clan because 'clan' is more for a family group than a club."

"Yes!" John said excitedly as his father was starting to make sense. The idea pleased him. Louis smiled broadly in agreement, although he honestly did not care.

"Right oh," Archie picked up the pencil and wrote something big and bold at the top of the page. "Langbourne Clan it is. Now, we will need people to run this Clan, and just like a business, we will need office bearers."

"What's that?" Louis asked.

"People who are important in the Clan and who make sure it runs properly. So, firstly we will need a chairman, who is head of the meeting and the main person, then we need a secretary, who keeps a record of the meeting; also a very important person, and lastly a treasurer who looks after the money. This is a very vital position. The treasurer must be honest and good with money."

"I want to be the chairman," John shot his hand up.

"Actually," Archie mulled briefly, "for now I think I should be the chairman, because I am head of the family, and I know how to run a meeting. After all, it is I who will teach you. One day, John, you can be the chairman."

John's shoulders slumped in sad disappointment.

"John, for now, you can be the secretary. The secretary's job is essential."

John's face lit up. "Yay! That's just what I want to be."

Archie almost rolled his eyes to the ceiling but controlled himself. "Louis, you can be the treasurer, and you can look after the money. Now, we as a clan must all agree on that. Do you all agree?"

The boys nodded.

"Raise your hands so I can see that you agree," Archie exerted his chairmanship authority.

His sons raised their hands high, and Archie made a show of counting two hands.

"I also agree," Archie raised a hand briefly to comply with his rule. "Therefore, we all agree. The resolution is carried," he grinned broadly.

"Dad," Louis piped up, "are resolutions heavy?"

Archie looked confused for a moment. "Oh, no, Louis. It's just a way of talking – like people in business. A resolution is an agreement that is made on a decision, and if we say it is 'carried' then it means the agreement, or decision, is accepted. That's all."

"Oh," Louis forced a smile while he tried to look as if he understood.

"John, as the secretary, you need to record the resolutions. Here, write down on this paper that we all agree to be called 'The Langbourne Clan'. Now, the first rule of the Clan is that you have to be a Langbourne to be a member of the Clan. What do you think about that?"

"That's a good idea, Daddy," Louis bounced excitedly in his chair. "Just for us only."

"John, are you alright with that?"

"Yes, Dad," John was wriggling with excitement. The idea that his father was asking his approval was almost too much for him.

"Right oh," Archie chuckled, noticing the full attention his children were giving him. "So, please record that too. Now, we need an objective. We need to decide why we are creating the Langbourne Clan and what our purpose will be."

"I know! I know!" John threw a hand in the air. "To make lots of money."

"No, no, no," Archie objected, shaking his head as he looked at the carpet for help. "No, we have businesses that will make money for us. The Clan should be to help people who need help. If we get any money in the Clan, we should give it away to people who need it. Don't you think?"

The boys concurred eagerly, smiles and nodding heads showing full support for the idea.

"Agreed then, our objective is to help others, and to help our own family if need be. Next, we need a motto, something we need to base our Clan on."

"What's a motto, Daddy?" John asked, confusion lining his brow.

"It's a short phrase that tells us what our principals are. Maybe two or three words only."

"What's 'principals'?" John asked, still looking confused.

Archie sighed. "Well, how do I explain it? It's what we believe in, what we strive to be or do."

Much discussion took place without a resolution before Kate walked in and put an end to the evening. "Bedtime, boys," she declared, much to the disappointment of the newly inducted clan members.

"Aww, Mom! We need a motto," John objected immediately.

"A motto?" Kate mused. "Well, how about 'Honesty and Truth'?"

"Wow, Mom," John exclaimed, "you should be the Chairman; you are so clever!"

With everyone in total agreement, the meeting concluded, and the boys were sent to bed. Kate knew they would not get to sleep for a good while because of all the excitement, but, as a good mother, she was insistent that her household rules were always respected.

Later, when Archie and Kate had closed the door to the boys' adjoining room and retired to their own, she asked Archie how the meeting had gone.

"Splendidly," he chuckled. "It was a good start, and when they see the minutes, the formality of it all will become even more exciting. John's writing is terrible, so I will type it up later."

Kate smiled fondly at her husband. "He is only ten years old, darling. One day they will look back on this and will be thankful for what you have instilled in them."

"I hope so," Archie mulled.

Little did he realise how significant their little Clan would become.

THE LANGBOURNE CLAN

A meeting of The Langbourne Clan was held in the Meikle's Hotel on the 18th March 1940.

PRESENT:
Mr A Langbourne, Mr John Langbourne, Mr Louis Langbourne.

ELECTION OF CHAIRMAN:
Unanimously decided that Mr A Langbourne be the Chairman.

ELECTION OF TREASURER:
Unanimously decided that Mr L Langbourne be appointed Treasurer.

ELECTION OF SECRETARY:
Unanimously decided that Mr J Langbourne be appointed the Secretary.

It was resolved that only members of the Langbourne Family could be members of the Langbourne Clan, and that the membership fee would be the sum of one penny per week.

It was decided the objectives of the Langbourne Clan were to assist in making all people happy, and in particular to do our best to increase the happiness of the Langbourne Family.

MOTTO
Decided that the motto of the Clan to be as follows:
H O N E S T Y   A N D   T R U T H

MEETINGS:
Decided that all meetings can only be held after giving 24 hours notice to all members. Such notice to be posted in a conspicuous position so that all members can see it.

The meeting then closed with a thanks to the Chair.

A Langbourne
Chairman
28/3/1940

* * *

Archie utterly underestimated the effects that his lesson of the Clan would have on his two young sons. It opened up a new world to them, and, apart from the teachings of running a formal meeting, it made them understand the importance of family and people worldwide. There were lessons on keeping a book of accounts for money, and taking responsibility, not just fiscally but personally as well. He taught his sons the importance of doing one's best, and that of helping others less fortunate than themselves, amongst a host of other life lessons.

Archie brought in the sense of belonging by creating the 'official' Langbourne Clan Crest, a green and blue shield with a sash and banner depicted within, and flanked by two flags with the words 'Truth' on one of them, and 'Honesty' on the other, inscribed in bold letters. He issued badges in the same shape as the crest, which the boys helped create from cardboard, glue and a safety pin, and then suitably coloured in with crayon.

There was a system of punishments for misdemeanours, which usually involved the non-issue of the badge at the meeting. Raising funds for a worthy cause and doing good deeds was a vital part of the Clan's membership. These good deeds became the cornerstone of the Clan. To report three good deeds in one week entitled one to wear the Clan Badge for the duration of the next meeting. It almost became a badge of honour and was worn with extreme pride. Whenever it was presented, it came with a formal citation greatly embellished by the Chairman, a tradition that Archie perfected beyond reproach.

Apart from the motto of 'Honesty and Truth', a sub-motto was created to include the ideals of helping your fellow man. As Archie had learned some Latin in his school years, he took the term 'Da Dextram Misero', which roughly translated to 'give aid to the unfortunate', or sometimes translated to 'give your right hand'. He also knew it was the motto used by an American medical corps during wartime. This motto was added to the crest, and therefore to the badge.

To go one further, both John and Louis joined a Wolf Scout group, a junior section of the more significant Boy Scout Association formed by Robert Baden-Powell. Baden-Powell had been inspired by his American friend, Fredrick Russell Burnham, a tracker, or 'scout' as he was known then, whom he had met during the various uprisings and wars in Africa. It pleased Archie immensely as the Scout motto was 'Do Your Best', and his sons were taught many life skills, adding to the lessons Archie was teaching them through the Clan.

The Clan meetings were scheduled to take place once a month, and the boys eagerly looked forward to each one. Secretly, so did Archie. The next meeting, therefore, was held almost exactly one month later as planned.

Salisbury

21st April 1940

Meeting of the Langbourne Clan, held in Meikle's Hotel on the 21st April 1940.

PRESENT:
Mr A Langbourne (Chairman)
Mr L Langbourne (TREAS.)
Mr J Langbourne (SEC.)

MINUTES:
The minutes of the previous meeting were read and confirmed.

Collection:
The following amounts were collected from the Members present
A. Langbourne three pence
J. Langbourne three pence
L. Langbourne three pence
Total : 9 pence.
Decided that from the first available monies a minute book should be purchased.

Punishment:
Decided that the Committee has the power to punish any member who wilfully breaks any rule or who might bring the name of the Langbournes into disgrace.

Badges:
The Chairman donated badges for the Committee. A vote of thanks was passed to A. Langbourne for his generosity.
Agreed that before any member could earn his badge, he must perform three worthy deeds, the worthiness of which must be decided by the Committee.
Should a badge be taken away by the Committee for any reason, it cannot be earned again before one worthy deed is performed.

The meeting then closed with a vote of thanks to the Chair.

A. Langbourne
Chairman 28/4/1940

The meetings continued every month for some time thereafter. John was the first to receive his badge for helping a friend who was being attacked by bees. He was stung in the process, three times no less, and received heartfelt condolences from the committee.

The Clan Committee went further in suggesting a secret signal or sign with which to identify themselves. Archie thought this was a bit excessive, but, to keep up the interest of his sons, he agreed with the proposal, and the secret sign was developed – again in total secrecy. Not even Kate knew the sign, although she wasn't concerned one way or the other. As it was, her involvement with the war effort was all-consuming.

In one lesson, Archie took the opportunity of explaining to the boys how Morris and David had invented the 'black rhino' code, and how each member of the family, each city and each country they dealt with had codenames of their own.

John put his hand up in excitement, slicing the air several times. "Can I have a code, Dad? I want to be a lion."

Archie chuckled briefly. "You can have a codename, John, but not Lion. That is Uncle Morris' codename."

John was immediately disappointed and lowered his hand despondently.

"Have you got a codename?" Louis asked.

"Yes, they called me 'Tsindi'. It's a local word for squirrel."

"Why?" John was curious as always.

"I don't know. Perhaps because I am always scurrying around. David is Eagle because he loves birds, and Harry is Badger. Again, I have no idea why they gave him that name. You boys think about a codename you would like and tell me in the morning."

In May 1940, Kate, much as she opposed it, was inducted into the Langbourne Clan.

Nguni rubbed his chin thoughtfully. "I can see Boss Archie's heart belonged to his family."

"Yes," David said in agreement, although there was a forlorn look on his face. "One day Paddy went to Salisbury to visit Archie to do some business for us, but as soon as he arrived, he became very sick. Archie rushed him to St Anne's Hospital, which is close to where the family live, and the next day Paddy died. Nobody can tell us why. The doctor thinks it was probably a sickness he got when he was serving in German East Africa. He was only 46 years old. Too young," David shook his head solemnly.

Nguni contemplated this for a moment. "Maybe he got that water sickness you got when we moved all those wagons? You nearly died, but our traditional muthi fixed you. Maybe he should have seen a Xhosa healer."

"Perhaps," David mulled as he cast his thoughts momentarily to those dark weeks trekking through the Transvaal, days which he tried to forget. He felt he had never really fully recovered from whatever inflicted him there, that it still lurked deep inside him.

"Did he take a wife?" Nguni asked.

"Paddy?" David smiled affectionately. "Yes, Adele is her name, and they had two lovely children, Richard and Sonya. They live here in Bulawayo; near-near. I miss Paddy; he was such a lovely man. When he died the service at our place of worship was filled to capacity with friends paying their respects. It was good to see."

David relaxed back in his chair. "Tell me, how is your brother, Nguni? What news of him?"

"Daluxolo?" Nguni cocked a wry eyebrow that complimented his mischievous smile. "He's an old buffalo now. He stays in his village with all his wives and children. He drinks beer and gets fat."

David stared at Nguni with a quizzical look on his face; he wasn't sure if Nguni was joking or being serious.

Nguni chuckled. "He is very well. Nkosazana has given him many, many children. Some boys, some girls. The cattle you bought for us have grown very plump, and there are plenty now. Our crops are tall and strong. Our village is very happy."

"That is good to hear, Nguni," David smiled contentedly, and helped himself to another piece of shortbread. "I hope he is not working too hard. He must indeed be an old man now, like you and me."

"Ghaw!" Nguni hawked in disgust. "Daluxolo has too many wives to do all his work. His belly is bigger than mine!"

David suddenly let out an uncontrolled laugh, catching some shortbread crumbs in his cupped hand. "Well," David grinned, "perhaps it is a good sign that he has had a good life."

"Yes, we have all had a good life," Nguni agreed. "Daluxolo and me, we were talking by the fire one night, and we said our best times were being in the bush with you. It was the times we laughed the most. Our favourite time was when you were trying to steal a feather from the vulture."

David laughed heartily at the memory. He had hidden in a hole in the ground with the putrefying carcass of an impala above him, hoping to snatch a feather from a live vulture as they fed on the dead animal. A Zulu tribal tradition, this was the right of passage for a young male, and David, rather stupidly, decided he wanted to test his manhood as a Zulu. When the vultures descended, the resultant feeding frenzy was so violent that the putrid entrails, ripped from the belly of the antelope, fell into the hole and onto David's head and shoulders. He had begun retching from the vile odour and had no escape.

"It was a bad day for me," David said between laughs, and wiped a tear from his eye. "I failed the Zulu ritual. In the Zulu tradition, I am not a man."

"You are not a Zulu," Nguni's belly shook with laughter. "Maybe a Xhosa, or a Matabele, but not a Zulu."

The banter and memories flowed, and their friendship re-bonded as if they had never been apart. David had not laughed this much in many a year – decades in fact. His work and travel had long been his life. It had been so intense that he and Hanna managed to visit their children at Cheltenham College but once a year if that.

When the laughter died down, David became pensive. "You saved my life many times over. I owe my life to you and Daluxolo. You know that?"

Nguni simply shrugged. "You are my friend. You would save me if I had a problem."

"That I would," David agreed, "that I would."

"Daluxolo is well, but not as strong as the young man you remember."

"Yes, not one of us is as strong as we were."

"When you last saw Daluxolo he was strong and a good tracker…"

"He was the best," David interrupted. "He tracked me down in the lost valley in the Western Cape when even a British army could not."

"That is true," Nguni reflected on his brother's skills. "There was a man in Port Elizabeth who came to our village one day. He had heard of the tracking skills of Daluxolo, and offered my brother a job to track a very big leopard that was killing his cattle."

"Did he take the job?" David asked.

"Yes, he took the job. He was offered many cattle in payment, but it was not because of the cattle he took the job. He wanted to go to the bush again. When he was with you, he was the happiest I have ever seen him. So, he went. It was very far away; they travelled for many days."

"Did he find the leopard?"

"Yes, of course!" Nguni almost looked indignant that David would question his brother's skills. "But they did not kill it. Instead, the leopard killed the hunter."

"Oh my," David was shocked. "What happened?"

"The hunter was not good. He could not shoot straight like you. Daluxolo took the man close to the animal, but when he shot, he missed. The leopard ran away. The hunter was very angry and made Daluxolo find it again. For a second time, Daluxolo tracked the leopard and found him. It was huge, the biggest leopard my brother had ever seen. The leopard was observing them carefully. Then the hunter shot at it again and missed."

"Oh dear," David shuffled in his chair; he could sense what was coming.

"The hunter was very angry again. He said Daluxolo was not taking him close enough to shoot it. But the leopard was very clever. He was watching everything and saw what the man was trying to do. The leopard was so angry he began to hunt the hunter."

"What happened?" David asked, now completely engrossed in the story.

"They followed the spoor for two days. The leopard was making the men walk very far, and making them tired. They came to a flat area of grass with just one tree in the middle, and the hunter told Daluxolo to walk ahead to see if the tracks went to the tree, because he believed the animal was resting there.

"Daluxolo said the leopard made his tracks to the tree, but he knew the leopard was cunning and was hiding somewhere else, but the man told Daluxolo to go forward. So my brother did. He could see the tracks going towards the tree, and was searching in the grass and the tree very hard but could not see anything. Suddenly Daluxolo remembered the cunning of the leopard and realised that he must be behind them, watching them. He turned to tell the hunter to be careful and saw the leopard crouching in the grass just behind the hunter.

"Before Daluxolo could shout to the hunter, the leopard jumped from the grass. The hunter turned, but was too late; the leopard came very fast and bit the man's neck. With the back legs, he cut the man's stomach completely open and killed him right away. But now, my brother was in big trouble because he was standing on the open ground with no gun, and the leopard was looking at him. He said the anger in its eyes was terrible."

"Oh no," David moaned. He knew Daluxolo would have been in serious trouble.

Nguni continued. "The leopard then ran to Daluxolo and bit him first on his arm, then on his leg, but then stopped, and let him go."

"Really?" David was intrigued, "I wonder why?"

"Because," Nguni said with an air of confidence, "the leopard was watching what the hunter did, and he knew Daluxolo was not the hunter, but he was teaching him a lesson. He was saying to my brother, 'I can see you were forced to hunt me, but you must never do it again, so I will let you go'."

"So was Daluxolo alright?" David asked cautiously.

"No," Nguni replied. "Daluxolo was very seriously injured. His arm was broken like a dry twig, and his leg had big holes in it. He could hardly walk."

"Oh, dear. So how did Daluxolo get rescued?"

"He managed to walk to a village where they looked after him while someone sent for me. I went to him along with his wife, Nkosazana, and our healer, and seven young men. When he was strong enough, we carried him home. Daluxolo has never tracked anyone or any animal since then."

David let out a heavy sigh. "That was a horrible story, Nguni. Daluxolo was very lucky."

"Yes," Nguni agreed. "You, Boss David, were the last person he tracked. He is happy with that. Now he watches his chickens and gets fat." Nguni chuckled at his joke.

"I must agree," David attempted a smile, "that Daluxolo was a first-class tracker. And he could hide his tracks even better!"

"He did a good job when we were running and hiding from those soldiers," Nguni said. "That man, the leader of those soldiers, I wonder what happened to him? And the farmer who was your friend. That was a sorrowful time."

"Oh," David suddenly looked Nguni in the eye. "I met Commander Reitz in Cape Town some years later. He had a great deal of admiration for you and Daluxolo. A great deal."

"Is that so?" Nguni asked.

The two friends on the veranda became pensive as they reflected on their escape from the Boer commando, silently reaching for their mugs simultaneously.

CHAPTER THIRTEEN
New York 1942

Morris stepped onto the sidewalk of his New York hotel. That winter's day in November of 1942 was unusually cold, and Morris shrugged deeper into his woollen overcoat, turning the collar up to try and protect the back of his neck from the icy chill. Hailing a cab, he gave the driver the address of a budget motel some ten minutes north and settled into the rear seat for the short journey.

For a change, Morris' thoughts were not on his business, but they were troubled by the news coming out of Europe. War had been raging for almost three years now; Germany had invaded Russia, Poland, France, Austria and a host of other European countries. The battlefront with England was fierce, with aerial bombings a daily occurrence on both sides of the Channel.

When the arm of war reached out and touched its icy fingers on London, Morris wasted no time. He insisted that all women and children of the Langbourne family evacuate and travel to America immediately. He would accommodate and support them in his 14-roomed mansion in Holmby Hills. Some family members grasped the offer; others didn't, leaving Morris somewhat perplexed at the decision of those who had decided to remain in harm's way.

A cryptic letter from his old friend and mentor in London, Yoni Goldberg, had Morris travelling from California to New York for a clandestine meeting, to which he was now headed. He would typically ignore a request for such a meeting, a meeting without a reason or agenda. However, coming from Yoni Goldberg, Morris wasted no time in making arrangements to accommodate this request, even if it was on the other side of the American continent.

Yoni's motel was well overdue for refurbishment. Paint was peeling from the walls, and, as Morris alighted from the cab, he noticed the roof over the two-story complex was missing some tiles. Crinkling his nose in mild distaste, he paid the cab driver, then strode over to Room 24, ignoring the reception office.

Morris didn't need to knock; as he approached the door he noticed the curtain in the window of the room shift slightly, followed immediately by the door opening wide, and none other than Yoni Goldberg stepped into the freezing air to greet his long-time friend. Arms outstretched, he gave Morris a brief embrace, then ushered him into his room and out of the cold.

While pleasantries were being made, Morris studied his mentor; he was shocked at how much Yoni had aged since he had last seen the man. Yoni's usually bushy black beard, a feature that made him stand out in a crowd, had thinned, patches of grey streaking it in parts. It was no longer as perfectly manicured as it had always been in the past, and even Yoni's thick mop of black hair had greyed and thinned significantly.

"How is your lovely wife?" Morris asked.

"Ruth is well, but the war is taking its toll on her. Life is not easy in London right now. There are many shortages, and our lives are very disrupted. How about you, Morris? Your wife and children?"

"We are divorced now, but that's alright," he quickly reassured his friend. "Most of my children are still in England. They don't seem to have an interest in the safety of America. My youngest son from my marriage to Rose Bertha, Derrick was his name, was tragically killed four months ago in Durban, South Africa."

"I'm so sorry to hear that, my friend," Yoni said with genuine shock in his voice.

"He was in the army, but it was an accident. He was a passenger in a friend's automobile; his death was not a result of the war," Morris became pensive for a brief moment. "You don't look well, Yoni," Morris frowned as he typically changed the subject.

Yoni's eyes were bloodshot. It looked as though he had not had a good night's sleep in months. The lines on his forehead were deep, and dark bags hung under his eyes.

"Things are not well, Morris," the learned gentleman's shoulders slumped as he sat slowly on a cheap fabric-covered armchair, motioning Morris to sit in the remaining seat. "The war in England is dreadful. The Germans are now flying bombing raids over the Channel and dropping bombs on us."

"So I've heard," Morris nodded forlornly as he took the proffered seat.

"Our problems are small in comparison to what is happening on the European continent, though. Hitler is exterminating the Jews in the tens of thousands. Every day! It's terrible."

Morris had heard that the Germans were rounding up the Jewish populations in all the countries they had occupied and deporting them to unknown destinations. Still, for him in California, news had a distinctly American slant and tended to focus on American wartime activities in various other parts of the world. Pearl Harbour in Hawaii had been bombed almost a year earlier, bringing the Americans into the war. Japan had invaded Singapore a few months later, and the entire Pacific was suddenly in conflict. What Hitler was doing to the Jews, gypsies, homosexuals and other minorities in the countries he had invaded was known, but not understood, and indeed the actual extent of it was fairly unknown to most of the world.

"Yoni," Morris reached over to the man and placed a firm hand on his arm. "Bring your wife. Bring Ruth, and you two must stay with me in my home in California until the war is over. I have plenty of room for your family. You check out of this hotel this very instant and come with me."

Yoni smiled his appreciation. "That's not why I'm here, my friend. I will not leave England and my people during the war. I am here to ask my American friends for their help."

Morris raised his eyebrows in surprise. "I'm not a fighting man, Yoni. It is against my principals. Besides, I am too old to fight."

"I'm not asking you to fight with your body, my friend, but with your money. We have many sympathisers who are secretly helping the Jews wherever they can. I'm asking you for financial help, to help them. We believe our people are being systematically rounded up and exterminated. People are disappearing. There is torture, rape, murder, suffering, and often it is done in front of their children. You have no idea what the Nazi regime is doing to our people." Yoni related several atrocities that were being committed against the Jews.

It shook Morris to the core; he had had no idea how terrible the reality was. "I don't want to know any more," Morris interrupted his friend and shook his head in sorrow, and for the first time in his life, a tear began to well on his lower eyelids.

"We cannot compete with the guns and bombs, or the tanks and military might. We have to rescue as many Jews as we can, we need to move them out of German hands and move them to safe countries; it takes money to do that. We must show the world what is happening, and get resources over there. It takes a lot of money."

"I have money," Morris said without hesitation. "I sold my shipping company just before the war started, you helped me with that, as you know."

Morris had enjoyed the fruits and the many advantages of a shipping company, which he bought at a very low price after the Anglo Boer War ended in 1902. It was a time when many companies had over-extended themselves as they profiteered at the British government's expense and demand. However, along with the abrupt end of the Boer War, came the end of the high shipping demand, and many businesses collapsed. Not just the shipping sector went into liquidation; the ramifications of the sudden end of the war was enormous. It was a perfect time for Morris to step in and pick up precisely what he wanted, using a massive windfall from the sale of second-hand army boots to the Russian military.

When, in 1938, Morris saw the signs of a possible war erupting in Europe, and the rise of Hitler, his concerns were focused on a new threat – the rapid development of Hitler's submarines, or U-Boats as they were commonly known. Underwater bombing machines, to Morris, were a threat he could not ignore, simply because they were a direct threat to his inventory – his ships. Morris had had a close shave with this threat during the First World War, or the Great War as it was called. He was no longer going to risk his vessels being destroyed and sunk, and besides, he had already made a fortune in the business. So, with Yoni's knowledge and contacts in the marine insurance industry, he sold his interest in his shipping company, for a healthy profit.

Morris pulled a cheque book from his breast pocket and then reached for a fountain pen in another. Removing the cap and, while resting the cheque book on his knee, Morris scribbled a number in the box allocated for numerals. He followed it by several zeros, signed it with his illegible scrawl and tore it out of the booklet.

"Will this help you? It's the entire proceeds from the sale of my shipping company. I don't need it. It is yours to do with as you feel necessary," Morris gave a curt nod as he handed Yoni the cheque.

Yoni took the cheque and studied it in silence. Then he lowered his head and began to sob uncontrollably.

"Come," Morris stood and helped his old friend up, embracing his shaking shoulders as he did so. "You need a good meal and a solid sleep. You will come to my hotel this very minute. I will not have you stay here a moment longer."

Morris was not used to emotional scenes, and he needed to get out of the third-rate motel, which had simply added to the unpleasantness of the day. He paid the bill, hailed a taxi, and bundled Yoni and his small tote bag into it.

Morris knew the subject of the war was not over. They would undoubtedly discuss it further in the morning.

When he returned to Holmby Hills in Los Angeles two days later, the first thing he did was book an international telephone call to David in Bulawayo. David's phone rang at half-past two in the morning, and Morris did virtually all the talking. It was brief, and very much to the point.

David hung up and returned to bed, almost stunned at what he had just heard on the telephone.

"What's the matter?" Hanna asked. She had turned on the bedside lamp and was already sitting up in bed.

"That was Morris," David said, almost in a daze. "Some terrible things are happening in Germany. Terrible things are happening to the Jews there."

"What?" Hanna asked, alarm tainting her voice.

"I'm not exactly sure, but they are trying to exterminate the Jewish race. The Jews in Europe need help and money. We can help with money, so Morris would like our brothers to contribute as much as we can. Morris has already donated all his profits from his old shipping company."

"Will you?" Hanna asked, but she already knew the answer.

"Of course, and I know Harry will too. I'll also talk to Herbert; Louis left him a lot of money when he died. We have to do what we can."

"Fighting is not good," Nguni rumbled softly. "The money Boss Morris gave; did it save many people?"

"We will never know," David answered as he poured fresh hot tea into their cups. "What those people are doing with Morris' money is very secret, but Mr Goldberg has told Morris that many lives were saved, and are still being saved, and many people are risking their lives to do this. Lots of people are giving money, not just us. The war is still raging, even today. It is a terrible war. I don't know what Mr Goldberg does with the money, but I know he is helping the cause. It is probably best we never know."

Nguni nodded solemnly, then noisily took a sip of his tea.

"In fact," David continued, "even Archie in Salisbury is raising money for the Jewish cause. His wife, Kate, is very active in some groups of people raising money to help. She is a lovely person. They have two sons, one called John and the other called Louis."

"Ahh…" Nguni smiled as he appreciated how Archie had passed Louis' name to the next generation. "That is good. And how is Boss Archie doing over there, in Salisbury?"

"Very well, actually," David took a sip of his sweet beverage. "He runs a very sound business, and we are all happy with him. He and Morris don't talk to each other much, but that's alright; it's normal for the two of them."

"What about Boss Hurry?" Nguni asked with a smile. "I remember his shoes were always so big."

"Harry?" David laughed. "Yes, he has big feet. He is very well. In fact, he will be here shortly. You will see him; he will stay for dinner. You will stay for dinner too. I insist."

Nguni's face became very sad, and he cast his eyes to the floor. David noticed his sudden change in mood.

"What's wrong, my friend?" David asked gently.

Nguni looked David in the eye; a dark cloud seemed to weigh him down. "It is not possible to see Boss Hurry. It is time; we must go now."

David stared at his friend, a puzzled look on his face. "We? Where are we going?"

"I have come to show you the way to Nomandudwane."

"Nomandudwane?" David exclaimed, completely puzzled. "Way out there in the bush? The place of the scorpion? Where I got stung by that scorpion when I was a young man?"

"Yes," Nguni said, still looking forlorn.

"Why must you show me the way there? I don't want to go there now."

Furrows of concern appeared between Nguni's eyebrows. "Once, when we were there, you said you wished for your spirit to return to Nomandudwane to rest when you reached the end of your life."

David laughed heartily. "Yes, I did, Nguni. At the end of my life, yes. I am amazed you have remembered that I said that. My spirit can rest there after I die. But I'm not ready to go there now."

Nguni remained silent, and David noticed his friend's deep concern. It was troubling, and David's jocularity very quickly left him. He wondered why Nguni would say such a thing, and why he would travel so far to insist on this journey.

"Nguni," David cocked his head, inquisitively, "what are you telling me?"

"It is time, Boss," Nguni said in his soothing, rumbling voice. "I have been sent to show you the way."

"Time for me to go to Nomandudwane?" David looked very puzzled and shook his head. "So, you are saying I have died. When did this happen?" he chuckled nervously. Something didn't seem right.

"When I came here to see you."

"Like, now-now?" David asked.

"Yes, Boss. Now-now."

David suddenly felt a little uncertain with the direction the conversation was heading. For a moment he thought Nguni was going a bit senile in his old age. He scratched his head, not quite sure how to handle what was being said.

"What makes you think I am dead, my friend?" David asked, but this time there was a nervous tremble in his voice; the conversation was taking on a bizarre tone, and David was becoming very uncomfortable.

Nguni cast a glance over David's shoulder and tossed his head very slightly. David spun in his chair and looked in that direction. A very odd sight greeted him, something he struggled to comprehend.

He saw himself lying on the lounger, asleep, covered by the light blanket Hanna had draped over him. His body looked at peace and very comfortable. He stared at the bewildering sight, his mind racing for answers, but he came up with nothing.

David turned back to Nguni. "Nguni?"

Nguni nodded his head matter-of-factly, a look of concern still on his face, and he slowly turned to stare at his feet.

"Well," David said as he slumped back in his chair, "That's not very convenient. I'm meeting Harry in a few minutes."

Nguni quickly looked up at David, their eyes met, unwavering and searching.

Finally, David broke the silence. "So, the time has come, has it?"

"Yes Boss," Nguni repeated, but this time a small smile hooked at the corners of his mouth.

David swivelled in his chair once more to reconfirm what he had just seen, then looked back at Nguni. "I have so much more I need to do. I can't go now. Morris needs me, and Hanna..." David trailed off.

"It is not for us to decide, Boss David. When it is our time, then it is our time," Nguni rumbled softly.

David stared hard at Nguni. "What are you saying, my friend? Are you... also...?"

"Yes, Boss," Nguni nodded with a broad smile.

"When?" David exclaimed.

"Two years ago. There was a big storm coming, so I ran to shelter under a tree, but the lightning came and struck the tree I was under."

"I am sorry to hear that, my friend."

"Ghah!" Nguni dismissed David's sympathy with a wave of his hand. "It was my time, and I am not worried. I had a good life. I am happy."

"My religion says my soul will go to a state of peace, not to a place," David frowned. "I'm not sure my soul is supposed to go to Nomandudwane."

Nguni contemplated what David has said for a moment. "When we were there, you named the place 'Nomandudwane', *the place of the scorpion*, because you said you felt at peace there, and that place made you think of Africa the way it should always be."

"Yes," David agreed, "even after the trauma of being stung by that scorpion, I still remember that place fondly. Funny how a place that can cause so much pain still brings back such fine memories."

Nguni shook his head slowly. "I think a part of you will always be in Africa, even if you were born in Europe. If where you are at peace is not a place, then I do not understand. Your culture is sometimes very confusing."

David grinned. "You know, I think I might have forgotten how to find Nomandudwane," he winked as he replaced his teacup on the table. "It has been a very long time."

"That is why I have come to lead you there," Nguni laughed, his voice rumbling down the veranda, "but I am not carrying you this time. You can walk on your own."

David burst out laughing. "I will walk, my friend, I will walk. But first I must say goodbye to Hanna."

Nguni suddenly looked pensive again. "That cannot be done, my friend. It is time to go. But she will see you soon, in Nomandudwane."

"How? When? Hanna doesn't know where Nomandudwane is."

"Four more years, she will join you. Daluxolo will come and show her the way."

"Four years?" David said softly. A tear rolled down one cheek, and he wiped it away with the back of his hand.

Reaching for his teacup, David peered into the bottom of it. The tea had gone cold, and as he swirled what was left, black tea leaves circled and turned lazily in the brown liquid. He watched Nguni lift his cup, take a small sip, then swirl the remainder of what was left. With a deft flick of his wrist, Nguni tossed the dregs of his tea and all the soggy contents out of the enamel mug, and into the garden. A small line of splashes dotted the veranda floor.

David smiled; this was their unspoken custom when, in the bush, a session of tea-drinking was over. In western culture, David would *never* throw out the dregs of his tea, but politely leave his cup in its saucer. In the bush, etiquette and table manners were left behind for the cities and suburbs to contend with. They were different, and they all had meaning.

He looked again into the bottom of his cup, swirled the remains and, in time-honoured bush fashion, he also tossed them into the garden. He grinned widely; he knew Hanna would certainly not approve.

Both men stood, and David squeezed his best friend on his shoulder.

"Then it shall be," David said. "Show me the way, Nguni."

Nguni gripped David firmly on his shoulder, a symbol of brotherhood and friendship, then gestured towards the garden.

"*Mashihambe!*" Nguni boomed in glee.

Both men were smiling broadly as they stepped off the veranda.

CHAPTER FOURTEEN
Bulawayo 1943

Pulling into the driveway in his black British made Rover Saloon, Harry cut the engine and applied the hand brake. He saw Hanna kneeling in the garden tending to her rose bushes. Retrieving his leather briefcase from the passenger seat, Harry alighted.

"Hello, Harry," Hanna called out cheerily as she stood up. Her joints were a little stiff, and Harry noticed she was trying to conceal the effort it took her to get up from her kneeling position.

"Hanna," Harry responded as he straightened his tie and patted his lapels down with his free hand. Striding up to her, they embraced briefly and exchanged a peck on the cheek.

"How's that lovely wife of yours?" Hanna asked kindly.

"Fit as a fiddle, thanks. Anne sends her love. She gets back from Johannesburg tomorrow now, not Friday."

"Oh, you'll be pleased with that. How was your day?" Hanna asked.

"It could have been better," Harry grumbled. "I wish this damn war would come to an end. Business is certainly affected."

"Come through," Hanna hooked her arm into the crook of her brother-in-law's elbow. "David is resting on the back veranda. I know he is anxious to see you. We have lamb stew for dinner, by the way."

"Excellent," Harry beamed. "Just what I was hoping for."

Hanna giggled; she knew Harry well, and truly enjoyed his

company. They gaily walked into the house, arm in arm, chatting about trivialities, before emerging onto the veranda at the rear. They saw David resting, eyes closed, but he did not stir.

"David," Hanna almost sang out, "Harry's here. Wake up, Dear." But there was no response.

"David?" Hanna's tone suddenly changed.

Harry felt a heavy rush in the pit of his stomach. He had a bad feeling and wanted to call out to his brother and rush over to him, but Hanna beat him to it. She touched David's shoulder and gave him a gentle push. When there was still no response, Hanna touched his forehead with her palm. Her sudden gasp sent a wave of nausea through Harry. Hesitantly he stepped over to Hanna, and, as she straightened, Harry held her around her shoulders; he didn't know what else to do.

They stood in silence, staring at David's lifeless body, both uncertain as to what to do or say next. Harry felt Hanna's shoulders begin to shake, and he held her all the more tightly. Harry wanted to cry himself, but composed himself, albeit with great difficulty. He knew he had to remain strong for her.

Stepping around to David's body, Harry felt David's wrist to press for a pulse, but the unnaturally limp feel in David's arm scared him, and he instantly knew his brother was deceased.

"We should call Dr Kotzen," Harry broke the tense silence. He noticed that Hanna was trying desperately to control her emotions and had covered her mouth with her hand, attempting to compose herself.

Hanna nodded. "Yes, if you wouldn't mind. There's a phone book under the telephone."

"I'll be right back," Harry assured Hanna as he quickly went inside to do the necessary. When he returned, he found Hanna sitting in the Morris chair looking composed and in control of herself.

"Look," Hanna drew Harry's attention to the little coffee table with a gentle wave of her hand. "David must have passed away only moments after I brought him his tea. He hasn't touched it. The teapot is cold."

Harry felt awkward and wasn't sure how to react. Instead he took a seat in the available chair and cleared his throat. "Ivor Kotzen is on his way. I just caught him."

Hanna and Harry sat in reflective silence waiting for the doctor. Dr Kotzen arrived fifteen minutes later and pronounced David dead. He contacted the Chevra Kadisha, a group of Jewish people who prepare the body before burial, and gave Hanna much needed support until some of her closest friends came around to offer more comfort.

Harry, once he had done all he could for Hanna, returned to his own home and booked a long-distance call to Los Angeles. He was dreading making this call, and, for over an hour, he sat staring at the telephone apparatus, trying to plan what he would say to Morris. He knew, however, that no matter how many times he rehearsed his speech, it would never come out the way he wanted it to.

Finally, the phone rang, and Harry gingerly picked up the receiver.

"Hello," his voice quaked uncontrollably.

The operator's voice sounded metallic. "Hello, is that Mr Langbourne? You booked a call to California, USA?"

"Yes, this is Harry Langbourne. Thank you," Harry confirmed.

"Hold on; I'll connect you shortly."

Harry listened to some clicks and inaudible chatter, before finally hearing Morris' familiar voice crackle quietly in the background as he accepted the call.

"I'm putting you through now," the operator said just as the line clicked and became slightly clearer.

"Morris?" Harry tended to shout down the receiver.

"Yes, Harry," Morris responded, his voice sounding very tinny. "What is it?"

"I have some bad news, Morris," Harry replied, and paused, he didn't quite know how to say this. "David passed away this afternoon."

There was silence. Then, "What happened?" Morris exclaimed.

"I went around to see David today. He passed away just before I got there, I think." Harry's voice faltered. There was an awkward silence, and Harry wasn't sure if Morris had heard him, so he continued. "Did you hear me?"

"David died?" Morris asked.

"Yes, this afternoon. He was resting on his patio, and he died in his sleep."

"No, surely not," Morris asserted.

"Yes," Harry said simply. "Hanna and I found him. It was a great shock."

"Was he in pain, was he sick?"

"No, he was resting on his patio, and he just slipped away in his sleep."

There was another long pause.

Morris finally broke the silence. "Alright, thank you, Harry. How is Hanna?"

"She is surrounded by friends."

"Good," Morris said. "I will phone you tomorrow. I have to think. I... I am in shock. Look after Hanna."

"I will. Good night Brother."

"I wish you long life, Harry. We will talk tomorrow." Morris ended the conversation with an abrupt click.

David was buried in the Bulawayo cemetery. At the service, the Synagogue had been packed to capacity, and the eulogies were emotional and touching. Morris did not come to the funeral; he was too far away and also deeply involved in a business venture that was taxing both his time and his money. Besides, most commercial flights that routed through Europe were suspended for the duration of the war, South African Airways in particular.

One week after David's funeral, Morris booked an international call to Rhodesia. He needed to ask Harry many questions, and the postal service would take far too long to get the necessary replies back to him. That just would not do. As expensive as the call might be, Morris needed to make some difficult decisions, and the conversation he would have with Harry, he knew, would be brief and to the point.

Morris' biggest concern was that suddenly, with David's passing,

Harry was the only one of the four original full brothers who remained in Africa. When the telephone call was finally connected, Morris was relieved to hear that it was relatively clear and free of the annoying static and crackles.

"Morning, Harry," Morris began, "let's be brief. This call is costing me a fortune."

"Good evening, Brother," Harry replied, getting in a dig that it was very late where he was.

"Can you handle Rhodesia and all of the South African businesses without Eagle?" Morris asked, referring to David in his code name.

"Under normal circumstances, yes. But without both Giraffe and Eagle, no," Harry had to be honest. Because of the war, the business was tremendously demanding as it was. Now, with the loss of both Louis and David, Harry was left feeling deflated.

"Meaning?" Morris said abruptly.

"I can't find staff. Almost every able-bodied person in both countries has gone to fight this damnable war."

"I didn't realise it was that bad in Rhodesia," Morris stated.

"It's far worse than you realise. Loxton and Johnson have gone off to fight, so I'm holding down Bulawayo on my own. All the managers in South Africa are fighting somewhere in North Africa, and I have heard that our manager of the East London branch was killed in action. The exception is Port Elizabeth; our manager there is still operative. All the same, it means I have to travel every fortnight, which leaves Bulawayo without leadership while I am away; and travel is hellishly expensive now, you have no idea! I had to close down Kimberley last week. The sales are simply not happening, and we only have one salesman employed there. I had to let him go."

The line went silent as Morris digested what Harry had said. To Morris, the situation was dire. It was evident to him that when David was in the mix, they were barely holding their heads above water, but now, well, David's death had changed everything.

"Alright, Harry," Morris began slowly, "you will have to close down the African operation. Close it all down, Langbourne

Brothers, Langbourne Coetzee, the warehouses, shipping office, purchasing, everything. I will phone Danie in Johannesburg and ask him to assist you. I want the shut-down finalised in three months. Terminate the leases, sell all commercial property and sell all stock. Discount like hell. Get rid of everything."

"Completely? All of it?" Harry asked tentatively. "What about Archie in Salisbury?"

"Give him the option of shutting down with you. I honestly don't care what he does; we have very little to do with him now anyhow. If he opts to stay open, he will have to find his own suppliers. If that is the case, make a deal with him to take over all your stock in trade, and sell him our 50% in his business; let him have the lot. He will do a deal with you, he thrives on negotiations. I'm sure, though, with those conditions, he will probably shut shop too."

"Do you know," Harry added, "that Langbourne Brothers have been operational for 50 years now. A closure will be big news here."

"50 years in Rhodesia, yes, and 52 years in Africa. It's time to close the doors, Harry. We have had a good innings."

"What do I do with the capital?"

"I'll structure some trusts and entities with Danie. We will invest in the stock markets. It will keep us liquid and earning without the stresses that commerce brings with it – staff, rent, purchases; those sorts of things."

"Very well, Brother," Harry sighed. He was truthfully quite relieved. "Are you planning to come out here?"

"Perhaps, after the war," Morris mused, "I'm involved in some big projects right now. I'm building some commercial properties in Arizona and financing a movie in Hollywood. It's taking a lot of my time. After the war I want you to fly over here and visit me. We have much to discuss."

Harry was intrigued. "What's the name of the movie?"

"The name is a secret, but I can tell you that it's story about a Christian Saint; Joan of Arc."

"Right oh," Harry shrugged while holding the receiver. "I will update you next week, then. Goodbye, Morris."

There was a loud click as the line disconnected. Morris was not in the habit of returning a farewell greeting, so, as always, abruptly hung up. Harry gently put the receiver down and stared, in deep concentration, at a painting on the wall.

Anne walked into the room and silently watched her husband for a moment. "Everything alright, Dear?" she asked.

Harry sighed deeply. "After half a century, Langbourne Brothers is closing down."

Anne walked up to Harry and gave him a loving squeeze. She recognised this as the end of an extraordinary era.

Barely four days later Archie alighted from the train and stepped onto the familiar Bulawayo platform. He wore his usual oversized day suit, the trousers held up by suspenders, and his felt Fedora hat. Archie didn't look to see if anyone had come to greet him. After all, it was just past six o'clock in the morning, and he had much on his mind.

The phone call from Harry concerned him deeply; his half-brother had sounded very upset, and he had refused to discuss anything over the phone. Archie had visited Bulawayo just a fortnight earlier, for David's funeral, and now he had been expected to return with a dash of urgency. Revisiting the distraught Hanna would be a welcome occasion, as he adored her, but his meeting with Harry held some trepidation for him. Something told him this was going to be a very testing day.

Archie felt in his gut that he was on the brink of losing his business, and he was going to have none of that. A deep-seated sense of anger was fermenting in the pit of his stomach. The emotions allied to the loss of David, and all the sentiment that surrounded the funeral, was bad enough, but, coupled with the abominable war in Europe, the awkward phone call from Harry was keeping Archie awake at night. His tightly-held anger was strung taut like the piano wire at 'Middle C'. Clasping his well-worn leather carry-all containing a change of clothes and his toiletries, Archie strode towards Abercorn Street.

Of course, being just after six in the morning, Langbourne Brothers was closed. It caused more frustration for Archie, but, realising it was nobody's fault, he walked over to a nearby hotel and ordered some breakfast. There was no one there that he knew, so he ate in solitary silence, and read through *The Chronicle*, the official newspaper of Bulawayo.

Just before eight o'clock, Archie paid his bill and made his way to the Abercorn Street warehouse. The door was still firmly closed. Impatiently, he checked the time on his wristwatch. Just as the minute hand hit eight o'clock precisely, Harry swung open the door.

Archie forced a smile. "Punctual as always, Harry."

"Since the beginning of time," Harry responded with a dry smile. "Come on in, Archie. Thank you for making the trip down here."

The boiling fury in Archie's stomach immediately reduced to a gentle simmer; this was not the greeting Archie expected. Harry seemed more relaxed than usual, almost pleased to see him. He served tea in the staff room, and the entire conversation seemed quite placid, much to Archie's surprise. Once the brothers sat down with steaming cups in front of them, Harry began, a deep furrow creasing his brow.

"Archie, thanks again for coming at such short notice. I'm guessing you have an inkling of what I am about to say."

"No," Archie replied bluntly, the molten lava in his stomach quickly coming to the boil once more.

Harry tilted his head slightly and looked at Archie quizzically. "Alright. Somehow I would have thought you would put two and two together," Harry slowly spread his hands, palms down, on the desk as if clearing a space. "With the sad passing of David, and without Louis, I cannot manage all the businesses in both Rhodesia – Bulawayo specifically – and South Africa. Not only that but, as you are well aware, all the menfolk are off fighting this abominable war.

"I have discussed this with Morris in America, and we have decided to close down all sections of Langbourne Brothers and Langbourne Coetzee."

Archie leaned forward in his seat, a look of determination starting to envelop his face. "What about me? Are you going to tell me to shut down as well?"

"No," Harry smiled. "You are Langbourne Trading, and nothing to do with us. We have no say in your business. You must feel free to do what you feel is best for you. Of course, we still have shares of your business, so we will need to negotiate what we do with those depending on the direction you take."

Archie almost let out an audible sigh. To cover his relief, he picked up his cup of tea and took a noisy sip, stalling for time to restructure the intended outburst that had been ready to erupt from his mouth.

"I must do what I want?" Archie asked, to confirm that he had heard correctly.

Harry's smile seemed to encompass some kindness at that question. "Indeed. You are your own entity. However, if you decide to continue, this decision will affect the agreement we have with you in that you won't be able to purchase goods through our offices anymore."

"I understand," Archie nodded, his mind now racing off on a new tangent. "Nor will I be able to enjoy the discounts and buying power of the Langbourne Group."

"Exactly," Harry agreed as he took a noiseless sip of his tea. "Indeed, you will be pretty much on your own from now on."

"What's going to happen to your staff?" Archie asked, genuine concern lacing his voice.

"I don't know, exactly," Harry admitted. "They don't know yet, obviously. We will give them a generous pay-out."

"I might be able to take some of them if they are prepared to move to Salisbury."

Harry sighed. "If you could make an offer to our bookkeeper, Ivy Collier, I would be very grateful."

"No problems there," Archie nodded curtly and leaned back in his seat. "If she is willing, I'll take her without hesitation."

"Do you remember Daluxolo?" Harry asked.

"Never met him, but of course I know all about him and his brother, Nguni."

"I'm employing his grandson; his name is Eric. He's young, but he is an outstanding worker, and very well presented. You would do

Morris and me a huge favour if you employed him. We owe a lot to his family."

"Consider it done," Archie nodded. "To be honest, I thought you were going to force me to shut down."

Harry chuckled loudly. "We may have had our differences over the years, Archie, but you are family, after all, and we look after each other."

Archie shook his head slowly but allowed a soft laugh to escape. "We are a complicated family, but I agree, we are family, and I do have a deep respect for all the brothers."

For a brief moment, both men wallowed in the warmth of a rare truce.

Harry grinned and shook a warning finger at Archie. "Admit it, Archie, you are the difficult one. You are stubborn, cantankerous and downright belligerent; but you are one of us."

"Be that as it may, Morris certainly doesn't indicate that."

Harry resignedly threw his hands in the air. "That's Morris for you; you should know that by now. I'll tell you one thing if you promise never to repeat this…"

"Go ahead," Archie grinned.

"Morris indeed has a great deal of respect for you. You've proven yourself – here in Bulawayo when you first arrived, and you have certainly proven yourself on your own up in Salisbury. You run a tight ship, and you have made a lot of money for us."

"That's nice to know," Archie replied, "but as I said, Morris doesn't show it. It would be nice if he did from time to time."

"And, as I said, that's Morris for you. Just accept it."

Archie slumped back in his seat again. "Well, I suppose I should return to the station and head home. It looks like my work is done here, and I have much to do in Salisbury."

"Absolutely not," Harry objected as he stood up. "You will stay with Anne and me tonight as our guest. We will invite Hanna to join us for supper. Perhaps Paddy's widow, Adele, as well. I know they would both love to see you again."

"And of course, me them too," Archie smiled. "I believe Louis's son, Herbert, has offered to put Adele's children through university.

A very generous gesture."

"Indeed, but Herbert is like that. Probably a little too generous, actually," Harry grumbled to himself quietly. "Anyhow, we have a lot to discuss and organise. Come, let's get some breakfast. You must be starving."

Archie had only just had breakfast but thought it only right to accept Harry's invitation. He stood and hooked his thumbs through his suspenders. "Thank you, Harry. That would be lovely. Now, when are you going to announce to the staff that you are closing down?"

"Probably next week, when I have my ducks in a row," Harry ushered Archie out the office. "I have to let the Standard Bank know, and I need to get down to Johannesburg and discuss this with Zebra."

"Danie Coetzee?"

"Yes, Zebra, Danie Coetzee."

"Does he know?"

"Oh yes, he knows everything about our business. Come now, we still have much to work through," Harry fussed as he ushered Archie outside the warehouse and into Abercorn Street.

Anne and Harry Langbourne politely led their guests through to the dining room. The dining table, draped in pure white cloth, was elegantly decorated with crystal and silverware, together with an ornate silver candelabrum in the centre of the table spotlighting the decor. The flames of the five candles flickered softly in welcome as the family entered, deep in earnest chatter.

"Oh, how beautiful, Anne," Hanna complimented her hostess when she saw the romantic setting.

"Look at that!" Adele followed up.

"Thank you," Anne smiled gently. She loved entertaining, and dressing her dining table was essential to her; something passed down by her mother.

"Where would you like us to sit, Anne?" Adele fussed.

"Anywhere you like. Let's put the men one at each end, and I'll sit here," Anne suggested as she pulled out a chair, leaving the awaiting chairs for her sisters-in-law.

As everyone took their seats, the aroma of roast beef wafted into the room, drawing several appreciative oohs and aahs. A man in a crisp white uniform entered with a large roast on a wooden platter; reflections from the candles shimmered off the succulent juices that coated the meal. Harry stood up and stepped over to the sideboard and, moving some carving utensils to one side, indicated where the feast was to be placed.

"Thank you, Eric," Harry said. "Eric, this is my brother from Salisbury," he pointed to Archie. "This is the man I was telling you about this afternoon, whom you can work for after I leave to go to Johannesburg if you so wish."

"Good evening, Eric," Archie greeted the young man, a strapping young fellow who carried a warm and welcoming smile.

"Good evening, Sah," Eric replied, his face lighting up.

"If you want to work for me in Salisbury, Eric, I can give you a job," Archie said kindly.

"Yes, Sah," Eric beamed. "I will go to Salisbury."

"Did you cook this meal?" Archie gestured to the delicious-looking roast.

"Yes, Sah," Eric's smile almost took over his entire face.

"Then I definitely would like you to work for me," Archie's chuckle was contagious. "Boss Harry tells me you are the grandson of Daluxolo. Is that right?"

"Yes, Sah. He is my grandfather. His brother is Nguni."

"I have never met them, but I know many, many stories about your grandfather and his brother, as told to me by my brothers."

Harry looked at Eric. "Then we will talk tomorrow and make arrangements for you to go to Salisbury, Eric."

After Eric left the room, Harry began carving the meat, which he did with gusto after slashing a large bone-handled knife across a lethal-looking steel sharpener. The evening was very jolly, with occasional memorable references to David and Paddy. Their two widows were very composed and laughed along with the conversations, but Harry and Archie could sense the ache in their hearts.

Archie leaned back in his chair and addressed Adele. "Harry tells me that Herbert has offered to put Richard and Sonya through university."

"Yes, indeed," Adele replied. "It is very generous of him. I have no idea why he offered that. He just came to see me one day and asked what I was going to do with the children. Of course, I had no idea. Paddy had recently passed away, and I was an emotional wreck. So, he just said, 'I'll pay for their university fees', and that was that."

"Well, take him up on it," Archie said firmly, and then cast his eye at Harry, who nodded silently.

"I'm afraid I'll have to," Adele said. "I will have little option when that time comes."

Harry cleared his throat. "We are all family. We will look after each other. Don't worry."

Archie stole another glance at Harry. He found Harry's statement to be a bit at odds with how he had felt himself to have been received over the years. Nonetheless, he was pleased to hear Harry's comment. Perhaps, Archie thought, Harry was softening with age.

CHAPTER FIFTEEN
London 1947

The war had raged, soldiers had died, cities became rubble, and the memories of atrocities committed against millions of innocent civilians were still raw. Brutal, senseless killings were perpetrated against women, children and the elderly, simply because of what they believed in, who they loved, or what race they were. Murder, rape, torture and indescribable hardship, physical and mental, became everyday events.

With the support of many, many people and organisations, donations were made to help the victims. These efforts were always dangerous and often deadly. Military, financial and scientific brainpower were tested to the limits; sometimes their plans worked in some small measure, but mostly they failed.

Then the tide turned: the belligerent nations overextended themselves, and the Allied forces began the reversal shift. The Americans dropped a massive bomb on Japan, which signalled the beginning of the end of the war. The 2nd of September 1945 dawned, and it was all over. Much damage had been done; irreparable, unforgivable damage.

An estimated seventy to eighty-five million people were dead, not counting the tens of millions more who were severely broken in body, mind, or both.

It was a full two years after the war ended before Morris felt it was safe to venture out from the new world. Flying to London first, he called in on Yoni and Ruth Goldberg and then went to view what remained of a building that was once his warehouse. Bombed and burnt to the ground, he turned his back on the structure and went in search of his youngest half-brother, Freddy, who was handling his affairs in England.

Freddy, a spritely young man with unusually curly hair, something not generally seen within the family, always seemed to wear an infectious smile, and therefore he was liked by all who came in contact with him. As Morris' salesman, he was very good at his job and often seemed to snare some almost impossible contracts. Morris could never find fault with him and quite enjoyed the fellow.

Freddy worked from home, a small double story brick house within the City of London area. As he was mostly a travelling salesman for Langbourne Coetzee, he didn't need a big office, and so a small room at the back of the house with a telephone connection did him proud. It suited Morris too as the rent Freddy levied Morris for this was quite insignificant.

Freddy jumped to his feet when he saw Morris push open the door of the tea shop that he was waiting in. "Welcome back to England, Uncle Morris," he greeted his eldest half-brother.

"How are you?" Morris pumped Freddy's hand. "I'm glad to see you have survived unscathed."

"I was never in any real danger," Freddy lied; it was the norm to say that these days. "The shortages are the worst of it all."

They sat and drank tea as they discussed business affairs, Freddy being careful to keep gossip about the war to a minimum. He knew Morris was only interested in his business, and, due to the short time they had together, he understood the conversation would be brief and intense. For that reason, Freddy kept a notepad on the table and a short pencil tucked behind his ear – which took advantage of the camouflage amongst his copious curls.

When company matters were concluded, Morris leaned forward and lowered his voice slightly.

"Freddy," he said, his tone grave. "As you know, we don't have any trading operations left in our business. Archie, in Rhodesia, is doing a great job, but he has other suppliers now besides us, so he is no longer as important a customer. All the other customers are more of a headache than a profitable deal. I have decided to close Langbourne Coetzee down – completely. It's already closed in Africa, and I see no reason to keep it open here. Besides, I'm 72 years old, and I wish to simplify my life."

"I've been expecting you to close my branch for a while now," Freddy smiled. "I agree, the profits don't necessarily justify the efforts any longer."

"I'd like to retain you, though. Not to manage Langbourne Coetzee, but to be my representative in England. I have many connections and loose ends that need managing, and I need someone I can trust to be my man here. Would you do that for me?"

"Of course," Freddy beamed. This offer was better than he expected, even without mention yet of a salary.

"For instance," Morris continued, "I need to ensure Rose Bertha continues to get her maintenance in accordance with the divorce settlement."

"Certainly," Freddy frowned. "I have been paying her every month as you directed, and have taken care of all accommodation and medical needs. She lives not far from here now, in a hotel complex. It's not luxurious, but she is comfortable. Would you like to see her?"

"No, I have no desire to see her," Morris said a little too quickly. "My grandchildren's schooling?"

Freddy accepted the sudden change in subject, so moved away from Rose Bertha. "Their schooling is going well, and all fees are up to date. Would you like to…"

"Good, good," Morris interrupted. "I leave for Africa tomorrow. I will see Harry in Johannesburg, and then Archie in Rhodesia. Anything you would like me to take to them?"

"No thanks, Uncle Morris. All is in order. I was thinking of visiting Archie in a few years. I might take Fifi with me. A holiday, if you will."

"I have absolutely no enthusiasm to visit Rhodesia again. I'm only going because Harry insists I visit Archie while I'm on the continent. Last time I was in Africa was in 1898."

Freddy allowed a soft whistle to escape his lips. "That was, what, about 50 years ago. You'll be sure to see some changes."

"Yes, I believe I shall," Morris went silent as a thousand memories flooded his mind. "It was a lifetime ago," he sighed softly, then stood abruptly, gathering his coat. "Good, thanks for the tea, and thanks for your willing service. I have prepared a list of tasks that I need you to carry out for me. I'll come past London in a fortnight when I return from Africa, and we can finalise our new arrangement."

Morris handed Freddy a folded piece of paper, and in the blink of an eye, Morris shook Freddy's hand in farewell, turned on his heel and strode out the door. Freddy watched him disappear from view before slowly taking his seat. He stared out the window as he contemplated how his life had dramatically altered course in the time it took to drink a cup of tea.

CHAPTER SIXTEEN
Johannesburg 1947

Harry admired the ornate ceiling of the Rand Club of Johannesburg. "Quite an amazing work of architecture," he mused.

"Quite," Danie agreed as he carefully placed his cup and saucer down on the highly polished coffee table before allowing his eyes to follow Harry's gaze. "This building has been demolished and rebuilt no less than three times."

"For heaven's sake, why?" Harry asked as he leaned back in his plush brown leather chair. It squeaked like a new saddle on a horse.

"It was outgrown, very quickly, twice. This one should last an eternity. Did you know that Cecil John Rhodes picked this location; an entire city block, bounded by Commissioner, Loveday, Harrison and Fox streets?"

"I'm not surprised," Harry grinned. "Rhodes never did anything in small measure."

Danie smiled at that comment, and settled into his equally grandiose lounger, the leather also squeaking comfortably under his weight. "The cocktail bar that I showed you when we arrived? It is said that Dr Leander Starr Jameson plotted the overthrow of the Boer Government there."

"Really?" Harry exclaimed, somewhat surprised. "I never knew the man, but Morris and David met him. He was a customer of ours. It seems our paths may have crossed in 1894; just as Louis and I were arriving in Bulawayo, Jameson's attempted coup was being thwarted down here."

"So you were there when the Matabele rose against the Rhodesian settlers?"

"Yes, literally the very morning Louis and I arrived in Bulawayo the Matabele impi surrounded the town and placed us under siege. It was quite a frightening introduction to Africa for me. It was a long time ago, but I recall we were under siege for about three months."

Danie rubbed his chin thoughtfully. "Yes, I recall the Siege of Bulawayo lasted that long. David never talked much about it."

"There wasn't much to talk about really," Harry shrugged and looked at his wristwatch impatiently. "I wonder what's taking Morris so long. He's usually very punctual."

"He will be here shortly, I'm sure," Danie nodded reassuringly. "It will be good to see him again. After 50 years, I wonder if I will recognise him."

"You will, he hasn't changed at all; still the same: a little less hair, and a bit more weight, but still the same. I used to see him almost every five years without fail, except during the war of course, so I think the last time I saw him was about seven years ago now."

"And there he is," Danie stood, beaming from ear to ear.

Morris walked into the lounge and immediately singled out his oldest friend and youngest full brother. Striding determinedly over to them with an equally broad smile, he clasped Danie's hand in a firm handshake.

"You're not the thin man I once knew, Danie," Morris joked at Danie's fuller physique. "Last we saw each other you were skin and bone."

"I would say the same of you, Morris, but I'm a little more polite!" Danie laughed.

"Harry, how are you, Brother?" Morris turned his attention away from Danie and shook Harry's hand vigorously.

"I'm well, thanks, Brother. Please, sit, sit. What will you have? Coffee? Tea?"

"Coffee, thanks," Morris smiled and sank noisily into the leather seat while Harry signalled a waiter, and, with simple hand gestures, ordered more coffee. The waiter nodded his understanding and immediately slipped through some white swing doors.

"So Danie, you never married?" Morris asked. He always started a conversation with questions, and at pace, no matter how personal they were. It was just his way.

"No, never married," Danie replied with a slight flush in his face.

"Why? A man like you? You would be quite a catch, my friend."

"No time, Morris. Always too busy to find a wife," Danie said with a faint chuckle.

"Perhaps very wise. I've had two wives, and both marriages ended badly. Cost me a fortune; both times. How's Anne, Harry?" Morris quickly shifted the direction of the conversation.

"Very well, indeed. Anne sends you her love and looks forward to meeting you later tonight."

"And your children? Dagmar, Sheila and… William is it?"

"Billy, yes, they will be home tonight. You will meet them too. I've asked Adele to join us. She is visiting Johannesburg from Bulawayo at the moment, with her children. Adele is making plans to put Richard in the Witwatersrand University. It seems he will start next year, and as you know, Herbert has offered to fund her children's education."

"Good, good, yes, I heard. He's a good boy, Herbert. Louis brought him up well."

Harry smiled contentedly. "It seems all our siblings brought their children up well, and gave them the best education available, thanks to your insistence and encouragement."

Morris nodded. "That is so, and I have provided for all my grandchildren likewise to attend the best learning establishments in England when they are of age." A frown suddenly crossed his brow. "What news of Sally's child, the one who joined that communist party here? What's his name again?"

"Michael," Harry said softly, dropping his eyes to the floor.

"Michael Harmel, that's right," Morris frowned. "Is he still involved with politics?"

"I think so," Harry nodded, "we haven't spoken for some years now, but I believe he is still mixing with the communist group."

"We Langbournes are businessmen. Capitalists by nature. We

171

can't be seen to be dabbling in politics. That's why I insisted we cut him off from the family," Morris directed this statement to Danie who nodded gravely.

"As I said," Harry gave Morris a stern look, "I have not seen or spoken to him in years. I don't even know where he lives anymore. It is sad, because Sally was my favourite sister, and, well, it's just a bit disappointing. After all, he is our nephew."

"Very sad about Hanna," Morris ignored Harry's statement and changed direction, "I would have loved to have seen her again. She was a charming lady. David was very blessed to have her as his wife."

"She had a very touching funeral, Brother."

"What happened?" Morris asked.

"Nobody really knows. She was visiting some friends for afternoon tea, and asked if she could lie down for a bit as she felt tired. She never woke up. Personally I think she died from a broken heart. Hanna never really got over David's death."

Morris was pensive. "I will visit their graves when I pass through Bulawayo."

"When do you leave Johannesburg?"

"Day after tomorrow. I have many business deals happening in California that demand my attention, so I can't give Africa much time."

Harry nodded his acceptance of this without objection; he had expected Morris' visit to be a fleeting one.

"So, Brother Harry," Morris continued as he sank back into the upholstery, "what keeps you busy these days? You have no business concerns to look after anymore."

Harry straightened up slightly when he noticed the wry smirk on Morris' face. "You are correct; all my personal affairs are invested in stocks, shares, bonds and the like, and Danie looks after my interests very well. I'm extremely involved in the Jewish Board of Deputies in Johannesburg. In fact, I am currently their Chairman. It keeps me very busy, indeed. My passion is raising funds to support Jewish survivors of the war."

"Excellent, excellent," Morris beamed. "I'm glad to hear that."

The coffee arrived, and the men took a break while it was poured and, observing a tray of creamy delights pass nearby, Morris quickly ordered a cake to go with their coffee.

Morris cleared his throat. "Danie we need to talk business. My business. Are my Africa affairs in order?"

Danie leant over to his right and retrieved a thick file from a black leather briefcase, which he placed on the coffee table in front of him.

"Yes, Morris, I just need you to sign some documents. I think you will find I have done all you have asked. After today, all going well, you should be completely free of Africa."

Morris knew there was very little chance of him ever returning to the African continent, so, for him, it was vitally important that all his African affairs were concluded and watertight. He signed several papers, Harry co-signed some, and Danie was given several instructions before the formal part of the meeting came to an end. Morris would spend his remaining days in Johannesburg visiting former friends and business colleagues, but now with the official part of the meeting over, it was time to catch up on old times over that coffee and cake.

CHAPTER SEVENTEEN
Bulawayo 1947

Painfully slow and tedious was how Morris later described the train journey to Bulawayo. Deprived of stimulating conversation from passengers, and having had to endure unacceptably lengthy stops at decrepit stations, Morris was pleased to finally arrive at his destination. He had considered travelling by air, but advice from well-wishers had convinced him that rail was the better option; flights were limited and unreliable. He regretted having taken their advice.

On arrival, well overdue and quite flustered overall, Morris made his way to his hotel where he checked in and immediately retired, hoping to face the new day refreshed. The following morning, after a hearty breakfast, he visited the grave of his much-loved brother, David, and that of David's wife, Hanna. Later, Morris walked the streets of Bulawayo and marvelled at the changes he saw; the town was almost unrecognisable.

The first place he visited was the old Langbourne Brothers warehouse that he and David had built in 1894. It was still there, and Morris glanced up at a lone brick that had been incorrectly set by David one morning, so long ago. David hadn't noticed, and by the time Morris had brought it to his attention, it was far too late to do anything about it. The two had decided to leave it as it was and trusted nobody would ever look up and notice. Nevertheless, Morris would remind David about that brick now and again, just for a laugh, when they stood on the pavement, as they often did, talking shop. And there it remained, half a century later. Morris wondered what stories that old brick could tell from up there if it were able to talk.

He pushed open the large wooden doors and looked inside. The interior was dark and dingy, and slightly dusty. It remained a warehouse but was now used to store agricultural items. A gentleman of Indian descent approached Morris and asked if he could be of assistance.

"I'm just looking, thanks," Morris said, intending to brush him off, but then found himself saying, "I built this place with my brother many years ago, and we ran a business from here."

"I believe this was the original Langbourne Brothers building," the gentleman said, his smile almost enveloping his entire face. "May I assume that you are one of the Langbourne brothers, then?"

"Indeed," Morris smiled back and shook his hand. "Morris Langbourne."

"I'm the manager here, Mr Naidoo at your service, Sir. Would you like to look around?"

"Oh, I won't detain you; you must be very busy."

"Not at all, not at all," Naidoo beamed, gesticulating at the deserted shop.

With hands clasped behind his back, Morris followed his guide through to the rear of the building in silence. His host nattered and chattered excitedly, thoroughly enjoying this unexpected diversion to his humdrum day. Occasionally Morris would grunt something in agreement, or nod his head, but he wasn't really listening; his thoughts were buried in reminiscences.

Morris popped his head into what had once been his office. The rudimentary shelf he had used to stack his all-important ledgers upon was missing, but he could see the holes that were left by the screws in the wall. The nail on a side wall, where David was wont to hang his hat, was, surprisingly, still there. It had since been coated with thick white paint, a globule of which was frozen in time as if gravity had tried, and failed, to free it from the nail.

The large, heavy wooden doors at the rear of the building were still coarse and rough, and the strong hinges attached to them with oversized bolts and nuts remained as they had always been. The fixings were excessive, but Morris recalled that was all that was available at the time. Outside, in the receiving bay, Morris' eye caught a brass tap attached to the end of a dull copper water pipe. The fixture was dripping, and, on the brickwork below, slimy green algae grew abundantly. He touched the tap and tried, without success, to stem the drip. Mr Naidoo was about to make an excuse for the leak when he noticed that Morris was staring at the brass valve almost lovingly. To Naidoo's surprise, Morris had a faraway look in his eye, and he almost seemed to be caressing the brass.

"I see you recognise this water tap," Naidoo said, humorously.

"Ahh, yes," Morris snapped out of his daydream. "When we first started here, this was the only source of water we had for the shop. It is where my brothers and I used to bathe ourselves. At that time we lived in the building as well," Morris explained.

"Really?" Naidoo said in surprise.

"Yes, it was a long time ago."

"I find that hard to believe, Mr Langbourne."

Morris chuckled. "Would you believe, then, that we shared this water with our horse? We had a trough for him just over there. For our own privacy, we used to hang a hessian sack across here on a piece of string. Look! The hooks are still in the wall." Morris stood on tip-toes and touched one of the old brass hooks buried in the brickwork.

"My goodness gracious, I never noticed that," Naidoo marvelled as he stared at the hook first, then at Morris in disbelief.

Morris tucked his shirt back into his trousers. "Yes, those were memorable days," he mused. "Later, my younger brother Harry took on the duty to close the shop at the end of the day. He would stand at the front doors and call out to the customers remaining in the shop that the doors would be closing." Morris laughed at the memory. "Sometimes, customers would stay longer just to hear him shout it out. It became a bit of a tradition, actually."

"I have heard that from some of our older customers, Sir. We don't do that now, but yes, I have heard that about your brother."

Morris thanked Mr Naidoo and left the premises feeling rejuvenated by a sense of nostalgia that the old building had revived in him. With a spring in his step, Morris found his way to Fife Street where the brothers had once had a retail outlet. He had never personally seen the store in full swing; Louis had just commenced operating it when Morris had returned to Ireland and England.

Sitting in his office in London, looking at the financials that came out of Fife Street, Morris had found the figures hard to believe. Louis had run a thriving operation out of that store and had certainly stamped the Langbourne name on the Bulawayo community.

On entering the shop, though, Morris' heart sank. It was in dire need of repair, and the merchandise was scattered throughout the store without much thought for presentation. The goods being sold were aimed solely at the lower end of the market. The Langbourne Brothers' business run from there had catered for all spectrums of society. It was a disappointing contrast to what Morris had been expecting, so he turned on his heel and walked straight out.

As Morris stepped quickly onto the pavement, he lightly bumped a very tall man walking by, and turned to apologise.

"I beg your pardon, Sir," Morris said quickly.

The man looked down at Morris with a friendly smile of forgiveness, but then he stopped, a frown creasing his forehead. "We've met before, haven't we? Aren't you David Langbourne's brother?"

"Yes," Morris beamed broadly. "Captain Dent, I believe. Captain Grant Dent."

"No longer 'Captain', I'm pleased to say," Grant laughed.

"Morris Langbourne," he shook Grant's hand vigorously. "So good to see you after all this time. You did us proud during the rebellion."

"Oh, it was nothing. I was very sorry to hear about the passing of David," Grant quickly changed the subject. "I was at his funeral. David and I became very good friends over the years. In the early days, we spent a lot of time on horseback between here and Mafeking. That was before the railway arrived."

"Those were the days," Morris almost sighed. "Thanks for going to David's funeral, Mr Dent. Sadly, I couldn't make it. I was in America, and it was just too far away. Not to mention the travel restrictions because of the war. I live in the States now."

"Then I count it very fortunate that we crossed paths today. And, please, call me Grant."

"Likewise, please call me Morris. Do you have time for a coffee, Grant?"

"I'd be delighted."

Grant led Morris to a simple hotel on Grey Street, close to the Central Police Station. They sat on garden furniture in a shady courtyard and enjoyed each other's company. While Grant chose a coffee, Morris settled for a most enjoyable creamy coffee milkshake.

Grant was an easy-going gentleman, tall and handsome with a full head of greying hair. His piercing eyes showed a deep interest in what people were saying; he preferred to listen rather than talk. Regarded as a gentle giant, his imposing physique and handsome looks commanded immediate respect when he walked into a room; Grant just seemed to be the kind of person who turned the heads of both genders, people comfortably warming to him on sight. In his day, he had been an exceptional and dependable soldier who had instilled loyalty and confidence in his subordinates.

"You haven't changed much, Grant," Morris noted as he took a sip of his milkshake. "Perhaps a little greyer on top, but I recall an image, as if it were yesterday, of you standing upon a wagon wheel with a rifle aimed into the distance, watching and waiting for a Matabele attack."

"Thank heavens they didn't attack," Grant allowed a laugh to slip. "The day we were relieved, I was down to my last seven bullets."

"I had no idea," Morris frowned with consternation as he suddenly realised just how close he and his brothers had been to death.

"I suppose we should thank Cecil Rhodes for saving the day," Grant mused.

"I met the gentleman on a couple of occasions. Rhodes had

charisma; I'll say that for him."

"I went to his funeral too, back in 1902," Grant frowned as he recalled that hot day in the Matopos Hills.

"In Cape Town? He died in the suburb of Muizenberg if I recall," Morris said.

"Oh," Grant put his cup down, "indeed he died in Muizenberg, that is correct, but he was buried here, in Bulawayo, in the Matopos Hills."

Morris cocked his head in surprise. "Really? I had no idea."

"Mmm… It's very beautiful there, and Rhodes declared it the most beautiful place in the world. The place where he is buried is called World's View; he named it World's View himself. You should see it. Are you doing anything tomorrow? It's Saturday, and my wife and I, along with some good friends, are taking a drive out to the Matopos for a picnic. You would be most welcome to come along. You won't regret it; it truly is a lovely day out."

"Well, I don't want to impose…"

"Not at all. I insist—the more, the merrier. You'll enjoy my friends too, a mixed bunch. Heather and I will collect you from your hotel at eleven o'clock; we'll be back by four."

The convoy of three cars trundled merrily along the strip road towards the Matopos Hills. Morris sat in the passenger seat of the leading vehicle next to Grant and admired the boulder-strewn landscape unfolding around them.

Interspersed with shrub and forest, the most striking features of the land were the massive outcrops of granite boulders, most rounded and smooth with many precariously balanced on top of each other.

"Incredible scenery," Morris mused. He wore a pair of light beige slacks paired with a plain white business shirt. The sleeves were rolled up to just below his elbow, and the collar was unbuttoned. He slouched comfortably in the seat, his left elbow resting on the windowsill.

"This is pretty much the start of the National Park," Grant explained. "It's called the Matopos National Park, but the correct name is Matobo, for that's how the Matabele pronounce it. It means bald heads, and you can see why. Mzilikazi, Lobengula's father, named this place."

"Fascinating," Morris replied as he stared at the unfolding scenery. "If I had known how beautiful this place was, I would have visited when I lived in Bulawayo. But then, I suppose, we didn't have automobiles in those days, and a journey on horseback would have taken half a day at least. I'm not partial to horseback."

"I understand," Grant smiled knowingly.

About thirty minutes later the party arrived at the base of a colossal boulder, almost a mountain in itself, and parked in a bush clearing designated for vehicles. With a gently sloping rock face ahead of them, Morris noticed a faint but distinct dirt track on the granite surface that meandered up the bare slope.

"We'll be walking up that path?" Morris inquired as he stepped out the car.

"Yes," Heather covered her eyes against the sunlight as she pointed upwards and seemingly beyond the crest. "It's not a difficult climb."

Tall for a lady, Heather seemed a perfect match for Grant. She was slightly older than Grant, but younger than Morris, with short fair hair fashioned into a loose bob reaching her shoulders. Heather had a calmness about her, charming wit and good sense of humour. Morris gleaned from her that Grant had been a bachelor up until she met him, and if it weren't for the advent of a leap year in 1944, he would probably have been a bachelor still.

"You proposed to him?" Morris chuckled.

"Well he wasn't going to get down on his knee, were you, darling?" she jibed at Grant with a sly smile.

Grant shrugged his shoulders in mock resignation. "I have bad knees; you know that, Heather."

"Well, just as well I proposed when I did," Heather beamed. "It's so unfair. We women only get one day every four years to propose to our man, when males can take any day of the year to propose. Preposterous!"

"I totally agree," Morris winked at Grant and laughed; he felt very relaxed in Heather's company.

As the other cars in the convoy pulled up and claimed what little shade remained in the dry grassy parking area, Grant and Heather introduced Morris to the other couples that alighted: Lindsay and Cath Collins, Ralph and Jan Kelsey, Peter and Debs Barron, and Mary and Bob Power. They were all lovely, happy people who made Morris feel very welcome from the start.

Between all the excited chatter and bursts of raucous laughter, Morris sidled up to Grant and nodded at the crowd.

"Good bunch of friends you have here."

"Yes, I've known the menfolk since I arrived in Bulawayo, back around 1890. We fought in all this country's wars together. I've been to all their weddings and watched their kids grow up. We come out to the Matopos every two months or so if the weather is fine. I think the womenfolk have an even closer bond than us men."

"Thanks for inviting me out with you." Morris looked up at Grant's impressive height and smiled. "It means a lot."

"You're very welcome, Morris. Such a pleasure to have you join us. I had a lot of respect for your brother. He was a good friend."

Several straw baskets of homemade biscuits, sandwiches and cake made appearances from the respective boots of the cars. Morris noted that some wicker baskets contained flasks of hot water for coffee or tea; it all bode well for a magnificent day.

"Right," Grant looked at the granite slope to his right when all the gear had been unpacked. "Let's go. We shall walk that way, up and over the top."

With idle banter from the men and cheerful conversation from the ladies, the party made its way to the summit. Only once Morris found himself physically standing on the rock face did he appreciate the enormity of what nature was presenting to him. He was awestruck. Looking at the size of the mountain that curved away and out of sight above him, Morris wondered how much of that one single piece of granite was below the surface of the ground, the base far below where any human eye would ever see. He contemplated the weight of a rock the size of a regular football, and then looked at the boulder they were ascending. He shook his head in disbelief.

There were lichens of many colours that clung tightly to the granite, decorating the rocks in Africa's glorious shades of green, red and gold. Grasses and shrubs invaded the granite, desperately clinging to any small crevice, living their stressed existence in the harsh conditions, and yet, somehow, thriving.

"Amazing how all that vegetation can prosper in such a small crack in the rock. It doesn't seem as though there's much water available," Morris commented.

"Nature is amazing, Morris," Grant said as he stooped and snapped off a dry twig from a haggard-looking shrub. The small dried leaves on the twig were dark grey, almost black; scorched and hard. Grant passed it to Morris. "Here, take this home with you tonight and put it in a glass of water. Although it looks dead, by morning, it will have burst into life; the leaves will be green and soft. It's called a Resurrection Plant."

"You don't say?" Morris took the twig and twiddled it between his thumb and forefinger before giving it a sniff. He carefully pushed it into the breast pocket of his shirt as a vibrant blue-headed lizard caught his eye. It suddenly dashed for a thin fissure and disappeared.

Morris remembered that David would often come to the Matopos. In his younger days, he would ride out on horseback with his friend, the now-famous Briton, Colonel Robert Baden-Powell. In later years he would drive out in a buggy with Hanna to picnic, just as he had done this day. Morris would listen as David told him how wondrous the Matopos was, but, in those days, Morris had little interest in the bush. His focus was entirely on business.

Of course, in his early 20s, Morris had moved to Europe and never returned to Africa, so he had not had the opportunity to see what David had enjoyed. Finally, walking up the gentle face of this magnificent boulder, he regretted not making an effort to come with David in his earlier years.

As they approached the summit, Grant veered slightly to his right and aimed for a large round boulder covered in orange lichen. It stood prominently, almost unnaturally, on the smooth face of the practically lunar-type surface they walked upon. It had a slight overhang on one side.

"We will set up our picnic under the shade of that rock," Grant told Morris. "My favourite spot, nice and cool."

"It looks as if it could roll down the hill at any moment," Morris sounded slightly nervous. "Is it safe to sit under it?"

Grant gave a hearty laugh. "It's been there for aeons. It won't move now, I can assure you. When we get to it, try to give it a push; use all your might and then tell me if you think it will move in the next million years."

Morris laughed. He knew Grant was probably right. Nevertheless, he secretly did lean his entire weight against the rock just to reassure himself. Not even a steamroller would budge it, he decided. The ladies immediately began to lay brightly coloured picnic blankets under the overhang, and, having done this many times before, took command of the various baskets.

"Gentlemen," Grant summoned his friends, "let's go for a walk while the ladies prepare the picnic. I'd like to show Morris the grave of Cecil John Rhodes."

"Splendid idea," Ralph called out. It didn't take much encouragement to get the menfolk to leave their wives to 'do their thing'.

Ralph had light brown hair combed tightly over the top of his head, and his face seemed to smile naturally under a close-cropped and well-manicured moustache. An Australian by birth, with a strong accent that held no secrets as to where he hailed from, Ralph was the fit and adventurous type. True to form, he was leading the pack of men up the hill.

A little further along, Morris noticed a massive cube-like monument, probably a little bigger than a double-story house. Constructed from granite, there were bronze panels near the top running the width of each sidewall. He couldn't make out what was depicted on them.

"Is that Rhodes' grave?" Morris asked. "It's a bit large for a grave."

"No," Lindsay replied. "That's the Allan Wilson Monument. We'll take you there in a moment."

Lindsay was almost as tall as Grant; well over six feet. An accomplished sportsman, he had once played rugby for Matabeleland and had also been a keen cricketer in his day. Although now in his 70s, Lindsay seemed to move like a twenty-year-old and Morris struggled to keep up with him.

Morris stared at the monument as they walked, racking his brain; the name Allan Wilson rang a bell, but he couldn't place it.

"There," Grant pointed slightly to his left. "Cecil John Rhodes' grave."

Morris had not known what to expect but found himself surprised by the simple grave. A flat rectangular granite slab the size of a large household dining table lay flat on the rock surface. The slab was about eight inches thick. Upon it was a smaller slab of granite of about the same thickness. A bronze plaque, almost covering the entire top slab, was held down fast with six large bronze rivets. It bore an uncomplicated engraved inscription in capital letters – 'HERE LIE THE REMAINS OF CECIL JOHN RHODES'.

The men gathered around and stood in respectful silence for a moment. Morris noticed the five men around him were deep in thought, as though many sad memories were playing through their minds.

Bob broke the silence. "He was a fascinating man. Even controversial some would say."

Morris couldn't remember what Bob Power's vocation was; he thought he was a Customs Official or perhaps worked with the Ministry of Home Affairs. He was a solid man and had a keen sense of humour. Right now, though, he looked quite forlorn. Balding slightly, Bob kept his hair trimmed short. It was only at this point that Morris noticed Bob had an artificial leg. It intrigued him that Bob hadn't broken into a sweat from the walk to the summit, yet Morris was dabbing perspiration from his brow.

"Why would that be?" Morris asked Bob. "Rhodes created a country that was named after him and negotiated the end of a brutal war."

"Yes," Bob straightened up, "but don't forget he was implicated in the failed Jameson Raid. Leander Starr Jameson cost him his Premiership of the Cape Colony."

Morris accepted this argument and fell silent.

Grant put his hands in his pockets and sighed. "They'll be writing books about this man well into the next century, of that I'm sure."

Ralph, standing next to Grant, reached down and gently nudged some dirt off the base slab. "I met Mr Rhodes; twice actually."

"Mmm…" Grant hummed softly in agreement, "I never met him, but I did see him in the Bulawayo laager during the '96 rebellion, quite a few times."

Morris cleared his throat. "First time I saw him I was 16 years old. It was in Port Elizabeth. My brother and I had only just stepped off the boat from Ireland. 1891 I think it was. We went to the Grand Hotel, and there was a large gathering of the railway industry happening. I believe it was when Rhodes made his famous announcement to build the Cape-to-Cairo railway line. Cecil John Rhodes was pointed out to me by someone. Then I met him again in Bulawayo. We didn't speak about anything significant. In fact, I can't remember what we spoke about, but I do remember his eyes; pale blue and striking. They seemed to bore right into your soul."

"Exactly right, mate," Ralph nodded, his Australian mannerisms very distinctive. "Exactly how I remember him."

Grant straightened and removed his hands from his pockets. "Talking about Leander Starr Jameson, that's his grave over there," he pointed a little way down the slope.

"I didn't know he was buried here too," Morris lifted an eyebrow in surprise.

"Come," Grant turned and walked down the slope. The group of men followed obediently.

"Do you know how Leander Starr Jameson got his name?" Grant asked nobody in particular as they walked casually down the hill.

"Pray, tell," Peter answered, somewhat curiously. "I'm assuming there is a story behind that."

Peter Barron had worked in the Rhodesian mining industry most of his life. He was an engineer and had travelled extensively around the country. His last posting was in Bulawayo, where he and Debs had decided to retire.

Grant smiled at Peter. "A little-known story, indeed. While Jameson's mother was giving birth in a small town in Scotland, his father was walking the streets in agitation, worried for the wellbeing of his wife and soon-to-be-born child. In all his anxiety, he tripped when he was by a canal and fell in. Mr Jameson didn't know how to swim and was flailing about, on the verge of drowning, when an American saw him and rescued the man. He pulled him out by his jacket collar. When Mr Jameson was safe and wringing out his jacket, he asked the American what his name was as he wanted to thank him. His name was Mr Leander Starr."

"Huh," Peter exclaimed. "Leander Starr Jameson. I always wondered why his middle name was spelt like that."

"Well," Bob said, "here's another bit of trivia for you. Do you know the poem titled 'IF' by Rudyard Kipling?"

Morris nodded. "'If you can keep your head when all about you are losing theirs and blaming it on you'."

Peter piped in. "'If you can trust yourself when all men doubt you, but make allowance for their doubting too'. Yes, we know the poem."

Bob smiled, "Kipling wrote that poem as a tribute to Leander Starr Jameson."

"Well, that's conflicting," Morris said, drawing some confused stares from the men. "It's my favourite poem. I have always tried to live by its principals. I know it by heart, and yet I have little respect for the man it was written for. A bit confusing."

Ralph sighed. "I wouldn't let that worry you, mate. You know, many great people do things that seem untoward by some, but overall they can be very sound people. People make mistakes."

"Perhaps," Morris agreed; he certainly could not argue that fact.

"Like you, I try to live my life by the principals in the poem," Grant said. "I think most Rhodesians live by those principals, simply because of who we are, what we stand for and what we have had to endure in this country."

Morris agreed. "You're right, gentlemen. Perhaps I have been somewhat insular in my beliefs of the man."

Morris wasn't sure if it was the mysterious sanctity of the Matopos, or the company he was in, or both, but he realised that he would respect Jameson's grave more than he had initially thought. The entire atmosphere of the Matopos mountains was enveloping him in a strangely eerie feeling, something he had never experienced before.

Jameson's grave was almost identical to Cecil John Rhodes' resting place, only this time there was only one slab of granite below the large bronze plaque. The inscription on this was a little more succinct – 'HERE LIES LEANDER STARR JAMESON'.

The group of men shuffled around the gravesite and studied the inscription.

"He was an interesting man, very difficult not to like," Grant said, then looked at Morris. "Did you ever meet him when you were in Bulawayo?"

Morris shrugged uncomfortably. "I knew him, yes. At first, I liked the gentleman. As you said, a very likeable man; I even negotiated a couple of deals with him. A curious and dynamic person, great sense of humour, and a man you tended to gravitate towards; but I must say I lost a lot of respect for him after the Jameson Raid debacle."

Bob tugged at his collar. "Despite his folly with the Raid, I actually have a great deal of respect for Dr Jameson."

"Why did you lose respect for him, Morris?" Peter asked, a curious eyebrow arching.

"Because he left Bulawayo undefended?" Lindsay answered for Morris.

"Yes, exactly," Morris nodded. "My brothers and I were in Bulawayo when the Matabele surrounded the town and put us under siege. You were there as well," Morris glanced at Grant.

"We were all there," Ralph looked at his friends in turn. "Grant was defending the laager with Bob. Peter, Lindsay and I were part of the Bulawayo Field Force, which was led by Fredrick Courtney Selous. Many lives were lost on both sides."

"It cost me my leg," Bob tapped his prosthesis. "Dr Jameson took it off after I was shot by a Matabele. He was an exceptional doctor; I can testify to that."

Morris stared at Bob, speechless.

"There were other reasons why the Matabele rose against the European settlers," Peter said. "The rinderpest plague, the drought, the locusts. All quite understandable reasons; I don't think we can put all the blame on Jameson, although I do agree he was foolhardy with the raid, and he held some fanciful ambitions."

Morris was about to say something when Grant suddenly cut him off.

"Gentlemen," he said, "it looks as though the ladies are about to call us to lunch. We should go back now."

As the group of men left Jameson's grave, they engaged in some idle chatter. The day was pristine, with a few pure white puffy clouds in the distance dotting the azure sky.

Ralph sidled up to Morris. "I'm assuming you were one of the Langbourne brothers, on Fife Street?"

"Yes, that was our business," Morris smiled. "We have had to close it down since two of my brothers, Louis and David, passed away. The war also played a part, of course; everyone was off fighting, and we simply didn't have the people to run the show. What's your line of work?"

"Me? I'm a dentist. I'll be retiring next year. Grant tells me you live in the USA. I would guess you are retired then?"

Morris laughed. "I don't think there's much chance of me retiring."

"So, what do you do these days?"

"Oh, not a great deal," Morris became vague, "a bit of this, a bit of that, property, movies; I have financed a couple of movies in Hollywood. Those were interesting times."

"Fascinating!" Ralph exclaimed. "Have you met any of the famous names we might know?"

"Perhaps. I've met Greta Garbo; have you heard of her?"

"Greta Garbo, of course, mate. She's one of my favourites."

"Yes, lovely lady. And Humphrey Bogart. I had him around for a dinner party the other night."

"Fair dinkum! Hey fellas," Ralph called to his friends, "this chap knows some famous people."

The menfolk ahead stopped and turned to face Morris and Ralph.

"Really?" Peter called back. "Like who?"

"Movie stars," Ralph shouted back.

Morris suddenly felt coy. He hadn't intended bringing attention to himself.

"Tell us about it over lunch," Grant smiled and waved his hand in the air, encouraging them to keep moving. "Come along."

"What does Lindsay do for a living?" Morris asked Ralph, trying to change the subject in the hope that the movie business would be forgotten. Morris had financed a few movies, none of which were box office successes, but it did allow him to mix and mingle with big names and personalities, something that gave him much joy.

"Lindsay works for the Ministry of Finance. The Tax Department."

Morris looked up at Ralph in horror. "He's a tax man?"

"Yes."

"I'm a businessman, I don't much care for the tax man, to be honest."

Ralph chuckled. "Well, if you pay your taxes, you have nothing to worry about. Anyhow, Lindsay is a good bloke."

"Oh, I pay my taxes alright – too much tax, in my opinion. That's the problem. I think the government takes too much tax off people. Anyhow, I don't have a problem with Lindsay, he seems like a sterling man, but I always appear to be in a fight with the Internal Revenue people in America. They always question my returns; they never leave me alone."

Morris paused for a moment then grinned. "I just have an inbuilt dislike for the Tax Department."

"Don't we all," Ralph laughed.

"Lunch is ready, boys," Cath's girlish voice drifted up the slope as the men sauntered down.

Cath Collins was an attractive lady with long blonde hair. She always appeared to be happy; there was even a joyful bounce in her stride. She and Lindsay seemed a perfect match, with her often finishing off his sentences, and him, hers.

The picnic lunch was delicious. Morris had never experienced such a variety of wholesome food, and the choices were vast; homemade pickles, jams, bread, sauces and relishes – Morris didn't know where to start.

He looked at the spread in total amazement. "Do you ladies go to all this trouble every weekend you come here?"

"It's no trouble at all," Debs chirped. "We love doing this."

Debs had short black hair and sported a healthy tan. Morris assumed she enjoyed the outdoors, and he conjectured that she was likely a keen gardener as Hanna had been.

Jan flipped back a cloth to expose a large, freshly-baked loaf of bread covered in several types of grains. "Ralph," she handed her husband a rather formidable stainless-steel knife. "Please slice the bread. Thick slices, and straight; don't mess it up like last time."

Morris smothered a chortle at that remark. Ralph took the knife and, casting a look at Morris, winked with a slight smile and rolled his eyes. Jan, Ralph's lovely wife, had sparkling brown eyes and silky honey-brown hair that framed her face perfectly. She wore a blue-and-white summer dress that enhanced her hourglass figure.

Jan had taken note of the silent humour between her husband and Morris. "Or perhaps you might like to slice the bread, Morris?" she interjected with a smile. "You can't do worse than Ralph."

"Oh no, thanks, Jan. I know I'd do a dreadful job," Morris exclaimed. "Please, Ralph, go ahead."

Mary reached for a pink cushion and tossed it at Morris. "Here, make yourself comfortable then, young man."

She was the shortest of all the ladies and the feistiest. Sporting neat brown hair and a radiant face, she oozed confidence. Morris had warmed to her very quickly.

Morris grinned as he caught the cushion, placed it on the rock by his feet and grunted as he made his way down to ground level. He tried to cross his legs, but they wouldn't cooperate as they had done in his youth, so he sat with his legs uncomfortably to the side. Furthermore, Morris was wearing patent leather shoes that he had just bought in England, and he didn't want to scuff them on the rough granite. He made a supreme effort to get his legs in front of him; sitting at ground level was not easy.

"What brought you to Bulawayo, Morris?" Cath asked as she buttered a cheese cracker.

"I came to see family. Last time I was in Bulawayo was about 50 years ago."

"Heavens!" I'm sure you have seen some significant changes. Here," Cath handed Morris a pale blue plate with a buttered cheese cracker on it. "Help yourself to whatever you want; nobody will help you from now on."

"Thanks," Morris smiled, taking the offering and promptly letting the cracker slip off the plate. He hurriedly caught it before it hit the ground, but it broke in half showering crumbs on the picnic blanket.

"Good catch," Debs exclaimed. "A glass of wine, Morris? Red or white?"

"Oh, I, well…" Morris started nervously, a little overwhelmed by the womenfolk's attention and generous hospitality.

Grant, realising Morris' predicament, quickly came to the rescue. "The claret is good, Morris. Have a glass of red."

"Good, alright, thank you. A glass of claret will be lovely."

Heather passed Grant a folding outdoor chair. "Sit, Grant," she demanded. "Get yourself down to our height, for heaven's sake. We'll break our necks if we have to talk to you up there all day. And you too, Lindsay. Sit!"

Grant grumbled something as he opened the chair and placed it precariously on the uneven surface while Lindsay gathered up a cushion and sat on it, seemingly quite effortlessly. Mary opened a garden chair for Bob and helped him into it. As everyone took their places, plates were passed around, and they all began picking at the delights the ladies had provided on the blanket.

The conversation bounced happily between them, the setting in the majestic Matopos lending an air of relaxed enjoyment. Much to Morris' dismay, though, the discussion soon turned towards him.

"What's America like, Morris?" Jan asked after a sip of her wine. "I've never been there; we hear a lot of stories, though."

"It's lovely, really. America is a huge country, so it is very diverse."

Ralph suddenly interrupted. "By the way, Morris tells me he is in the movie industry."

"Really?" most of the ladies sang out in a chorus.

"And he knows some big names, like Humphrey Bogart, not so, Morris?"

Morris blushed. "Well... You could say that."

"Tell us more," Mary said, her smile was contagious and suddenly everyone's attention was firmly fixed on Morris.

"I don't have much to do with the actual making of movies; my role is purely financial. They are currently working on a movie called 'Joan of Arc', which is about to be released. It stars Ingrid Bergman. Have you heard of her?"

"Oh yes," two of the ladies sang out.

"Have you met her?" Mary asked.

"Yes, a couple of times."

"Who else have you met?" Mary persisted.

"Zsa Zsa Gabor," Morris' smile was genuine. "She's lovely."

"You lucky man!" Peter chuckled, which promptly elicited a hard slap on his upper arm from Debs.

"Yes, she is a lovely lady," Morris confirmed. "Then there is Humphrey Bogart, of course. Actually, two of my children are in the arts and entertainment business. My son, Leslie, is a film producer and screenwriter. He married a lady named Effie Atherton."

"I've heard of her!" Cath exclaimed. "Isn't she an actress in London?"

"Yes, she has done some film and stage work, she's also on the BBC. My eldest son, Cecil, is an impresario in London; he works a great deal with stage and plays, that sort of thing. He believes he has discovered a young lass whom he thinks will be a great movie star one day, so he is trying to promote her. If he can get her to come to America, he is hoping I might use my contacts to introduce her to some movers and shakers in the movie industry."

"What's her name?" Ralph asked.

"Oh... I can't remember offhand; he did tell me. Hmm...

Hepburn, that's it! Audrey Hepburn."

"Never heard of her," Ralph shook his head. Everyone shook their head in unison.

"Any children?" Jan asked nonchalantly.

"Five from my first wife; Derek, Cecil, Leslie, Harry and Dagmar. All in England. I lost Derek, in an automobile accident during the war."

"I'm sorry to hear that," Cath said with genuine sorrow in her voice.

"Thank you, Cath. Then I had a daughter, Anne, with my second wife, and a step-son, John. Cecil, incidentally, won the Navy League Sword of Honour at Cheltenham College." Morris beamed proudly.

"Crikey!" Ralph exclaimed in his thick accent. "That will make you proud. I hear that is a very prestigious award."

"Apart from financing Hollywood movies, what else do you do?" Debs asked inquisitively.

Morris began to blush. "A bit of this, and a bit of that, nothing really," he tried to change the subject.

"You had Langbourne Brothers here in Bulawayo, didn't you?" Mary questioned.

"Well, yes, it is where my brothers and I began our business careers. I had to close it down during the war when my brother David died. It was too much for Harry to run on his own."

Ralph clicked his finger and pointed at Morris. "Your brother, Harry Langbourne, he was a patient of mine. I remember him now. Where is he these days?"

"Johannesburg," Morris smiled fondly. "Happily married to Anne and has two daughters and a son."

Morris successfully managed to divert the attention away from himself before busying himself with eating some of the delights that were provided. He listened to his new friends joke and tell stories about nothing much in particular. Finally, the coffee flasks were produced, and to Morris' absolute joy, Mary opened a cake tin that was filled to the brim with little square slices of shortbread.

"Oh," Morris couldn't contain himself. "I love shortbread. My absolute favourite!"

"Mary makes the best shortbread in the world," Bob smiled at his wife, "and because I love shortbread too, I insist you all eat as much as you can, or I will have to eat what's left for the remainder of the week. I can assure you that it is not healthy for me."

"I've never had a problem with shortbread," Morris grinned, and without waiting for an offer, reached over and helped himself to two squares.

When lunch was over, the men stood, some with a fair amount of difficulty and stiff joints, and began to pack up the picnic site. It was then that Morris discovered that the men would traditionally carry the remains of the picnic, or *katundu* as Grant called it, down to the cars while the ladies walked up to the memorial and paid their respects.

"Did you boys tell Morris the story about Allan Wilson?" Cath asked Lindsay.

"No, we didn't get the chance," Lindsay replied.

"Come on, Morris, join us and we'll tell you a most fascinating story of bravery and courage, and the amazing military tactics and might of the Matabele nation."

The story of Major Allan Wilson would be the most fascinating historical tale he would ever hear. Morris felt very fortunate that he had met Grant the previous day; his visit to Bulawayo had turned out far better than he had imagined it would.

A strange sense of hollow sadness washed over Morris as he turned to walk up the massive granite slope with the ladies. The day was almost done, and he could not understand how, in just a few hours, total strangers could make him feel as though he belonged, as though he was at home; his true home. Then, in the blink of an eye, it was over; from warm happiness and joy to an empty sadness. Perhaps, Morris thought, it was the unexplainable magic of Mother Africa.

CHAPTER EIGHTEEN
Salisbury 1947

Another train station, copious billows of steam, pungent smoke and the ear-splitting screech of metal, but this was to be his last stop.

The first-class compartment on Rhodesia Railways was, this time, comfortable enough, and the service and amenities were quite acceptable. The overnight journey from Bulawayo to Salisbury could have been tedious, as there had been nothing to see in the pitch black of the African night, but Morris slept well through the monotonous clattering of the wheels on the iron track.

Glancing out the window as he retrieved his leather duffle bag from the overhead netting, Morris saw Archie leaning against the red-brick station wall. Archie was wearing a heavy-woven pure wool jacket that was slightly too big for him, and sported his traditional fedora hat with a broad black silk band. His narrow tie was plain black, thinner than the hatband, and the Windsor knot was tied so tightly that it was unrecognisable as a triangle, and looked more like a ball.

"Huh," Morris muttered to himself. "Little seems to have changed here."

Gathering up his umbrella, duffle bag and briefcase, Morris left the carriage and alighted. Archie spotted him right away and strode over to greet his eldest half-brother.

"Welcome to Salisbury, Morris," Archie beamed, his hand outstretched in greeting. "Pleasant journey?"

"Yes, thank you," Morris put his duffle on the ground and quickly shook Archie's proffered hand. "Glad to be here at last, though."

Morris was pleased to be in Salisbury, mainly because it marked the final destination of his African trip and his soon-to-be return home to California.

"May I take your bag?" Archie asked, retrieving the duffle bag from the floor before Morris could answer him. "How many suitcases have you?"

"Five," Morris answered as he looked around the fast-emptying platform.

"Five?" Archie was taken aback.

"I would think they are in the boxcar at the rear. Well, I would hope so anyhow."

"Let's have a look, then." Archie immediately strode off towards the far end of the platform. Morris quickened his pace to keep up with him.

Archie continued the conversation when Morris caught up. "We'll walk to Langbourne's, I mean Langbourne Trading," Archie corrected himself. "It's only four blocks north of here."

"We can't walk four blocks with five pieces of luggage," Morris argued, horrified at the thought. "They're heavy."

Archie chuckled, and it caught Morris by surprise; his laugh sounded just like David's and brought a flood of nostalgic memories back.

"Never fear, I will organise some porters to carry your bags to the hotel. I have booked you into the Meikle's Hotel. It's very nice there."

"Thank you," Morris was secretly relieved. "I know Tom Meikle from the old days. A good man. I was told he built a fine hotel. Most of his equipment came from Louis in Johannesburg, did you know that? I hope Tom will be there; it will be good to reconnect with him."

"Ahh," Archie looked Morris in the eye momentarily. "He died just before the war. David kindly gave me an introduction to Thomas Meikle when I moved to Salisbury in the hope he might give me a good rate; I was without a place to live for three months, as you may recall. Sadly, Mr Meikle died just before I arrived here. I never met him, but his family were very hospitable and accommodating, and I was given a very favourable rate."

"How sad," Morris lamented. "He had an astute business brain. I used to enjoy our discussions. He had a brother, Stewart; also a sterling gentleman."

"Here we go," Archie said as they arrived at a wagon that contained numerous boxes, crates, bags and trunks. "Identify your belongings, and I'll look for some porters. I shan't be long."

Morris took his bag back from Archie and watched him quickly disappear. He grumbled to himself. His trunks were very heavy, and the thought of dragging them out of the hodgepodge of other passengers' belongings seemed a little daunting. Morris walked to the soot-stained red-brick wall of the station building and carefully put his duffle bag, briefcase and umbrella down. Then, stepping over and past numerous items of bedraggled and haphazard cargo, looked for his belongings, constantly casting a beady eye back at his property to make sure nobody walked off with it.

Dragging four of his five trunks noisily between other baggage and passengers to the vicinity of the station wall, Morris craned his neck to see if he could find the last of his trunks amongst the hectic activity by the open carriage door. Casting a glance up the platform in the hopes of seeing Archie, Morris checked his wristwatch. It had stopped, and, in frustration, he began winding the little button while searching for a wall clock. He spotted one, but as it indicated the time to be something after quarter past three, and knowing it was closer to six o'clock in the morning, Morris grunted in frustration.

Another look at the open door of the luggage carriage showed that the baggage handlers had finished their work and had left. Scanning the rapidly diminishing pile of boxes and crates, and not seeing his remaining trunk, Morris' heart began to sink.

"Right you are," Archie suddenly announced from behind his left shoulder. "We have some porters. My goodness, is this all yours?"

Standing behind Archie were five Mashona men wearing

westernised civilian clothing. One man, who seemed to be their spokesman, was wearing the khaki uniform of the Rhodesia Railways.

"Yes," Morris said sheepishly while eyeing the group of porters standing attentively. They looked thin and malnourished. "Do you honestly think these men can carry my luggage?" Morris glanced at Archie.

"I wasn't expecting trunks, no. I will have to engage more porters; two to a trunk should do."

"I'm afraid one of my trunks appears to be missing."

"Wait here, I will look for it. Does it look like these?"

"Yes," Morris grumbled.

Archie walked over to the open carriage door and momentarily peered into the dark interior. Turning back to Morris, he was beaming. "It's in here. The last one." He waved to the porters and pointed behind him. He flashed two fingers in the air, indicating the number two. The leader understood and sent a couple of his men into the carriage to retrieve the last trunk.

"Five more men, please, Joshua," Archie indicated to the lead porter, who nodded and immediately trotted off to find more help.

"What's the time?" Morris asked Archie, a little relieved that all his belongings had stayed with him for the duration of the journey.

Archie looked at his wristwatch. "Just gone six o'clock. I thought that while the porters are taking your bags to Meikle's we would walk to the shop and I'll show you around. Then we can walk over to Meikle's for breakfast and settle you in. Meikle's is only four blocks east of Langbourne's."

"Splendid," Morris said, trying to sound pleased. He was famished and felt that a nice hot bath would be most welcome too.

Five more porters arrived, and, with two to a trunk, Archie explained to Joshua where to go and gave him some money to pay the porters after the job was done. After following them out of the station building, Morris and Archie then broke away from the procession of porters. They walked towards the corner of Speke Avenue and Inez Terrace, to the building from where Archie now ran his thriving wholesale business.

"What happened to Paddy?" Morris asked as they crossed over South Avenue. "That was tragic and very sudden."

"Yes," Archie said sadly. He had been very fond of his older brother. "Paddy came up from Bulawayo to see me on business matters. He did that regularly, as you know, and he would stay with us, that is Kate, the boys and me. We always kept a room ready for him. One day he arrived and suddenly took ill during dinner. His health deteriorated quite rapidly, so I took him to St Anne's Hospital; it's close to my home. By morning he had died. The doctors have no idea what he died from, although Kipps Rosin, a renowned surgeon and a good friend of the Jewish community, seems to think it was as a result of something he picked up in Tanzania during the First World War."

"I heard he was very sickly after the war," Morris said.

"Yes. He was shot in the lower back, but typhoid and malaria and whatever other dreadful diseases thrive in that jungle seem to be worse than a bullet. I couldn't believe how fast he went down and then perished. Almost in my own home. It was devastating for us all."

"I had a similar experience with Louis," Morris shook his head sadly. "We knew he was sick but didn't realise how ill he was. He died in the guest room of my apartment. Horrible stuff."

"I heard," Archie commiserated, then changed the subject to Morris' relief. "How's Badger, and Anne? I haven't seen them in about six months."

"Well, thanks. They send their regards. As does Zebra."

"Interesting man, Danie Coetzee."

The two men chatted easily as they walked north along Angwa Street, then turned left into Speke Avenue. Being a Sunday, the streets were empty, and at that hour, Archie and Morris stood out very much like lone figures. At the end of the next block, Archie stopped and pointed across Inez Terrace. There, on the opposite corner, was the two-story building he had constructed using money loaned to him on the back of a Langbourne Brothers guarantee.

"There you are," Archie smiled as he admired his building. "You gave me the means to build it, for which I am most grateful."

"Very nice," Morris smiled. He was genuinely impressed. "Because you paid the loan back in record time and released us of the guarantee, we too are grateful. I didn't realise the building took up a quarter of a city block."

The building was painted in an off-white colour with olive-green lines highlighting protruding brickwork as a decorative design. It stretched south along Inez Terrace up to an alleyway, and east for half the block until it abutted the next building. The corner had been cut away with the entrance embedded within. It effectively allowed access to the doorway from two streets. The lettering of the name 'Langbourne Trading Co. Ltd.' was cast in concrete and painted in the same olive-green colour. It sat proudly about halfway up the walls on both Inez Terrace and Speke Avenue. If that wasn't enough, the name was yet again emblazoned on not one but two massive signs with huge olive-green lettering above the roof. Like the door, one sign was boastfully mounted across the corner of the building. The final touch was a tall flagpole on the very edge of the roof, but it bore no flag.

"Very nice," Morris repeated. "Where's the flag?"

"The pulley at the top has jammed, and I can't get anyone to shimmy up there to fix it. A couple of men have tried, but they were overcome with fear before they even attempted to climb up that pole. It's a little thin and bends under the weight of an adult man. A child would manage, but Kate won't let me send our son up there. I'm working on that, though," Archie laughed.

"I don't blame her," Morris didn't see the humour.

"I should have put the pole on a hinge mechanism or something. Nevertheless, that's the way it is. Let's go inside, and I'll show you around."

As they crossed the empty street, Morris looked at the surrounding buildings. On the opposite corner was a sign for 'Kaufman and Sons Wholesalers'.

"Is that Abe Kaufman's building?" Morris asked.

"I think so," Archie looked across at the pale-yellow building with blue trimmings. "I know the sons, but have never met Mr Kaufman. They give me stiff opposition, but they are nice enough people. Opposition in business is healthy."

It needed three keys to open the chunky locks on the main door. Morris stood patiently, enjoying the cool morning breeze. On entering the warehouse, Morris was reminded of his own warehouse during his younger days in Bulawayo. The first few yards of floor space were designated for office work, and the desks, partitioned from the public access by a low wooden barrier, were strewn with copious amounts of scattered paperwork. Thereafter, the remainder of the store was laid out with large, heavy wooden rectangular tables that were piled high with all manner of goods.

The first row of tables was stacked with bolts of colourful fabric; cotton, polyester, nylon and silk for clothing, rows of darker material for suits and formal wear, countless heavier bolts for drapes, curtaining and many types of upholstery and coverings. There was an empty cutting table, the same size as the others but with a small trough depressed at one end to accommodate a bolt of fabric to prevent it from rolling away. A brass ruler along one side, with imperial feet and inches engraved into it, ensured accurate measurements. A massive pair of lethal-looking iron tailor's scissors lay threateningly on the table, ready to attack any fabric that came near it. A dirty, and much frayed piece of string attached to the loop for one's thumb guaranteed the scissors remained at the cutting table, preventing it from being borrowed for any alternative purpose. The row of tables behind the material displayed hundreds of varieties of glassware, and behind that, enamelware of every description. In the distance, the display tables were chock-a-block with clothing, neatly folded, and behind the clothing, high stacks of shoeboxes.

"Looks as though you have a good variety of merchandise, Archie," Morris congratulated his half-brother. "If I could make one suggestion, simply based on how Harry designed the warehouse in Bulawayo, I would move the bolts of material to the back of the warehouse. As it is, they make a high barrier, so customers coming in have to walk past them to see what's beyond. If you move them to the rear, the depth of the shop and all the smaller merchandise will be more visible."

Archie scratched his chin reflectively. "A good suggestion, thank you."

"Perhaps move the glassware right to the front. Make the most of the light from the windows and let them sparkle."

"Thank you, Morris. I like that idea. I'll make your suggested changes tomorrow. Now, let me show you the storeroom and despatch area."

As they walked deeper into the warehouse, Morris looked back at the office area and the mess of papers and files strewn over everyone's desks. It reminded him of his old friend, Julian Weil in Mafeking, who had had the most disorderly office Morris had ever seen. It had always intrigued Morris as to how anyone could work like that. He was about to say something to Archie but felt it might be best not to interfere too much and keep the peace. He knew that Archie had as quick a temperament as himself, so decided silence was a sound decision, all things considered.

Half an hour later, Archie was locking the doors, and they were striding off to Meikle's Hotel, both anticipating a hearty breakfast.

"David's son, Leslie, visited Rhodesia last year," Archie said as they crossed First Street. "He is the most delightful man. And his wife, Millicent, certainly stole the show. A captivating lady; such beauty and charm. She made quite an impression on Salisbury's society when they were here."

"Yes, I believe so," Morris smiled. "He lives not far from me in Beverley Hills. A very nice man. Leslie works for me now, you know? Looks after my affairs and all."

"So I heard," Archie replied. "Millicent was telling us – in fact, she gave an interview to the Rhodesia Herald when she was here – about her life in Hollywood and the famous names she mixes with at the shops or in markets."

"Really?" Morris seemed amused. "Like who?"

"Oh, Greer Garson, Gregory Peck, Lana Turner and Robert Taylor. There were others, but I can't remember them offhand."

"Well, that's true. Millicent should be an actress herself, she is certainly very beautiful, but she has no interest in that sort of thing. The day Millicent first met Leslie, she knew she would marry him, but he had no idea. She was patient and waited several years before he came to his senses. I'm happy for them."

"We inducted them into our 'Langbourne Clan' when they were here. It's a type of club I formed when my sons were young, ostensibly to teach them how to run a business, board meetings and committees, that sort of thing, but it has since grown into something entirely different."

"I was told about that," Morris said with genuine interest. "Tell me more about this... clan."

"Well, we have a motto, and objectives, like a constitution, and we give out good deed badges; even bravery badges now!" Archie chuckled. "But the main point of the Clan is to report on family matters and keep up unity, closeness and contact within the Langbourne Family. We also raise funds for charity."

"Splendid idea," Morris nodded his approval.

"The sole criteria to be a member is that you must be a part of the Langbourne family. We started with three members, myself, John and Louis, and now we have 19 members. On that note, we have arranged to have you for dinner tonight, as you are aware, but we have also convened a meeting of the Langbourne Clan where we will officially invite you to join, and, if you accept, you will be our 20th member."

"Sounds wonderful. I would be delighted and honoured."

"Tremendous!" Archie exclaimed excitedly. "Harry, and Louis' son, Herbert, are already members. Harry is quite active in the Clan. Even David became a member before he died."

"Well, I never! I had no idea. Leslie told me you had a club for the family going, but I never imagined it was so structured."

"A *clan*, not a club. You will find out all about it tonight. We have quite a gathering in your honour; every available Langbourne in Salisbury today will be there. Meanwhile, here we are," Archie grinned as he gestured towards the entrance of the hotel.

The life-sized statues of a pair of lions graced the entrance to the most prestigious hotel in the land. Morris admired them as he walked through the main doors that overlooked Cecil Square, a nature park with an extravagant fountain in the centre. The walking paths inside the park were laid out in the shape of the markings on the Union Jack when seen from above. On the other side of the park was the Anglican Cathedral, which was still under construction.

Morris, as was the case with all guests checking in, was treated like royalty, and he was suitably impressed.

"Tom Meikle did well," Morris quietly commented to Archie as he gazed admiringly around the foyer.

"Indeed, he did. As I said, I was very fortunate to spend three months here when I first arrived. We never had a complaint. The food was outstanding, and the bedrooms well-appointed. The place nearly burnt down while we were resident here, and we would never have known until a reporter with The Rhodesia Herald wrote something about the incident almost a month later."

"I am very sorry to hear that Tom passed away. I would have liked to have been able to congratulate him."

The receptionist returned with Morris' key and gave him directions to where he would find his room. To Morris' relief, his five trunks had already been taken to his suite.

Breakfast over, and much enjoyed by both men, Archie then arranged to collect Morris at the main entrance at six o'clock that evening before bidding him farewell. Although Archie suggested some activities to bide his time, Morris had already formed plans to try and contact some old acquaintances, and so they parted company until the evening.

11 Philips Avenue boasted a double-storey house that Archie had proudly built as a home for Kate and their two boys. Intricate wrought ironwork displayed inside decorative arches depressed slightly into the walls, marked the home as unique, as did the large windows on both levels. The windowsills were but one foot off the floor, and the glass panes reached almost to the ceilings. It had the effect of bringing the lush green garden into the home, especially from the upper level.

Copious sunshine, perfect temperatures and fertile soil, together with just the right amount of summer rain, meant flora in Salisbury thrived almost wherever it was planted. It seemed especially so for the creeping ivy that had practically invaded the decorative ironwork completely, and which now clung with a vice-like grip to the concrete splatter-dash finish on the outer walls. It even threatened to attack the eaves of the roof.

Kate loved her roses, as did many of the Langbourne women, and her rose garden was spectacular. As Archie drove Morris through the gate, their lone dog, a mongrel called Flash, lost interest in whatever he was burying in a rose bed and ran to greet them.

"Does he bite?" Morris asked Archie with some trepidation.

"No, he's quite friendly. We are down to one hound at the moment. We usually have three dogs, but one was killed by a passing car last week, and the other one, Edgar, is in the kennels. The stupid dog won't stop fighting with other dogs in the neighbourhood. The police got involved in the last incident, so Kate finally had enough and put it in the dog kennels on the other side of town in the hopes of finding it a home on a farm somewhere."

"Goodness," Morris frowned as he watched Flash bound after the car.

"Well, here we are," Archie chuckled, once again unintentionally reminding Morris of David. "I owe thanks again to Langbourne Brothers for securing the collateral for the mortgage so that I could build our home."

"Our pleasure," Morris said as he alighted gingerly, hoping Flash was not interested in newcomers. Sadly though, Flash seemed to be *only* interested in strangers.

With a great deal of shouting and threatening, Archie finally tamed Flash's interest in Morris by throwing a grubby ball at the gate. His aim was true, and the ball bounced through the gate and out onto the street. Archie quickly led Morris to the front door, which opened before they reached it and Kate emerged smiling, wearing a long formal black dress as if she was about to attend an opera.

"Morris," Archie beamed at his beautiful wife, "this is Kate. Kate darling, meet my brother, Morris."

Morris smiled broadly. "Pleased to meet you, at last, Kate. I have heard much about you."

"And I about you, Morris. It is such an honour to have you in our home finally. Do come in."

Kate wasn't sure if she should hug Morris, shake his hand, or even curtsy for that matter, such were the fearful stories she had heard about him, but her conundrum was resolved when Archie hurriedly bustled Morris through the door and past Kate.

"Quick, let's go in before that blasted dog comes back," Archie muttered. "Please close the door, Kate."

The entrance hall boasted a wide staircase hugging the right wall as Morris stepped into the subdued gloom of the hallway. Family photos in black and white prints were hung on the walls in simple, narrow black frames. The parquet flooring was polished to a high shine and, coming from somewhere deep in the belly of the house, a low rumble of joyful voices could be heard, punctuated by merry laughter.

Kate took Morris' jacket and hung it on a chunky black wrought iron hook before leading him through to the waiting guests. The rich aroma of a roast beef dinner caused Morris to flare his nostrils in anticipation. As they entered the lounge, Archie called for everyone's attention.

"Good evening, Family," he said proudly. "I'd like you to meet my brother from America, Morris. Morris is the most senior member of the Langbourne family."

The gathering went silent.

"Firstly," Archie gestured to a well-presented gentleman in his mid-30s. "I believe you two have met."

The man stepped forward, beaming broadly. "Hello, Uncle Morris. I'm Cyril Langbourne, David's youngest son."

"Good heavens!" Morris almost laughed as he pumped Cyril's hand. "I would never have recognised you. You must have been about four or five when I met you."

"Yes, back in England. I still remember when – November 1916."

"You have a good memory," Morris joked.

"Cyril has a thing for dates," Archie said, "Don't you?"

"November the 18th to be precise Uncle Morris," Cyril said to a chorus of laughter. "This is my lovely wife, Eve."

Eve was dressed in a full floral dress that billowed around her as she stepped over to Morris and gave him a peck on both cheeks. "Welcome," she said simply.

"And this is Adele," Archie gestured to a lady who reclined elegantly on a sofa. Before she could stand, Morris stepped over to her and, bending forward slightly, kissed the back of her hand.

"Lovely to meet you, Uncle Morris," Adele smiled sweetly.

"I'm so sorry for your loss, Adele. Archie and I were talking about Paddy this afternoon. Such a lovely fellow. I had a lot of respect for him."

"Thank you, Uncle Morris," Adele said sadly as her eyes began to water up.

"You must be Sonya," Morris quickly moved to a young lady who sat beside Adele. He knew she had to be Adele's daughter as the likeness was uncanny.

Sonythe black sheep of thea lightly jumped to her feet and kissed Morris on the cheek. "Lovely to meet you at last, Uncle Morris. Welcome to Rhodesia."

"And this is Richard," Archie tapped a young man on the shoulder. "Paddy's son."

"Pleased to meet you, Uncle Morris," Richard shook Morris' hand firmly.

"My word," Morris looked Richard up and down. "I can't believe the resemblance. You're Paddy's son alright. Very pleased to meet you too."

Richard was 17 and a delightfully polite young man. Dressed in smart slacks and a short-sleeved open-neck shirt, the shy tilt of his head belied his muscular forearms and vice-like grip. Even to Morris, Richard was a very handsome young man.

"You're at University, right?" Morris asked.

"Yes," Richard answered, a broad open smile stretching across his face. "Wits University in Johannesburg."

"What degree are you after?"

"Accounting. I have a love for numbers and arithmetic."

"A man after my own heart," Morris gave Richard a knowing nod and smile. The young man's already broad smile seemed to become impossibly bigger.

Archie, in his somewhat impatient manner, interrupted the conversation. "It seems like most of the Langbournes are numbers people. Here is my youngest son, Louis. He adds up telephone numbers in the phone book for fun. He's just turned 12."

"Do you?" Morris looked intrigued as he shook young Louis' hand.

"Yes, Uncle Morris," Louis replied, casting an uncertain look at his father. "It's become too easy for me now, so I add the columns up with the book upside down."

Morris gave Archie a curious look. "Is he serious?"

"Yes," Archie laughed. "We test each other by adding up the phone book; I sit on one side of the table, and Louis sits on the other. We flip the phone book open, select a column and race each other. I use an adding machine, but Louis invariably beats me and is always correct."

"Well I never," Morris smiled broadly. "It reminds me of when I was your age and living in Ireland. My father would set tough numerical challenges for me. I never found them difficult, though," he laughed.

"Last but not least, my son, John," Archie beamed.

"Pleased to meet you, Uncle Morris," John smiled and shook his uncle's hand firmly.

"I can see you and Richard are cousins. You look very similar."

"Oh, we are, Uncle Morris," John cast a pleasing smile at Richard. "We are the same age, our birthdays are only days apart, and we go to the same university in South Africa; only I want to do a business degree rather than accounting."

"They are like brothers," Archie agreed. "They also get up to a lot of mischief, not so boys?"

"No, never!" John and Richard said in unison and burst out laughing.

It had only been the previous weekend that they had attempted to climb up a downpipe of the neighbour's house to visit their daughter and her sleep-over friends for an innocent 'midnight feast'. The gutter had come loose, sending the boys crashing back to earth and a piece of wayward galvanised piping walloped the neighbour's new car. It was not their finest hour, nor Archie's for that matter; he had seriously considered sending the boys to join Edgar at the kennels for onward transfer to a distant farm. It didn't take long for Archie and his neighbour to realise it had been merely innocent teenage fun, something either of them might have done in their youth, and so, after an appropriate financial settlement, the matter was put behind them all.

"Gentlemen," Morris clasped John and Richard on their shoulders, "do me a favour and bring in the trunk that's in your father's boot. I have bought some gifts for you all from America."

The two young men left immediately, trying hard to suppress a run.

"And don't let the dog in!" Archie barked after them.

Morris had indeed brought gifts – many of them, and all of exceptional quality. Archie joked about the number of trunks Morris was travelling with but now realised why. When it came to generosity, Morris was outstanding. The family members, particularly the ladies, were humbled by the gifts Morris presented them. From French fragrances and European fashion accessories to Eastern ornaments and home decorations from around the world, the women were lavishly spoilt by Morris. The younger generation was equally overindulged, almost to the point of Archie becoming embarrassed. John received a very upmarket pocketknife that was just perfect for his love of the Boy Scouts Movement, and Richard's Swiss wristwatch with 17 jewels had him beaming uncontrollably.

As the excitement and chatter began to ebb, Archie brought the gathering to order and called for some attention.

"Firstly, let me thank Morris for his wonderful generosity, and also for making the time to come to Salisbury during his international travels. It is a privilege to have you here, Brother," Archie said as he received a nod of thanks from Morris.

"We have gathered here tonight," Archie glanced around the room at the expectant smiling faces, "to hold a meeting of the Langbourne Clan in the presence of our honourable guest. Perhaps we should begin, as I know Kate will be ready to serve dinner soon, and I'm sure we don't want to keep her waiting."

A soft laugh went around the room with some gentle humour directed at the matriarch.

"John, as you are the Chairman, perhaps you would begin the meeting for us."

"Certainly Dad," John nodded his agreement and then looked over at his father. "Mr Secretary, do we have a quorum?"

Archie, pulling out a pad and pencil, nodded once. "Yes, Mr Chairman, we have a quorum."

"Mr Treasurer," John directed his comment at Louis, "would you kindly read the previous minutes and confirm them."

"Huh!" Morris exclaimed.

"Something wrong?" Archie asked.

"No, I just didn't expect such formality at a family meeting. My apologies for the intrusion, Mr Chairman," Morris raised a hand apologetically towards John. "I'm just very impressed. If you don't mind me asking, how old are you boys?"

"Richard and I are 17, Uncle Morris, and Louis is 12," John replied.

"Well," Morris glanced at Archie in astonishment, "I began holding formal meetings like this with my brothers when I was in my early 20s. I offer my deepest respect to you, Archie. You have instilled the basic principles of business in your children at a very young age." Morris nodded his head in approval at Archie, then returned to John. "Please, forgive my interruption Mr Chairman."

"No apology necessary, Uncle Morris," John responded, then turned back to Louis. "Please continue, Mr Treasurer."

Once the formality of reading and approving the minutes of the last meeting was over, Louis continued with the welcome.

"On behalf of the Langbourne Clan," Louis stood proud, puffing out his chest, "we would like to welcome our distinguished guest from America, Uncle Morris Langbourne. The secretary has asked me to explain the objectives of the Clan.

"The main objective of the Clan is to bring the Langbourne Family closer together. Nowadays we are a far-flung family, with Langbournes in Rhodesia, South Africa, England, France and

America. Postage being what it is, and members proving to be slow to write, often important family matters go unrecorded.

"The Clan has a motto, which is 'Honesty and Truth', and we abide by the principle of making humanity happy, in particular the Langbourne family. We have a coat of arms, or a crest if you will," Louis held up a small cardboard badge that had been coloured in by hand with blue and green crayons, "which has our motto inscribed on it, 'Honesty and Truth'. There is also a Latin inscription on the top that says 'Da Dextrum Misero', which roughly means 'give your right hand', or in other words, 'help others'."

Morris stared at Louis in awe. He had not expected such formality, organisation or structure at this family gathering, nor to enjoy such a well-presented lecture from a 12-year-old. He was fascinated.

Louis put the badge down and continued with his speech. "The Clan also has a subscription that members are required to pay at each meeting, usually a penny. These are looked after by the Treasurer, who is me," Louis said proudly and fixed his stare on Morris. "When we have enough, we give the money to charity.

"Finally, all members of the Clan are expected to perform regular good deeds. It is an important part of the membership. If a member performs three good deeds in one week, then that member will get to wear the Good Deed Badge at the next meeting." Louis held up the slightly grubby cardboard badge and handed it to Morris.

Morris noticed that a small silver safety pin had been glued to the back. He nodded his genuine approval, raising his eyebrows at the small home-made badge before passing it to Eve who sat to his right. He held his silence; he wasn't quite sure what to say.

"As the Treasurer, I would now like to nominate Uncle Morris as a member of the Langbourne Clan. Do I have a seconder?"

Eve raised her hand. "I do. I second the motion."

Morris smiled; he was enjoying the proceedings immensely as it reminded him of the meetings he would hold with David, Louis and Harry back in the old warehouse in Abercorn Street. These formal meetings had held him in good stead when he was elected the inaugural Chairman and President of the Bulawayo Zionist

Movement when he was just 22 years old. He thought back to his father, who had taught him all he knew of business when they lived in Ireland. Jacob was an excellent teacher and brilliant businessman before he was overcome with grief when his first wife passed away. It soon transpired, though, that Morris was a great deal smarter even than his father.

"Splendid," Louis beamed. "Uncle Morris, would you accept membership into the Langbourne Clan?"

"Indeed, I would be honoured."

"All those in favour of Uncle Morris joining The Langbourne Clan, please raise your hand."

Everyone raised their hand in unison.

"All against," Louis scanned the room theatrically as everyone dropped their hands to their laps.

At this point, John took over the proceedings. "Uncle Morris, the Langbourne Clan duly inducts you into the Langbourne Clan and welcomes your membership. Congratulations."

There was a round of applause and some nods of appreciation from Morris before John continued. "We are honoured to have you within the Clan. You are the eldest member of the Langbourne Family, and it is, therefore, fitting that we recognise you today. I need to let you know that Uncle Harry is one of our keenest members. Even though he does not live in the colony of Rhodesia, his contributions are especially recognised by us. We were blessed to have had Uncle David as a member for a short while before he passed away. We would ask that you make every effort to keep in touch with the family members and keep us all abreast of family news in America."

Morris wriggled his way out of the plush sofa and stood, casting an appreciative eye over his relatives, their gazes now fixed intently on him. He stood silently for a brief moment before addressing the family.

"It is a great privilege to be elected a member of the Langbourne Clan, and I will endeavour to render good service. With my connections to the family in America and England, I believe I can add value to the Clan."

Archie raised his hand to say something and John nodded his approval. "In welcoming my brother to the Clan, I would like to thank Morris for agreeing to add to our membership. We are very isolated here, both as a country and, with the recently ended war, as a branch of the family. We have lost touch with events that have happened within our extended family around the world. If you would give us addresses of all the brothers, sisters, cousins, etcetera, we will endeavour to send minutes of all our meetings."

"I might suggest," Morris said as he took his seat, "that you make a list of everyone's birthdays and send birthday cards to them from the Clan. Also, any big achievements should be recorded, and congratulatory letters sent to them too."

"Splendid idea," John exclaimed. "May we carry that motion?"

Everyone mumbled their agreement, some raising their hands as well.

"We now move to the presidential address," John said officially. "As I have been at University in South Africa, and am only back for the holidays, Louis has been Acting Chairman. Therefore, I feel it is in order for him to take this honour today."

Louis stood again. "Thank you, Mr Chairman. It is with sadness that I must report the deaths of our grannies, Mrs Helena Langbourne in Dublin, and Mrs Jenny Hart in Johannesburg. I ask the meeting to stand in silence for a few moments."

Everyone obliged, and the room fell silent for a short while. A cricket trilled outside, followed by a hoarse croak from a frog.

"Thank you," Louis broke the silence, and everyone retook their seats.

Morris reached past Evelyn and took Kate's hand, giving it a gentle squeeze. "I'm sorry for the loss of your mother. I didn't know. I wish you long life."

Kate smiled sweetly at Morris and returned the squeeze. Morris realised then how important this little clan was; it was indeed a perfect avenue to keep the family members informed and, essentially, close.

Louis went on to congratulate a distant cousin on his marriage, Herbert and Josette on the birth of a son, Brian, and John and

Richard for completing another year at University. Then Louis became more serious and complained that he was disappointed that more meetings of the Clan were not held during 1947 and hoped the situation would be rectified in 1948. He reported that due to the lack of meetings, hardly any subscriptions were collected and that they had barely one shilling to give to charity, which was unacceptable. Louis felt that after one year, they should have had at least a pound or so.

Morris, realising how insignificant their funding levels were, suggested that the subscriptions should be increased for the adults, but remain the same for the younger generation. With that, he donated 25 pounds. This was more than the clan had raised in its entire existence, and immediately discussion took place as to whom to give the money to.

As the meeting drew to a close, Cyril stood and formally asked Morris to record some history of when he and his brothers came to Africa. He said his father, David, had done this exercise before he died, but the documents had gone missing. Morris agreed he would do this as soon as he had time. The meeting wound up with the mentioning of all good deeds done in the family. Archie was singled out for donating a trophy to the Boy Scouts Association, and another to Prince Edward School, a very prestigious establishment in Salisbury. Kate was commended for her work with several charities, and Morris was thanked for all the marvellous presents he had given to every member of the family in Africa.

It was then time to eat, and the family adjourned to the spacious dining room. It was an evening to remember, especially for Morris. After dreading the Rhodesian leg of his journey, the time with Archie and Kate had proven to be a delightful highlight. The entire trip had awoken some awkward emotions within his soul, something he had never previously experienced. It was almost a little uncomfortable.

Almost.

The following day found Archie and Morris standing on the railway platform again, staring at a large Rhodesia Railways locomotive. It was a cloudless day with nary a breeze in the air.

"Looks like a fine day for travelling," Archie covered his eyes with his hand as he gazed at the sky.

"Indeed," Morris said pensively. His mind was not on the weather. "Archie, I must thank you for all you have done for me while I have visited, but more importantly, I must thank you for all you have done for this branch of the family."

"It is I that must thank you for coming out here. It has been marvellous for the family and our morale." Archie beamed. "I originally started the Clan to teach my boys how to run a formal business and formal meetings, but it somehow developed from there. I realised we were losing touch with our international family, so I steered it to a family clan thing. It just grew bigger than I ever expected it to, and now, with your genuine endorsement, this really has been a great development for the family. No, I wholeheartedly thank you, once again."

Morris nodded, accepting what Archie had said. Both men stared in silent thought down the tracks.

"I have never been much of a family man," Morris mused, still staring into the distance. "My family has been David, Louis and Harry, and of course my sister, Bloomy. I have never felt the necessity to get close to anyone else, as you undoubtedly know. However, the war changed that for me."

"Really?" Archie looked at Morris quizzically.

"I'll tell you something you probably don't know. Our father was the only member of the family to leave Poland, back in 1879. Everyone else stayed behind." Morris sighed forlornly. "After the war I tried to find any relative we might have; aunt, uncle, cousin. I couldn't find anyone. I think every member of Father's family was killed when the war came to Poland."

Archie looked horrified. "I can't believe that. What about that cousin in Warsaw?"

"Gone. All of them murdered. I think we are all that is left; I can't find anyone alive. We are all that remains of our line of the family, and that's why your Clan touched a chord with me last night."

Archie stared at Morris in disbelief.

Morris shook his head sadly and continued. "I don't think people will truly understand the scale of death and destruction that war caused. I give thanks every day to our father's intuition, or whatever it was, that made him leave Poland. Because of him we live today, and so do our children and so will our grandchildren and their children after them."

"I had no idea," Archie almost whispered.

"Even though we argue amongst ourselves, we are all that we have. We need to remember that."

Archie laughed nervously. "You and I are not the easiest of people to get along with. We have to admit that. Certainly, you and I have tested our boundaries on many occasions, but still I hold you in the highest regard."

Morris gripped Archie on the shoulder and gave him a gentle nudge. "I struggled with you for many years, but you did well, and you have proven yourself over and over again. Yes, we had our days, that I cannot deny, but I have always respected your determination and *chutzpah*. You have gall; I'll give you that much. Now that I see how you care for our family, I have even more admiration for you. I've been wrong about you for many years. I've been wrong about many members of our family, but last night touched a chord, and I felt a belonging I have never felt before. Thank you."

Morris offered his hand, and Archie shook it firmly.

"You'll come back, Morris?" Archie asked apprehensively.

"I'll be back, Brother," Morris smiled and gripped Archie's hand with silent determination.

CHAPTER NINETEEN
Los Angeles 1949

Harry walked through the large glass doors of the hospital. A young nurse dressed in white, her blonde hair tied in a neat bun behind her head, was at the reception desk. She greeted Harry warmly.

"Good morning, Sir. How can I help you today?"

"Good morning," Harry replied, forcing a smile. He was jet-lagged. The journey from London to Los Angeles had been gruelling, and he had missed a lot of sleep. "I'm here to visit my brother, Morris Langbourne."

"Oh," the nurse said cheerily, "you must be Mr Harry Langbourne. Someone is waiting to see you. Sir?" she called to an elderly gentleman who was seated reading a newspaper.

The man quickly folded the newspaper and approached Harry with his arm extended. "Alwyn Pichanick," he spoke with a soft voice.

"Good to put a face to a voice," Harry returned the greeting. "Thanks for meeting me here, Mr Pichanick. Have you seen Morris today?"

"Not today, no. I thought I would wait for you and we could go in together. I was expecting you to arrive about now. Come, I'll take you up. He's in Room 402, on the fourth floor." Alwyn nodded at the nurse. "Thank you, Sister."

"I got in late last night," Harry grumbled as the men walked down a long corridor that smelled heavily of disinfectant. "The flight from New York to Los Angeles was the worst I've ever had to endure, and to top it off my damn hotel is right outside a bus depot. I hardly slept. How's my brother?" he asked belatedly.

"Grumpy," Alwyn chuckled trying to lighten the atmosphere, but then became sombre. "I spent some time with him yesterday finalising his affairs."

"And you have sorted out those documents we discussed over the phone?"

"Yes. Just a couple of signatures needed and then all will be in order, and hopefully to his liking." The lawyer then became sombre. "To be honest, Mr Langbourne, I don't think your brother has long to live, so you need to prepare yourself. He's lost a lot of weight. Cancer will do that to you."

"Thanks, Mr Pichanick," Harry said as they began to climb a flight of stairs, their footfalls echoing ominously around them.

Slightly out of breath, the two men stepped onto the fourth floor. Two doors away was a room, the door of which was shut. A group of younger people sat quietly outside on mismatched chairs. Harry instantly recognised Morris' children. They had matured since he last saw them; the three boys, Cecil, Leslie and Harry were now fine young men; Eunice had blossomed into a delightful young lady.

They greeted Harry fondly, but the tension was evident in their expressions. Introductions were made to Alwyn, and then some quick, pointless conversation ensued before Harry began to feel flustered. The doctor was in with Morris, though, and he simply had to wait. However, ten minutes later, the doctor emerged with a young nurse. The family gathered around him instantly.

"He's doing better today, but is still in a fair amount of discomfort," the doctor said with a reassuring smile. "You must be his brother?"

"Yes," Harry nodded as he shook the doctor's clammy hand. "Harry Langbourne."

"Good morning Mr Pichanick," the doctor shook Alwyn's hand too. "Mr Langbourne has asked to see both of you the moment you arrived. I'm afraid only two at a time if you don't mind," he addressed the rest of the anxious group.

Harry nodded at his nephews and niece and took a deep breath, steadying himself for what he might see. "Shall we, Mr Pichanick?"

The two senior men stepped into Room 402, Alwyn gently closing the door behind them. Harry looked at his brother lying comfortably on a hospital bed with his eyes closed and walked to the bedside. Morris appeared thin and fragile.

"Hello, Brother," Harry said gently.

Morris opened an eye and looked at Harry. A small smile appeared on his lips.

"I thought you wouldn't get here in time," Morris said quietly. He rolled his head to the left to look at his lawyer. "Morning Alwyn. Thanks for coming back."

"Only a pleasure, Morris,"

Morris turned back to Harry. "How was the flight?"

"Good thanks," Harry lied. "Gruelling, but good."

"Thanks for coming," Morris reached up and clasped Harry's hand in a traditional African grip. "Sorry you had to see me this way. They said they got it all last year, but obviously they didn't. The colon cancer has spread all over. Metastasised, they call it. Anyhow, enough of me. Open your briefcase, Alwyn, and let's get this over with. Harry, lift my bed so I can sit up. This bed's on hinges, just pull, there. Alwyn, help him!"

Harry cast an amused look at Alwyn. It was just like his brother, instructing people to do things his way, and immediately. Propped up and going through documents and papers with Alwyn, Morris seemed to regain some of his old energy. Harry smiled inwardly; this was Morris through and through. He was doing what he loved – business.

Alwyn got straight to the point as he knew that Morris would prefer that. "I have made the alterations you wanted, which should conclude everything. I just need you to sign this as a witness, if you don't mind Mr Harry," Alwyn handed a sheaf of paper to Harry, indicating a blank space for his signature.

"What am I signing?" Harry asked nobody in particular.

"Sign it, Harry," Morris commanded irritably. "It's just

paperwork to get my affairs in order. You don't seem to have noticed that I don't have much time. I've adjusted my last will and testament to donate a quarter of a million dollars for the construction of a convalescent care facility. My trustees will make sure it is built after my demise. Having experienced all this illness, I feel a convalescent centre is sorely lacking in Beverly Hills."

Harry raised an eyebrow at Alwyn, then scribbled his signature as required. After that, Morris seemed to relax a bit, and the conversation became more general with Morris moving off business matters to more personal issues.

"How was Rhodesia, after you left me?" Harry asked, hoping to change the subject.

"It was good. Archie is a good man."

"Goodness, I didn't expect you to say that of him," Harry said sarcastically. Alwyn raised an eyebrow at that unexpected comment.

"No, really, he is. That Clan of his? It's a good thing. You must support it when I'm gone, Harry, you really must."

"I do," Harry said uncomfortably at the reference to his brother's death. "And I will. Archie makes an effort to visit me in Johannesburg every time he is down that way. He even makes every Rhodesian family member call on me; the university teenagers included. I wish he would stop doing that. I'm expected to take them to lunch and show some interest in what they are up to. It was novel at first, but has begun to pall."

"Good, good," Morris said softly, closing his eyes. "Listen, I'm getting tired. This morphine is dreadful stuff, but necessary. Give me half an hour, will you."

"Your children are outside waiting to see you. Even young Harry flew in just this morning. Shall I send them in quickly?"

"No," Morris said firmly. "I'm too tired to deal with anyone right now. I'll just be grumpy and irritable." He opened one eye slightly. "Half an hour, give me half an hour, then I'll see them. And I want you here too."

"Certainly," Harry said as he and Alwyn lowered the head of the bed. They then slipped quietly out of the door.

Morris sighed and waited for the morphine to deal with the pain that had re-emerged in his abdomen. He heard a gentle knock on the door, but he ignored it. It came again.

"What is it?" he grumbled cantankerously.

The knock came again.

"What? Not now," he tried to bark angrily. A sharp pain shot through his stomach.

Morris heard the door creak open and then shut softly. He could sense two people standing beside him, but he decided to pretend he was asleep.

"Hello, Boss Morris," a deep baritone rumbled over him.

Morris opened one eye in surprise. "Nguni?"

Nguni laughed; it came from deep within his belly. He stood in his traditional Xhosa robe and held a staff.

Morris looked to his left and couldn't believe who he was staring at. "Daluxolo? What in heaven's name are…? How did…? Where…?"

"How are you, Boss Morris?" Daluxolo smiled sheepishly.

"I'm fine. I'm fine. Did Harry bring you all the way from South Africa? No wonder he took so long to get here. Help me up, help me up," Morris insisted.

The brothers pulled Morris by the arms until he was sitting. Morris' surprise was so great he completely forgot about his pain and discomfort.

"Ghaw," Nguni hawked, "you are too thin. Do the women not feed you here in America?"

Morris laughed. "Of course they do, but I don't have an appetite anymore, you see…" Morris began as he swung his legs off the bed and stood, clasping his old friends' hands in the traditional African handshake. "So good to see you. I don't understand…"

"Ghah!" Daluxolo exclaimed from behind Morris. He pulled at his gown, exposing his bare buttocks. "What are these torn women's clothes they give you in America. What kind of place is this?"

Morris pulled at his gown indignantly. "This is hospital gear if you don't mind! I've just had an operation. What made Harry bring you two? I mean, I'm terribly pleased to see you, but such a long way?"

"Boss Hurry didn't bring us," Nguni grinned mischievously.

With a puzzled look on his face, Morris stared hard at the two brothers. His mind was turning over in confusion. Then he began to smile knowingly. A chuckle started to rise from within, which caused Nguni and Daluxolo to join in with Morris. In no time they were all laughing uncontrollably.

"I know why you are here," Morris wiped a tear from his cheek.

Nguni composed himself. He smiled but did not say anything. Daluxolo rubbed a tear from his eye as he too checked his laugher.

Morris nodded as he cast his eyes around the room. "Perhaps we should go. Yes?"

"Perhaps," Nguni agreed.

Morris waved a warning finger at his friends. "But I'm not going out that door. Not dressed like this. There are too many people out there."

Daluxolo looked pensively at the window. "That way?"

Morris studied the view outside. "That is better, yes! I will need some help, though."

Nguni laughed. "I'm not carrying you today."

Morris shrugged and smiled. "Alright then, show me the way, Gentlemen."

A huge smile appeared on Nguni's face. *"Mashihambe!"* he bellowed, and strode towards the window.

CHAPTER TWENTY
Johannesburg 1950

It had been over a year since Morris had died. Harry, back in Johannesburg, was having his usual monthly lunch with Danie Coetzee. The conversation drifted between business and family matters.

"Are you planning another trip to Europe, Harry?" Danie asked after the meal was over.

"No, I don't have any desire to travel great distances anymore. That last visit to California almost broke me physically. Do you know it can take four days to get there? The worst is waiting at airports for planes to connect, and most often, if they are not cancelled, they are delayed. No, I'll remain right here if I have any say in it."

"What of Rhodesia? Would you visit Archie sometime?"

"Not even Rhodesia," Harry stifled a laugh. "I have seen enough of Archie, and every time he sends a relative down here I have to entertain them for lunch. Frighteningly boring! But Morris wanted me to keep the family connection going, so I oblige."

"I suppose you are the oldest surviving Langbourne brother now," Danie smiled.

"Yes. Head of the African Clan, I suppose. Bloomy, my sister in America, should become the head of the family if she were here, but otherwise, Archie takes that mantle after I die."

"Maybe Bloomy should be your Matriarch in America, and

Archie in Africa? Whatever happened to your nephew," Danie changed the subject, "the one who joined the communists?"

"Michael Harmel? I don't know. Still mixed up with the wrong people and getting himself into trouble with the police. I believe he even got himself placed under house arrest once for politically motivated shenanigans."

"I hear the members have disbanded the Communist Party and they will join another group, the African National Council, or ANC they call it. They are bigger and more powerful."

"Something like that," Harry grimaced. "He'll end up being charged for treason and locked away for life if he is not careful. I find that the saddest thing, because his mother, Sally, was my favourite sister. I adored her, and I feel I need to counsel and guide my nephew. I feel some responsibility towards him."

"You can help, though," Danie said sympathetically.

"Not really. It was Morris' wish that the family abandon him; cut him off completely. I find that very hard, albeit understandable. I don't want to be associated with him, to be honest. We are a family of businessmen, after all, not politicians."

Danie sighed and slumped back in his chair. After a long pause, he looked Harry in the eye. "Without sounding disrespectful, Morris died a year ago. He doesn't have to control you after his death; nobody can rule from the grave, you know."

"No," Harry objected, "I have no intention of reconnecting with Michael. Our views, in every aspect, will be poles apart, although I do feel I should have been there to give him some worldly guidance, for Sally's sake."

"Well," Danie frowned in deep thought. "I have a solution, perhaps."

"Pray, tell," Harry cocked an ear towards his friend as he nonchalantly wiped a bread crumb from the white tablecloth.

"You could leave him some money in your will, anonymously, after you die. Enough to give him a decent nest egg, to perhaps encourage him to abandon the wayward life he leads. Nobody needs to know, but it might settle your heart."

Harry drummed the table with his fingertips as he thought about

Danie's words for a moment.

"That's worth considering, at the very least for my sister's sake," Harry smiled faintly. "I'll give it some thought, Danie. Thanks."

CHAPTER TWENTY-ONE
Johannesburg 1954

Commissioner Street was a hive of activity that Monday morning. The sky over Johannesburg was grey and threatening, which mimicked the feelings of the couple headed for the upcoming meeting.

Ray Harmel put a hand on her husband's shoulder and prevented him from walking any further. "I thought you said you knew where to go," she scolded. "We are lost. Typical," she reprimanded him.

Ray, a Lithuanian Jewess who had escaped the war by the skin of her teeth, was relatively short, had wiry hair, and sharp features with an attitude to match. On arriving in South Africa, she got a job in the textile industry and wasted no time in joining the Textile Workers Union. Her abrasive attitude created numerous headaches for many of the men she worked under. It was through her association with the Communist Party that she had met Michael.

"It's near here," Michael sounded defensive as he pulled a neatly folded piece of paper from his jacket pocket. "Ja, look, we are here. Just look for a sign that says Coetzee and Coetzee Accounting. They are on the first floor, so the sign might be on the top of the building."

"There," Ray grunted. The signage was only one floor above street level. "What do accountants want with you anyway?"

"I told you, I don't know," Michael brooded. "The only thing I can think of is that it might have to do with my uncles' businesses.

The only Coetzee I can remember ever coming across is some chap who was somehow involved with them. That's all."

"Your uncles closed all their businesses down a decade ago," Ray muttered. "They're all dead now, anyhow."

"Well, we don't know that," Michael scratched at his chin.

"Think about it. Your uncle Harry, he died years ago in the war somewhere over Germany."

"No, I think that was a son of one of the other brothers, so my cousin. He was an airman. I think it was a car accident he died in, not a plane, though."

"Two died before the war, so they are long gone, and what of that idiot who went to America? Boris?"

"Morris."

"Yes, him. He turned out to be a horse thief and was hung from a tree. Serves him right."

"We don't know that, Ray. We don't know anything about the family."

"Well, I don't care anyhow. Miserable family. Abandoning us like that. Do you call that family? The Police Special Branch has just finished interrogating you, and now this?"

"I have already told you that I have no idea what this is about. Let's go; we are late enough already."

"You should have worn a suit," Ray nagged. "Look at all these people in the city, all smartly dressed."

"I don't have a suit," Michael absently reminded her as he crossed the street.

"Then you should have put on a tie."

Michael ignored his wife as he strode off in the direction of the firm of accountants. He was not one for dressing up. In fact, Michael was quite comfortable in corduroy trousers, loafers and an open-neck shirt; his favourite had a frayed collar, and that's what he had just happened to put on that day. He knew his strength was in his brain, not in how he dressed. He raised many eyebrows with his choice of attire, especially with his good friend and fellow activist, Nelson Mandela, who found it inconceivable that a man with a university degree would dress so poorly. However, when people engaged in conversation with Michael, they quickly upped their opinion of him.

Michael had a pleasant personality and was usually quick to find humour in any situation. Although his opinion on human rights and government oppression were viewed avidly by a large majority, that was not the case within certain quarters of lawmakers and law enforcers, which caused persistent problems for him and his family.

"Just don't say anything to annoy them," Ray warned. "They are more than likely spies for the police."

Michael again ignored Ray as they entered the stone brick building and made their way to the top of a flight of concrete stairs. He knew she might be right; the strange letter from Mr Coetzee didn't give much away and sounded official enough to be a demand, not an invitation.

On entering the reception of Coetzee and Coetzee, Ray, as was her way, talked over her husband and gruffly announced their arrival. They then took a seat while the receptionist made her way down the corridor to alert the man who had arranged this meeting. A few seconds later she emerged from an office and called the Harmels through.

Danie greeted them with a friendly smile and a firm handshake before offering them seats. He then took his seat on the other side of the substantial, polished desk. Michael and Ray both looked around the office at the various certificates hanging on the walls. A painting of a luscious green landscape that seemed to be somewhere in England shared some space with the certificates.

On one wall was a set of shelves with numerous box files lined up in neat rows. Michael made a mental note that Mr Coetzee was methodical, professional, and liked things to be in perfect order – all the time. The accountant was even dressed in an expensive pinstriped navy suit and wore a silk tie with motifs from a club or association. His desk was clear of all paperwork, except for one sealed white envelope that lay perfectly positioned in front of him. Danie rested a hand on it expectantly.

"Thank you for coming to see me, Mr and Mrs Harmel," Danie began. "I appreciate your taking the time."

"Our pleasure, Mr Coetzee," Michael was polite, but couldn't help casting a quick look at the ominous envelope, which he was sure did not escape Mr Coetzee's notice. "I must say we are somewhat perplexed as to why you would have written to invite us to meet with you." His eyes strayed once again to the envelope.

Danie cleared his throat. "Nothing sinister, I can assure you. I was appointed the executor of a client's last will and testament. Sadly my client passed away some months back, and in the will, some money has been left to you, Mr Harmel. It is incumbent upon me, now, to disperse these funds to you."

"Oh," Michael exclaimed in surprise. "Who was it?"

Danie smiled. "Sadly, I am not at liberty to disclose that."

"Was it a relative?" Ray pressed the question.

Michael put his hand on Ray's lap. "My relatives don't acknowledge me; you know that."

"As I said," Danie continued, "I cannot disclose that information. My client has expressed strict anonymity must be maintained."

"Maybe somebody appreciates what you are doing for the Party," Ray suggested.

Danie remained silent and pokerfaced.

"Mr Coetzee," Michael ventured cautiously, "how much was left to me?"

Danie pushed the white envelope to Michael. "Five thousand pounds sterling."

"Heavens!" Ray exclaimed as Michael cautiously took the envelope off the desk.

"There is a cheque in there for the full amount, and a receipt, which I would like you to sign and leave with me please," Danie instructed. He took an expensive fountain pen from his jacket pocket and offered it to Michael. "I'll need some identification. You did bring your passport as I requested?"

Michael looked at the cheque and handed it to Ray. He then read the contents of the receipt and nodded his approval before signing it with Danie's pen and returning them to him with his passport.

"Thank you," Danie accepted the pen and receipt and glanced at the passport before returning it. "I believe that concludes my commitment to you. Any questions before you leave?"

Michael took the cheque back from Ray and studied it momentarily. It was Danie's company cheque, so it provided no means by which he might trace the origins of the inheritance.

"Are these funds cleared? Can I bank this today?"

"Of course," Danie smiled.

"Apart from you, does anyone else know I have received this money?" Michael asked with some suspicion.

"Yes," Danie frowned at the question. "This is all legal and above board. You will need to declare this to any authority that asks."

"Like?"

"Well," Danie cocked his head curiously, "an official from the taxation office, for example."

"Of course," Michael nodded. "Well then, no, I have no further questions, Mr Coetzee. Thank you."

Ray quickly spoke. "And you cannot give us a hint as to who would bequeath all this money to us? It is substantial, you know."

"Sadly, no."

"A person, or an organisation? You know this will leave a burning question in our lives?"

"I'm afraid I can't help you," Danie stood, signalling the end of the conversation.

Ray looked at Michael with daggers in her eyes. "Who would do this?"

Michael shrugged and got to his feet. "Thank you, Mr Coetzee. I certainly didn't expect this meeting to end in this way."

Danie escorted the Harmels out of the office and bid them farewell with a firm handshake. As he walked back to his office, he gave his receptionist the instruction that he did not want to be disturbed. Closing his office door, he walked over to a redwood sideboard. Very experienced artisans had made the exquisite piece of furniture; it made quite a statement. On Danie pressing a lever hidden on the underside of a drawer, a secret compartment sprung open. Inside were three envelopes, a crystal decanter, and an expensive-looking cut crystal goblet.

Danie poured himself a generous splash of whisky and walked to the window that overlooked the mad rush of Commissioner Street below. He held the glass up in the sunlight, and let its rays sparkle gloriously with brilliant diamond, ruby and gold flashes.

"To you, Harry," he said softly, "the last of my greatest friends. May your dear soul rest peacefully now."

CHAPTER TWENTY-TWO
Salisbury 1978

With barely a rustle of leaves in the nearby poplar trees, the soft spring air drifted lazily over the gathered crowd that sat expectantly on steep wooden benches. These old benches would ordinarily be used for spectators to watch a rugby match at the Police Sports Grounds, but today, the grounds were hosting the 1978 Pass Out Parade of the British South Africa Police recruits.

In the distance, on the far side of the parade ground, a lone police instructor turned on his heel, slammed his right foot into the ground, and marched briskly to confront the recruits. They were formed up in perfectly spaced squads, dressed in formal khaki tunics and starched jodhpurs. The highly polished leather boots, leggings and belts flashed the sunlight as if they were new mirrors. When the inspector reached the assembled squads, he came to an abrupt halt, and again slammed his heel into the ground. The dull thud could be heard by the invited guests on the distant rugby stands; the tension was mounting on both sides of the parade ground.

Violently spinning 180 degrees, as if the instructor had been wound up like a clock spring, he again pummelled the earth with his boot and stood eerily quiet, still and rigid. A deafening silence enveloped the vast parade ground, and the spectators did not dare breathe, let alone move.

Suddenly three deep booms from a massive drum rolled out over the ground. It repeated three times and then went silent. In the distance, the lone voice of the instructor pierced the air.

"Squaaaaaaad... Forwaaaaaard... March!" he barked.

Immediately a cacophony of brass instruments and drums erupted into military music, with the ranks of police officers marching in perfect synchronisation with its beat. The newly commissioned troops had been practising for this day long and hard. They were therefore in perfect formation as they traversed the perimeter of the field, heading towards the assembled mass of dignitaries, officers, relatives and friends. It was a big day for everyone involved.

Archie leaned slightly over towards John, who stood to his left and whispered into his ear. "Where's my grandson?"

John was craning his neck to get a better view. "Alan said he was in the middle squad, middle rank, third from the front."

"Alright," Archie mused, but his clouded eyes could not see that far.

"They'll turn left in a minute and walk past us, and should stop right there in front of us. Alan said when that happens, he will be in the middle squad, middle rank and third from the right."

It sounded all too complicated to Archie, so he resigned himself to simply watch the display of marching men until they halted in front of him. John's wife, Winsome, sat at Archie's right and she squeezed Archie's arm. He smiled back at her. He enjoyed Win very much and cherished their relationship. A quiet lady, she oozed love and compassion for everyone she came in contact with.

Having lost both his wives to illness, Archie particularly enjoyed his daughter-in-law. Win was always there for him, bringing him homemade meals from her kitchen, decorating his small flat with flowers on the weekends and offering love and friendly company when he needed to escape his loneliness.

Archie was proud of his sons, too. John was doing a tremendous job in his wholesale business, Langbourne Trading; so much so that Archie had handed the reins to him entirely. Not only that, but John had entered the world of politics and was a Member of Parliament, while still running the wholesale business. Politics was not something Archie would have encouraged, but John felt strongly about serving his country.

John was extremely energetic, heading the country's Boy Scout Association, and serving as a territorial officer in the army with the rank of major. If that wasn't enough, he was an international rugby referee and the national coach of Rhodesia's growing baseball team. Despite all his commitments, he managed to run a profitable business, which made Archie smile secretly with pride.

After handing the reigns to John, Archie had become bored. He tried his hand in the industrial sector with his youngest son, Louis. Archie built a factory in the industrial suburb of Workington, manufacturing enamel pots and pans. These items sold well; he was selling so many enamel pots, pans, teapots and mugs from his wholesale company that he could barely keep up. Therefore, Archie had decided that the next best thing would be to make them himself. He called his factory Tool and Equipment Company, or TECO for short.

When global sanctions were placed on Rhodesia, Archie was invited by the government to find ways to side-track these restrictions on trade, and spent a period in Paris, France, secretly setting up deals and systems to keep Rhodesia ticking along. Unfortunately, his mission was exposed, and he was deported. His passport was blacklisted, and he was sent back to Rhodesia. So severe was his banning order that Archie was prohibited from travelling to any country in the world, including Ireland, his country of birth. Only South Africa would allow him in.

When his second wife, Olive, took ill and died from an asthma attack in London, Archie was not able to attend her funeral.

Like his father, John later headed up a team, known as the 'Sanctions Busters', to circumvent the crippling sanctions on behalf of the government, taking Win and his two boys to Switzerland as a family. The Rhodesian government had set him up with false foreign passports, fake names and pseudo foreign business entities. His children went to the Geneva English School, with the surprising surname of Van Niekerk. John's family were technically spies.

He had done well in Switzerland, setting up secret barter deals, but after six months, the French secret police exposed him too, and he had to bolt back to Rhodesia with his young family before he was arrested. Nobody, least of all Archie, knew what John had done in those six months, but what became evident were the lasting effects of the Sanctions Busters. Somehow, they kept Rhodesia in essential supplies, such as fuel, medicines, machinery and even military equipment, despite the world sanctions and a raging civil war, for almost a decade.

Mining and agriculture boomed, despite the tense situation, and the products of these industries were used, in part, to barter for essential supplies. The strength of the Rhodesian Dollar increased until, quite surprisingly, it became twice the strength of the American Dollar.

Because of all the pressures of doing business in a country at war, and with international sanctions against them, Archie did not have much time to spend with his grandchildren. He only saw them occasionally for a Sunday lunch, or when John would bring them into the office after their monthly haircut or a dental appointment. It was not that he didn't enjoy family, it was just that he was so busy. Like so many other captains of industry, commerce, miners and farmers, Archie was desperately innovating, streamlining, compromising and solving problems of his operations to keep the businesses, and the country, alive.

Now that he had retired, however, Archie had set aside some time to get to know his grandchildren better. He felt he had mellowed a little since handing his businesses to his sons. Supporting John's eldest at his Pass Out Parade was something he would not miss.

As the ranks of recruits passed by, Archie spotted Alan, and his pride swelled. He almost regretted waiting so long to get to know him better. Now the boy was off to participate in the war that had been raging for over a decade.

The formalities of the parade didn't last long. There were speeches by high ranking police officers, and an address by an African politician, the Honourable Mr Zindoga, who was the Minister for Justice, Law and Order and Public Service. The grand finale was a march past by various men, who were no longer recruits, but officially qualified members of the British South Africa Police Force.

When the ranks of police officers were dismissed into public service, the gathered invitees gingerly stepped down the rickety rugby stands. They made their way to the refreshment tent, waiting anxiously to meet the young police officers who were being dismissed by their instructor at the far end of the field.

As John ambled over to a fellow member of parliament to discuss some pressing matter, Archie led Win and her youngest son, Rob, to where a set of waiters were serving copious cups of tea. He noticed Win dab a tear from her eye with a slightly damp tissue.

"Is that a tear of pride?" Archie asked with a smile.

Win sighed and forced a smile. "Yes and no. I'm proud of Alan, of course, but now I will have two of my three boys in the war, and it saddens me rather."

Archie put a comforting arm around his daughter-in-law. "I wouldn't worry too much, Win. Alan has chosen to be a policeman, not a soldier; I'm not worried about him. He'll be fine."

Win sighed and forced an unconvincing smile. She knew all too well that within a year her entire family, her husband and two sons, would be involved in a war that was escalating in brutality with every passing day. And while they were out doing their bit somewhere in the bush, she would be at home, on her own, for many a long night. The worry would be crippling.

"A cup of tea would be nice," Win changed the subject. "Milk with no sugar please."

Archie took the hint and joined a small queue. Collecting the required cups of tea served in government-issue crockery, he joined Win and Rob a little way from the milling throng. John had rejoined them, but Archie felt John was quite able to get his own refreshment. Handing Win her tea, and taking a sip of his own, Archie noticed a group of young policemen walking towards them, chatting happily, obviously pleased their big day was over and that it had gone flawlessly. Bit by bit, the young men peeled off to join their family groups. Alan arrived, beaming, together with three of his fellow squad mates.

A round of handshakes and hugs ensued as Alan introduced his friends.

"May I introduce you to my fellow police officers," Alan gestured to his friends. "This is Woman Patrol Officer Betty Bone, Patrol Officer Jim Harris, and Patrol Officer Skippy Morley. Guys, this is my mother, Win Langbourne, my grandpa, Archie Langbourne, my father John Langbourne and my *boet*, Rob."

"G'day," Skippy said with a distinct Australian accent, hand outstretched in warm greetings. "Pleased to meet youz fellas."

Skippy stood proud in his formal uniform; with dark cropped hair, his strongest feature was the broad smile that dominated his entire face.

Jim, tall, handsome and with sharp facial features, was a little more conservative in his introduction, confidently engaging John and Archie as if their equal. Win struck up a conversation with Betty, her tailored blue uniform, stunning beauty and blonde hair turning many a young recruit's heads in her direction as they walked past. After six months of intense daily physical training, these young men and women were in peak condition. With highly polished brass buttons, badges and insignia, the country's newest police officers certainly looked like a force to be reckoned with.

"Where are you being posted?" John asked Jim.

"Bulawayo, Sir. A good portion of us have been posted there."

"I'm posted there too," Betty confirmed. "It should be an exciting chapter in our lives."

Jim nodded in agreement. "I believe the day after we arrive the boys are going on a 'partoo' selection course, probably in the Matopos Hills."

"Oh no," Alan groaned loudly. "I didn't know that."

"What's partoo?" Archie looked confused.

"Police Anti Terrorist Unit, or PATU for short," Jim explained. "It's an elite branch of the Police. Bush work, bush survival, surveillance, weapons, that sort of thing. It's where our COIN training comes in."

"Sorry," Archie shook his head again, "what is coin training?"

"Counter-Insurgency," Betty smiled. "It's the type of warfare Rhodesia is engaged in at the moment."

"Jeez," Alan looked down at his highly polished boots. "I hated COIN training. It was the pits. I dread to imagine what the PATU selection will be like."

Skippy turned his beaming smile on Alan. "You did alright, Cobber. You survived COIN training."

Alan frowned. "Hardly. But you seemed to thrive in it. No, not my scene to be honest."

Jim laughed. "Well, I'll see you in Bulawayo, Gecko. Gentlemen, Mrs Langbourne, pleased to meet you, but please excuse me; I have spotted my parents. Betty, you coming?"

Jim and Betty left the gathering to join their families, but not before arranging to meet Skippy later in the afternoon for a celebratory drink at the camp's Blue Lantern Bar.

"Do you know where you have been posted?" Archie asked Skippy.

"Not exactly sure, Sir. Somewhere in the *shateen*; in the outback somewhere. It looks like I'm going bush."

"Oh, dear. Well, do be careful," Archie said before looking at Alan. "And you, do you know where you're going to be posted?"

"Sort of, Grandpa. Somewhere near Bulawayo. I leave tomorrow on the train."

Skippy noticed John didn't have a cup of tea. "May I get you a cuppa, Mr Langbourne?"

"Thank you," John smiled his appreciation.

"Too easy, mate," Skippy grinned as he turned to walk towards the tent, "I'll have one myself; it will be good to have a cup of tea without bluestone in it at last."

Archie looked curiously at the bottom of his empty teacup. "Bluestone? What's that?"

Alan blushed. "It's err... nothing really," he said, quickly changing the subject. "Interesting bloke, Skippy. A few of us somehow got nicknames. Like that bloke there," Alan waved to a redhead walking past. "He's my roommate. Really nice bloke. His name is Mike, but we all call him Paddlefoot."

"I can see why," John smiled as Paddlefoot walked off in his enormous boots.

Alan continued, pointing out his comrades. "That's Lizard, and that short bloke over there is Bog-Fly."

"Heavens!" Win exclaimed, suppressing a laugh. "I heard Jim call you Gecko?"

"Sadly, yes. It's a long story; don't ask. Unfortunately these nicknames seem to stick."

Just then Skippy returned, holding a cup with strong tea that was slopping freely into the saucer.

"There you go, Mr Langbourne," Skippy handed the beverage to John. "Sorry about the spillage, but some of it is still in the cup."

"Very kind of you," John accepted what was left of the tea with a laugh.

"If youz fellas will excuse me, I have been summoned by Batters," Skippy nodded courteously and turned on his heel.

"Quite an accent, that lad has," Archie waved his empty teacup at the retreating Australian.

Alan smiled in agreement. "Skip came out here from Australia without any friends or family; just arrived and joined the police in a country at war. That takes courage, I reckon. None of our squad has ever met an Australian in the flesh, so we just call him Skippy, after that Australian TV program, *Skippy the Bush Kangaroo*."

"Never heard of it," Archie grunted.

"I'm not sure what his real name is. Dave Morley, I think. But he answers to another first name and surname too, so I have no idea. He's very confusing, and his humour is very different. Everyone simply knows him as Skippy; I only know him as Skippy... or Skip."

Archie raised his eyebrows, not too sure if he was amused, impressed or dumbfounded. "Well, I must say, it does take some courage to leave your country, and your family when so young and start on your own. Especially when the country is at war. You know your great grandfather and great uncles did almost exactly that about a hundred years ago."

"They did?" Alan asked in surprise.

Just then, a group of John and Win's friends joined them, and much chatter and laughter erupted, effectively ending that conversation. However, after only five minutes, Archie tugged at Alan's tunic.

"Alan, come for a walk with me. I want to have a chat with you."

Alan immediately obeyed, and the two sauntered away from the crowd. Nobody noticed them walk off.

"Has your Dad ever told you about your great grandfather or your great uncles? My half-brothers, Morris, David, Louis and Harry?"

"I've heard him mention Uncle David and Uncle Harry," Alan replied, now very curious as to where this conversation was leading.

"Morris and David came to Africa in 1891. Just like your Australian friend, Skippy, they had no relatives here, and no friends. They just arrived, and with great determination, they dealt with it."

"I didn't know that," Alan said, although he recalled his father telling him a story about them once. "I thought they bought a cigarette factory or something."

"No, no, no," Archie shook his head resignedly. "They started their own factory, making cigarettes. How old are you?"

"Me?" Alan asked in surprise. "I am 19. Why?"

"Your Uncle Morris was 16 when they landed in Port Elizabeth in 1891; he was younger than you are now. Uncle David was only 15. When Louis arrived in Africa, he was 14, and Harry only 13. They were all younger than you. I followed them out years later when I was also 13 years old."

Archie's mind seemed to drift into the past; he became pensive and stared at the grass on the parade ground as they strolled in silence. Alan held his tongue; he had never seen his grandpa like this.

Reality slowly came back to Archie. "Your father knows all the stories of the original brothers, Morris, David, Louis and Harry. You make sure you pester him to tell you about their beginnings. Now I'm going to tell you the story, and I want you to tell your children and your grandchildren. Will you do that?"

"Yes, Grandpa," Alan nodded eagerly.
"Promise me you will tell them."
"I will, Grandpa. I promise."
Archie's eyes became dreamy, and he sighed deeply. "Ahh... It's a grand story..."

The following day Alan caught his train to Bulawayo. Unbeknown to him, the memorable conversation he had with his Grandpa Archie, while walking around the parade square that long-ago day, would be the last time he ever spoke with him. Archie died from colon cancer less than a year later.

Once the war had ended, Alan went on to work for his father, continuing the Langbourne tradition. Forty years on, he made good his promise to his Grandpa Archie.

And that is where this story begins.

THE END

AUTHOR'S NOTES

The Clan Minute Book

The original Minute Book of the Clan contained excellent records of not just family matters, but local and international issues affecting the family at the time. What is intriguing is that the first office bearer, at the first meeting, was only six years old. This is in keeping with the family's tradition of teaching their children the principals of business from a very young age.

Archie's idea of good deed awards transcended generations. To this day his grandsons still compete for token good deed badges.

Sample Room (Bulawayo 1893) & Landau Trading (Salisbury c.1950)

The Sample Room, constructed in Bulawayo in 1893, was replaced by a brick and mortar building in Abercorn Street after the overthrow of King Lobengula. In 1907 Fergus W Ferguson published a book entitled 'Southern Rhodesia' wherein he discussed several businesses that operated in that country at the time. He gives mention to Morris and David's business wherein he states, in part:

Primary consideration must be devoted to the large business, in these premises, measuring 120 feet by 100 feet, are to be seen the commodities of every market in the world. Like the establishments of most of their contemporaries, the external appearance of this noted house does not by any means convey an adequate idea of the stock in trade centred therein. This can only be obtained by an inspection of the ramifications in the interior, and in the stores at the rear for reserve stocks. To describe these fully is out of the question, as an undertaking of that kind would weary our readers, and occupy many pages of our book.

When Morris instructed Harry to close the business after David's death, the existing stock was sold to Archie in (then) Salisbury. The building was sold to none other than the Thomas Meikle family.

When I was six years old, my father tried to get me to climb the flagpole of Archie's building to untangle a knot. I got half way up, but fear overcame me. My best friend, Martin Robinson, then did the deed. He is the only person ever to climb to the top. (His parents never found out!)

OK Bazaars : Eloff Street Opening Day
(Photo: Johannesburg Heritage Foundation / CC BY-SA)

It is often thought that Morris' biggest commercial mistake (and probably regret) was not taking the offer of shares in the OK Bazaars venture. The story depicted in this book is true, and it was done on a handshake alone. After Mr Cohen and Mr Miller paid back the loan, Morris told his brothers to walk away from the deal, despite being offered a substantial share of the business.

OK Bazaars continued to expand, opening over 200 stores in several African countries and listing on the Johannesburg Stock Exchange. His family often reminded Morris that he should have taken up Cohen's offer, but he stood by his decision.

In the 1980s, the retail environment in South Africa began to change, and OK Bazaars fell into financial difficulty. In 1997 a corporation called Shoprite bought OK Bazaars for 1 Rand (valued at approximately 10 cents at the date of this publication).

Perhaps Morris did make the right decision. Later, however, Shoprite managed to turn a corner. According to their website, they state that in December 2019, they operate in 15 countries in Africa with 2998 corporate outlets. Shoprite engages over 147 000 employees and serves over 35 million customers per day.

Holmby Hills Home
(Photo : Tavo Olmos : Library of Congress)

Paul Revere Williams, the architect of Morris' home in Holmby Hills, was born in Los Angeles in 1894. Despite the racial prejudices that existed at that time, he chose to become an architect against the advice of his teachers. Nevertheless, he persevered.

With his charismatic charm, flair and determination, he excelled and finally opened his own business, designing homes for big Hollywood names such as Lucille Ball, Frank Sinatra and Bill 'Bojangles' Robinson, amongst many others. Some of his homes were used as backdrops to popular TV series, such as 'Dallas' and 'The Colbys'.

Racial issues at that time were a massive hurdle for Mr Williams. However, because he understood human nature on an extraordinary level, he knew that many of his clients would feel uncomfortable with him sitting beside them during consultations. He, therefore, learned to draw upside down so clients could watch him draft from the other side of the desk, where they felt more comfortable. Mr Williams would later comment on the irony that house constructions he oversaw were in areas that he, himself, was forbidden to purchase.

With his popularity soaring, he was engaged to design and oversee many large state buildings, libraries, government offices and hotels. The dome-shaped structure that can be seen at the Los Angeles Airport (LAX) was designed by Mr Williams, including other state buildings such as military bases and hospitals.

In all, there are over 3000 buildings in the USA that can be attributed to his design. He earned the nickname of "The Architect of Hollywood". At least two documentaries were made about him, and he received several American architectural awards.

Photographs of Morris' 'mansion' can be found on a website dedicated to Mr Williams at www.paulrwilliamsproject.org.

After Morris' death, his Holmby Hills home was sold to Zsa Zsa Gabor at the time when she was married to George Sanders. The house changed hands several times after that. Revlon CEO Ron Pearlman and LA Kings Hockey Team owner, Bruce McNall, were among some of the notable personalities who lived in the property at one stage or another. It is believed the famous ice hockey player, Wayne Gretzky, learned to ride a motorbike in the driveway.

Later, the Harvard Westlake School, which was built on the next property, wished to expand and offered to purchase the house with a view to knocking it down. There was heated objection due to its Paul Williams heritage. Eventually, it was bought by Ann-Marie Villicana and her husband, Robin Salzar, for $1 with an agreement to relocate the heritage-listed house. It was dismantled into six parts and transported to Pasadena where it was reassembled. At the time of publication, Ann-Marie and Robin are living happily in the Morris Landau Home.

Reuben Jacob

Born in 1852, Rywen Bratsztajn grew up in Pounka, Poland. He married Esther and opened a successful business in the textile trade. Rywen later changed his surname. Some years later he dropped the name Reuben and adopted his second name of Jacob only. His death certificate in 1925 records his first name as Jacob.

Because Jacob decided to leave Poland in 1879, he may have been the only member of the Breitstein family branch to survive past 1945 as no death certificates of his extended family can be found after the Holocaust of World War Two. However, because he lived in Ireland and had 13 children (12 of whom continued to have families of their own) the genealogy of Jacob's line has survived.

A very religious man, Jacob passed away in Ireland at the age of 73.

Bloomy

Affectionately known as Bloomy, she spent most of her young adult life as the matriarch of the family after her mother died. Hers was not an easy start in life. With three younger siblings and a father who was suffering from depression, her mother's young niece, Helena, was invited to Ireland to help bring up the children.

As was probably accepted custom in those days, Bloomy's father, Jacob, ultimately married Helena and they went on to have six more children. Bernard Zeider began courting Bloomy and soon married her. She went on to have seven daughters and a son.

Bernard was a hopeful businessman, always looking to do "deals" or start a business that would make a lot of money. (His very successful brothers-in-law likely influenced him.) Sadly, he was not business savvy and the business ventures he undertook often failed dismally. He was asked by a friend to join him in a furniture business, a type that today we call 'flat-pack furniture', and he immediately left for America, leaving Bloomy and his entire family behind to fend for themselves.

Bloomy moved in with Jacob and lived there for several years, during which time it is believed that Morris supported her. Bernard eventually called the family to join him in Pittsburgh. Bloomy packed up her children and duly left for America. However, it was not long after she was settled into her new home that Bernard once again abandoned his family to pursue his fortune in California, along with his son, Al.

The potential business failed, and Bernard never returned to Pittsburgh or his family, his whereabouts becoming a mystery forevermore. Bernard died alone at the age of 56 in Denver, for reasons no one has been able to discover.

Bloomy, being very resourceful and competent, brought up her large family on her own. When Morris discovered her plight in life, he continued to supplement her living expenses in America. She remained very close to her children, who gave her five grandchildren and 11 great-grandchildren, several of whom live in the USA to this day.

Her great-granddaughter, Nancy, once told me, *"Uncle Morris was extremely generous to Granny, and my family would like to acknowledge the benefit he bestowed on all of us."*

Sally

Sally, also known as Sarah-Sally, was born in 1888. When she was 20 years old, she married Arthur Harmel, a pharmacist, and moved to South Africa. It was known that she had a very close relationship with her older brothers, but in particular with Harry, and Harry, likewise with her.

In 1915 Sally bore a son, Michael Harmel, and only three years later she contracted the deadly Spanish Flu, a pandemic that is thought to have killed up to 100 million people around the globe. Sally succumbed to the virus and died in 1918, leaving behind her husband and son, Michael. At the time, Michael was just three years old.

Arthur, being so distraught from the sudden death of his lovely wife, made some irrational decisions. Fearing future heartache that might inflict Michael when he was older, he decided to destroy all documentation, photographs and memories of Sally. His thoughts, I was told, were to prevent Michael hankering after a mother he never knew. Fortunately, some photos of Sally survived.

Michael attended Rhodes University in Grahamstown, South Africa. He moved amongst friends who were radical socialists, and he became outspoken in his views, joining the South African Communist Party (at the time it was a legal organisation). His ideas were extreme, and he was deeply committed to the liberation of all humanity and passionately opposed to racism.

As a result of his activities, he was subject to many banning orders, arrested or placed under house arrest. Because the brothers were, by that time, prominent members of the South African and Rhodesian commercial and social societies, with very capitalistic ideals, Michael's connections with the communist party went totally against their principals. Failing to convince him to change his ways, the brothers disowned him and cut him off from the family.

Harry, feeling he had some moral responsibility to care for his favourite sister's only son, was particularly torn by the wishes of his brothers. Still, as his loyalty to them were foremost, he too disowned Michael.

Michael married Ray, a Lithuanian Jewess who escaped the war and fled to South Africa, where they had a daughter, Barbara. Ray was a revolutionary, also joining the Communist Party, and was very involved in the Garment Workers Industry of South Africa, fighting for workers' rights. When Barbara was older, she too joined the cause. She befriended many of her parents' comrades, who included notable names like Nelson and Winnie Mandela, Walter Sisulu, Oliver Tambo and Govan Mbeki.

In 1954 Michael received a sum of money that had been bequeathed to him in a will. He did not know who bequeathed the money, or why, but he believed it came from one of his uncles. He was never able to find out. Through interviews with surviving members of the family, it was recently discovered that it was Harry who left Michael the money in his will; it also tied in with the date of Harry's death.

The inheritance, at that time, was substantial and enabled the Harmel family to purchase a plot of land in Johannesburg and build a house. In an interview with Barbara, she said there was some contention with the decision to build the house as Michael wanted to give his entire windfall to the Communist Party. However, Ray put her foot down and insisted charity began at home in this instance; they were always struggling for money. Ray won the argument, and so the house was constructed.

As it happened, their home was used on several occasions as a safe house, hiding and harbouring many of the Harmel's colleagues when the Police were hunting them down. One of their closest friends asked if they could have their pre-wedding photos taken in their home, so in June 1958, the Harmel family hosted a wedding dress rehearsal for Nelson and Winnie Mandela. Little did they know at the time that Nelson Mandela would one day become the President of South Africa, and Winnie, the First Lady.

When the apartheid situation became too difficult for Michael, the Communist Party insisted he go into exile and continue his actions from abroad where he would have more freedom of movement. In 1974 Michael slipped out of South Africa and established himself in Prague where he died at the age of 59. He never returned to South Africa.

Barbara remained in South Africa and continued in her father's footsteps, secretly distributing anti-apartheid and communist propaganda, amongst other covert activities. Eventually, Barbara was also forced into exile, basing herself in the United Kingdom, and spending some time in the USA.

Shortly after Michael's death, Barbara received a letter from Helen Joseph, a prominent anti-apartheid activist, that enclosed a second envelope and letter from Nelson Mandela. The letter was addressed to Barbara and offered his deepest condolences on the passing of her father, Michael. The correspondence had censorship stamps on it.

Barbara showed me this letter during an interview in her home. In her own words, she told me the following:

"When Nelson wrote this letter, he was about ten years into his life sentence. When he was arrested, he was classified as a 'D Class' prisoner, which meant he could only write two letters a year. I have no idea what class he was when he wrote this letter, so I don't know how many letters per year he was permitted to send. Whatever it was, and it couldn't have been many, it showed me how important it was that he felt the need to use some of his precious allocation to express his condolences to me."

There was a coded message in the letter, it had no meaning to me but seemed exceedingly significant to Barbara.

Many years into her exile, Barbara was giving a lecture in London when members of the South African government approached her. Suggestions were made that if she returned to the new South Africa, she would be warmly welcomed. She eventually did return and settled in Johannesburg.

Barbara continued: *"I had been living in Johannesburg for a while when I made an appointment to visit the President. I had not seen Nelson Mandela for many decades, since well before he was arrested. As I sat in this large foyer waiting for my appointed time to be ushered up to the President's office, I heard a sudden commotion at the lifts. When I looked over, a mob of people, security guards, reporters and dignitaries exited the lift, and in the middle of them was Nelson himself. The instant he saw me, he immediately broke away from the crowd, striding over, arms outstretched and calling out my name. He had the biggest smile and gave me an even bigger hug."*

Barbara's eyes welled up as she stared lovingly at the condolence letter on her lap.

"Oh, what a moment," she said tenderly.

Because of the significance the 'Harmel Home' played in the anti-apartheid movement, the house at 47 High Road, Gardens, was declared a National Heritage by the Johannesburg Heritage Foundation. In 2013, for the part Michael played in the anti-apartheid movement of South Africa, Barbara accepted the Order of Luthuli (Silver) posthumously on behalf of her father from the President of South Africa, His Excellency, Jacob Zuma.

It could be said that, despite the brothers disowning Michael and his policies, Harry unwittingly and unknowingly played a small part in the anti-apartheid movement by bequeathing enough money for Michael to build 'Harmel Home', which occasionally became a safe house for Mr Mandela and many of his colleagues.

In Mr Mandela's book, *'Long Walk to Freedom'*, (Little, Brown and Company, 1994) Michael Harmel is mentioned several times. Mr Mandela specifically discussed Michael's poor dress sense at the end of Chapter 9. He states in part:

'At one point in the evening I was introduced to Michael Harmel, whom I was told had a master's degree in English from Rhodes University. I was impressed with his degree, but when I met him, I thought to myself, 'This chap has an MA, and he is not even wearing a tie!' I just could not

reconcile this discrepancy. Later, Michael and I became friends, and I came to admire him greatly, in no small measure because he rejected so many of the other foolish conventions I once embraced. He was not only a brilliant writer, but was so committed to communism that he lived in the same manner as an African, though he could have lived on a grander scale.'

I have no doubt that Sally, had she lived long enough, would have been exceedingly proud of her son and granddaughter's civic accomplishments. Sadly, Barbara, a warm and truly wonderful lady, passed away before this book could be published.

Freddy

Freddy continued to represent Morris' family in the UK for many years, ensuring Rose Bertha received her maintenance and his grandchildren's education was paid on time.

He married Ophelia and had a daughter, June, who moved to Arizona where she married Jose. Then June did something she would never realise the ramifications. As a way to introduce her new husband to family members, June wrote to Archie in Rhodesia in 1977 asking for information on all the brothers and sisters.

Archie dictated his reply into a cassette tape recorder and posted the cassette to her. For some unknown reason, many years later, June posted that cassette tape to my father just before she died; I currently have that tape recording.

What is interesting is that Archie reconfirmed in that cassette many of the stories he and my father had told me, but more important is that he described the brothers' characters in great detail. It enabled me to capture not just the story, but the brothers' actual personalities. For me, this was pure gold.

If it wasn't for June's decision to post that cassette to my father, I believe this series would never have been written.

June had no children, and died in Phoenix, Arizona. Freddy died in London at the age of 62.

Paddy

Very little is known about Paddy, as he died when his children were relatively young. Fortunately, just one year before this book was published, Paddy's granddaughter, Laura, now living in the USA, found Paddy's passport in some old family files. Within the passport was a letter Paddy wrote to his aunt in pencil from his hospital bed in Tanganyika. Written in 1916, it is over 100 years old. Part of this letter was reproduced in this book by kind permission of the family.

At the time of publication, Paddy's son, Richard, at the age of 90, is a wonderful and caring gentleman who had many stories of his own to share with me.

Richard became an astute accountant; his grasp on numeracy is outstanding. Richard became a very successful businessman, forming several high-profile commercial ventures, and was an accomplished pilot.

With a sharp mind and delightful humour, Richard's contribution to these books has been an absolute godsend.

Archie and Kate

Archie lost two wives to illness; Kate, in 1951, and Olive in 1974. He handed his wholesale business to his eldest son, John in the 1960s. He turned his hand to industry, commissioning a factory that made enamelware called Tool and Equipment Company, or TECO for short. He ran this for many years with his youngest son, Louis. The story about Louis adding up the telephone book upside down is true!

In the early 1940s Archie was appointed the Rhodesian Trade Ambassador to Japan and in June 1950 was elected President of the Rhodesian Chamber of Commerce and Industry.

When international sanctions were imposed on Rhodesia in 1965, Archie was asked by the government to find secret ways to beat the restrictions in trade. He was exposed during a visit to France and had his passport blacklisted, thereby prohibiting him from travelling anywhere in the world, except South Africa. (He was even banned from entering Ireland, his country of birth, so severe were the sanctions against Rhodesia.) As a result, he was unable to attend Olive's funeral when she died suddenly in London.

His son, John, took up the mantle and helped establish a group called the Sanctions Busters. He successfully continued Archie's work in Switzerland, ultimately taking his family with him under a pseudo name and fake passports. The French secret police eventually exposed him too, and, like Archie, he was forced to return to Rhodesia in a hurry. He later made a name for himself in the business, political, sporting and Scouting movements. He retired to the UK with his second wife, but with failing health, he was moved to an unknown location in South Africa where he died. At the time of publishing, his family do not know where his final resting place is.

In his younger days, Archie was feared by those who knew or worked for him; he had a quick temper and didn't suffer fools, but once he retired, he mellowed and became quite likeable. He is buried in Harare, Zimbabwe.

Nguni and Daluxolo

The Xhosa brothers, Nguni and Daluxolo, were both fictitious and real people.

According to family stories, they indeed existed; however, no one in the family could remember their surnames. The closest connection I could find was that Archie employed Daluxolo's grandson in Salisbury. Archie would refer to the man as 'Eric', although that was not his real African name.

Often, in those days, if a man's traditional name were hard to pronounce, or difficult to say, they would adopt a westernised name for ease and simplicity. As a result, my research ended there when trying to locate these gentlemen or their families.

One thing is sure, though, these two brothers existed, and without them, Morris and his brothers would not have achieved what they did. This was recognised by Morris, David, Louis and Harry, and they were not shy to let it be known within the family.

For instance, in *'Langbourne's Empire'*, the story where the wagons were lost in the bush and protected by Nguni and Daluxolo for an entire year, is very much a true story. The perishables were eaten while they planted crops and reared the livestock. When the wagons were found, the Xhosa brothers had developed a fully functional village with a sustainable population of chickens, goats and other livestock, as well as some small fields of crops. They were

Langbourne's Legacy

concerned, however, that they would get into trouble for eating the perishables, a concern that both perplexed and amused Archie for as long as I knew him.

What is often overlooked is that while these wagons were lost and being cared for in the bush, prices of commodities hyper-inflated during the conflict in the country at the time. What these Xhosa brothers did, saved the brothers from financial ruin. The gravity of Morris' financial situation was mentioned briefly in Marvin C. Arthur's biography, *'It's Been a Wonderful Life'* (Arthurhouse 2005).

It was the unconditional loyalty these Xhosa brothers gave to their 'European family' that led me to title the fifth book, *'Langbourne's Loyalty'*. It is this policy of loyalty, friendship and family values that were instilled and encouraged amongst the descendants.

This loyalty was also the catalyst for Archie to create and form the principals of the 'Clan'; to foster family values, honesty, and care for fellow humankind. Having interviewed a number of the original brother's descendants, together with the contents from the Minute Book, old dictated tape recordings and other documents discovered in the research of this book, it is abundantly clear that Nguni and Daluxolo made a massive impression on Morris, David, Louis and Harry. As such, their values were passed down to future generations.

Harry

The Bulawayo Chronicle (4th September 1943) reported on Harry's keen interest in business and stated he travelled from Salisbury to the Congo on one occasion to drum up business. The distance between Salisbury and the Congolese border is around 900kms or 560 miles – a hazardous journey at the best of times. One family story suggests he made that journey on a bicycle.

The South African Jewish Times (26th November 1948) stated that Harry was the single biggest contributor to the Jewish Community Governor-General Fund, and worked tirelessly for the Jewish War Survivors Appeal. This he did at the cost of his own health.

After Harry's death, glowing obituaries appeared in various newspapers. At that point, he and his descendants seem to have disappeared from the history books. I am still searching for them.

Louis

During the First World War, Louis joined the Rhodesia Volunteers Reserve and gained the rank of Lieutenant. During his lifetime he was very active with his civic duties, being elected onto two Town Councils, Bulawayo and Salisbury, where he was highly regarded.

As a religious man, Louis continued to actively participate in the Zionist Organisation of Bulawayo, the organisation that Morris chaired at its inception. When Louis died, he left substantial amounts of money to the community of Bulawayo, which included, amongst others, money for an education bursary, the construction of a war memorial hall and a Hebrew school that was named after him. He also donated a large sum of money to the Jewish National Fund in Johannesburg, South Africa.

Louis was buried at Willesden Cemetery in London in 1934.

David

David had four children, Ettie, Ernest, Leslie and Cyril.

Little is known about Ettie, however Ernest became a renowned anaesthetist and wrote a well-respected paper on anaesthetics and pioneered the use of epidural anaesthesia. For many years he was the head of the Anaesthetics Department at the St. George's Hospital in Hyde Park. He was slated to anaesthetise King George V when he had his left lung removed, but Ernest contracted tuberculosis just before the operation and therefore could not attend. (The surgery was a success and was depicted in the television series *'The Crown'*: Series 1 Episode 1.) All doctors in attendance received a knighthood from King George V. Ernest, however, did not.

Leslie became a renowned barrister in London. He practiced law in Palestine and worked with a number of dignitaries. Leslie also worked closely with Emperor Halie Selassie of Ethiopia to negotiate a treaty, and was part of a legal team that formed the constitution of the new state of Israel after WW2. During his time in Southern Africa, Leslie sat on the Board of OK Bazaars looking after the family's interests. He later migrated to the USA where Morris engaged him to manage his American properties. He was a man of many talents; an accomplished Jazz pianist and playwright.

Cyril worked in Paris and New York before returning to Rhodesia to work in the family business. He later moved to Salisbury and entered the manufacturing industry. Cyril retired to

Cape Town with his wife, Eve. Leaving Eve in Cape Town, Cyril took a trip to London to visit his son, David, where he died peacefully in his sleep after a round of golf. It was the first time in his married life that he and Eve had been apart. Eve died in Cape Town at the age of 104.

Morris

Morris' divorce from Evelyn was of public interest in the Los Angeles newspapers, however his business affairs always remained confidential and close to his chest. Confidentiality was paramount to him, and the story of the 'black rhino' code is a fine example of how Morris operated. His desire for secrecy, or to mislead those who pried into his origins or business interests, can best be described in two newspaper articles:

The Los Angeles Times (November 22, 1936) suggested Morris was English or South African, however they admitted they weren't sure, but correctly stated that Morris arrived via London in 1936.

The St. Petersburg Times (August 28, 1937) states that society writers speculate *'Morris was the scion of an old South African goldmining family or a diamond magnate.'* They go on to state that financial journalists believed Morris *'was an international merchant and managing partner for an important London shipping firm. No one was certain.'*

Morris was very concerned about the events unfolding during the Second World War. Apart from inviting family members to stay with him at Holmby Hills (some accepted the offer, others did not), it is thought he may have given significant financial assistance to an organisation in the UK to assist the Jews affected by the war. This cannot be proven and will probably never be known, although there are suggestions within the family that this was the case.

In his Last Will and Testament, Morris bequeathed a large sum of money for the construction of a convalescent home in Beverly Hills. However, construction of this establishment cannot be found. The funds earmarked for this endeavour also cannot be traced, as was much of his other assets. A more thorough and intriguing analysis of what happened to Morris' estate after his death can be found in a biography soon to be published by his grandson, Robert Landau.

Morris is buried in Los Angeles, USA.

ACKNOWLEDGEMENTS

In the constantly changing world we live in today, I am cognisant that specific terms or phrases might offend some readers. Because of the period this series of books covers, I have had to consider issues regarding religion, race, gender, beliefs, politics and nationalities that occurred during those historic times. In so doing, I have tried to keep terms and language as neutral as possible, but still reflect the sentiments of that time. It has never been my intention to cause any offence to anyone, and if I have done so, please accept my apologies.

Many people helped me in the research of this series, of whom I am gratefully indebted. Special mention must be made to Richard Landau, Robert Landau, David Landau, Steve Landau, John S Landau, Pam Sussman Landau, Nancy Rich and Clive Stapley, all descendants of Reuben Jacob's family. I give special thanks to Nancy Rich, whose committed research into the family's genealogy is truly appreciated.

My thanks also to Rabbi Moshe Silberhaft for his guidance on certain Jewish beliefs, and a special thanks to the Head Librarian and staff at the Jacob Gitlin Library and Holocaust Centre in Cape Town, South Africa. My thanks also to my incredible proofreading team, with special mention to Martin and Trevor Robinson, Sue Arkell, Ashley Wilkinson, Melissa Muller, Steve Landau, Mary Power, Nancy Rich and my lovely wife, Sharon.

As always, my deepest gratitude to Cindy Kramer, my mentor and primary editor, who has been with me from the very first to the very last word in this series. Posthumously, I thank my father and grandfather for taking the time to tell me all the old stories. (In my grandfather's case, it was more of a series of lectures!)

I am grateful to Laura Landau, who found Paddy's handwritten letter in the USA over 100 years after he wrote it. I am also thankful to Laura and her father, Richard Landau, for permitting me to reproduce part of the contents in this book. My thanks again to Robert Landau and Ann-Marie Villicana for their information on Morris' Holmby Hills mansion.

Finally, I thank you, my readers, for your support. I wrote this series to preserve the story of some remarkable brothers, but I know there are many other stories out there that might soon be forgotten too. They need to be remembered and passed down the generations. On the same token, I urge you to record your own experiences; let it be your legacy.

ABOUT THE AUTHOR

Alan Landau was born in Salisbury, Rhodesia (now Harare, Zimbabwe) in 1959. In 1978 he joined the British South Africa Police (formally the BSAC). At that time Rhodesia was entangled in a civil war that ended in 1980. After serving in the new Zimbabwe Republic Police for a short time, Alan retired to enter the commercial world.

Alan worked in Zimbabwe's widely known tobacco industry for five years before joining his father and ultimately taking over the family business when his father retired to the UK. Later on, Alan was involved in the travel, tourism, hotel, property, financial, and retail sectors. His service to his community took the form of Rotary International with a committed focus on the Rotary Youth Exchange Program.

Having migrated to Brisbane, Australia, in 2001, Alan bought a franchise in the retail sector, which he successfully ran with his late wife and two children. In 2012 he sold the business and went into semi-retirement. He now pursues his hobbies of writing, travelling, wildlife safaris and ornithology with his wife, Sharon.

More about the author can be found as follows:
Web: www.landaubooks.com
Twitter: @landaubooks
Facebook: www.facebook.com/landaubooks
Instagram: landaubooks